Films on art

Films on art

A Source Book Compiled and Edited by
The Canadian Centre for Films on Art
for The American Federation of Arts.

Published by
Watson-Guptill Publications, New York,
in association with
The Canadian Film Institute, Ottawa.

Distributed in Canada by
The Canadian Film Institute.

First published 1977 in New York by Watson-Guptill Publications,
a division of Billboard Publications, Inc.,
1515 Broadway, New York, N.Y. 10036

Library of Congress Cataloging in Publication Data
Main entry under title:

Films on art.

    Includes indexes.
    1. Art—Film catalogs. 2. Art in moving-pictures.
I. Canadian Centre for Films on Art. II. American
Federation of Arts.
N368.F54 1977   016.7   77-21339
ISBN 0-8230-1780-X

Manufactured in U.S.A.

First Printing, 1977

The Canadian Centre for Films on Art received financial support
for this project from the National Film Board of Canada and
gratefully acknowledges a grant from the National Gallery of Canada.
The American Federation of Arts received financial support for
this project from the National Endowment for the Arts, Washington, D.C.

Project staff:
Dorothy Macpherson, Director, Canadian Centre for Films on Art
Jean Cleinge, Film Consultant and Cinéaste
Barbara Munro, Project Coordinator

Project advisers:
William Sloan, Supervising Film Librarian, The New York Public Library
Margareta Akermark, Associate Director, Department of Film
The Museum of Modern Art

Edited by Donna Wilkinson
Designed by Jay Anning
Set in 10/11 Press Roman by Copy Prep Company
Printed and bound by Book Press

Contents

Foreword

It was in the late 1930s that the film genre generally known today as the film on art achieved a status which earned it the right to independent recognition. Till then it had been swallowed up in the broad mass of documentary, the term invented by John Grierson to cover "the creative treatment of actuality" of which, for the "Father of Documentary," art was an essential part.

In 1951, in Florence, Professor Carlos Ragghianti produced his *Répertoire général international*, which listed and described more than a thousand titles. In 1960, under the imprint of the University of Pisa, he and the International Institute of Films on Art presented a revised and enlarged edition, bringing the volume up-to-date.

UNESCO, too, published three consecutive listings, 1949, 1951, 1953, covering most of the filmmaking countries in its international membership. The unique "actuality" of the film on art had become apparent. The films made from 1939 on were vastly different from the picture postcard sequences of scenery and famous buildings for which the name was at first used. Among the most original were the films made by two young members of a film society in Milan, Luciano Emmer and Enrico Gras, who joined forces to shoot a film from the paintings of Hieronymus Bosch which they released as *The Terrestrial Paradise*, 1948. A triumph of ingenuity, it was made with a very old camera, the shutter operated by a piece of string. Their second production, from the Giotto frescoes at Padua, was called *The Drama of the Son of Man*, with extracts from the New Testament as commentary and a specially composed music score. The method gave the viewer a sense of being taken right inside the painting, and there was all the excitement of being present at the dawn of a wonderful day of initiation into the greatest masterpieces of the ages.

Emmer's films were taken over by a large company and relaunched in the United States with considerable éclat and advertising, with Vincent Price as impresario. Sad to say they lost most of their rather childlike charm in the process, but it was a worthwhile survival operation: some can still be found in distributors' listings. Many others that deserved continued use were made from 1939 on, notably in the Low Countries, by such directors as Storck, Cauvin, Haesaerts, and later Haanstra. In the United States, enthusiasm and adequate funding were fast overtaking the European countries which had pioneered the film on art. In 1956, Professor Theodore Bowie of Indiana University issued a *Critical Guide* to the film on art. This listed about 300 films in six related categories. Here, possibly for the first time, a clear distinction was drawn between the "art film" and the "film on art," an important step in clarification: he stressed the value of his "Guide" to purchasing organizations.

American enthusiasm for the film on art was brought to the attention of the English-speaking world, as never before, by means of two important festivals. The first of these opened on Labor Day, 1951, at Woodstock, New York. Backed by The American Federation of Arts, it attracted an astonishing 1,200 visitors to a superb program selected by the wide-ranging talent scouts of Film Advisory Center, whose inaugural program, not long before at The Museum of Modern Art, had elicited a unanimously favorable response from critics, distributors, and the public. It was necessary to recast many screenings in duplicate and arrangements were also made for another festival to follow up during the next year: the second U.S. International Art Film Festival. Forty-four films were shown, "twenty-eight for the first time in America" as the program announced; several of the most interesting have survived to be included in this catalog.

In 1963 the writer of this Foreword was working as liaison officer with the National Gallery of Canada for the National Film Board of Canada. She was warmly urged during a visit to UNESCO headquarters in Paris not only to undertake editorship of an English edition of an international comprehensive catalog listing new films and their sources, but to organize a festival and seminar similar to those of the second U.S. International Art Film Festival. It was to be held preferably in Ottawa but would invite cooperation from other countries, including the U.S. and the U.S.S.R. Cooperation was obtained from the National Gallery of Canada, which lent its auditorium and committee rooms, and from the National Gallery Association, which undertook the local arrangements, giving delegates an unforgettable experience of the capital city at its best during the Tulip Festival. It was at first understood that twenty-five representatives from across the country would be invited and entertained, but the Woodstock experience was repeated and it was with difficulty that official delegate participation was limited to 100. Discussion was passionate and intense. When all the argument had died away it was clear that, as in the United States, there were many audiences of many different types for the film on art: one comparatively small and exacting in galleries, museums, and university art departments; others much larger in university and college extension courses, in public libraries and elsewhere; and, at the other end of the scale, an almost unlimited potential for purchase in the school system at all levels. Many were not satisfied by the occasional screening but wanted to arrange series, which often developed into small festivals.

In the same year, 1963, the well-known British writer and thinker, Sir Herbert Read, made a speech which has relevance to our current concern with the increase of violence in daily life. Taking issue with anthropologist Robert Ardrey, who believes in the basic ugliness of human nature, "We believe," he says, "that we possess in the principles of art . . . an antidote to the forces of destruction that now threaten the existence of the human race. The instinct for order is the only natural instinct that can control the instinct for destruction, the mortal instinct. Art is the name we give to the only human activity that can establish a universal order in all we do and make in thought and in imagination."

This book, produced with the help of the National Gallery of Canada and the National Film Board of Canada, is offered as a contribution to those engaged in art activities of all kinds and at all levels. May it help you find the film you need.

Acknowledgments are gratefully extended to the many who will recognize their own intuitions and even words in one or more of our descriptions: we have drawn on the whole range of distributors' and reviewers' film notes. To single out a few may seem invidious, but we are especially indebted to the following: William McK. Chapman, Editor, *Films on Art, 1952;* Professor Theodore Bowie; Perry Miller Adato, formerly of the Film Center, then NET; Rosalind Kossoff, first of AF Films, then of Film Images until 1969; Arthur Knight, film critic; William Sloan, Editor of *Film Library Quarterly*, and Rohama Lee, Editor of *Film News*, and their lively contributors; Margareta Akermark, consistent supporter of films on art at The Museum of Modern Art; and, outstanding among other perceptive distributors, Leo Dratfield of Films Incorporated, Tom Brandon of Brandon Films, Wesley Greene of International Film Bureau, Eva Kroy Wisbar of Visual Resources, and Christian and Michael Blackwood of Blackwood Films.

Dorothy Macpherson
Director
Canadian Centre for Films on Art

Preface

Those of us who have worked on this book in Canada and the United States aimed at bringing together a selection of films on the fine arts that would help programmers and teachers make wise decisions. Although there are other catalogs and indexes that identify art films, none are designed to provide this evaluative service. Existing major indexes attempt to catalog everything in the film field on a nonselective basis; it is both a strength and a weakness. The result is that the inaccurate and poorly-made film is listed alongside the film of merit. In addition major film indexes often overlook works from independent filmmakers and small distributors—works which are included here. Our intent has been to bring together films which make exciting teaching and exciting programming possible.

At the time when The American Federation of Arts was planning to bring out a new and updated version of its original 1952 book, *Films on Art*, it was fortunate in securing the services of Dorothy Macpherson of the Canadian Centre for Films on Art. She is well known as the foremost authority on the subject in North America and has built an outstanding basic collection of films on art at the National Gallery of Canada.

Mrs. Macpherson secured the services of filmmaker and scholar Jean Cleinge to carry out, under her supervision, the work of compiling titles, putting together bibliographic data, and writing annotations. When they had completed gathering a large number of titles and information, they sent the material to us in New York to review and make suggestions.

As the two of us considered the hundreds of titles, we evaluated the entries from our experience in the film libraries of an art museum and a public library. In carrying out this work we have been asked what criteria we used. Our answer is that we looked for films that were appropriate subjects for such a listing, that were effective with audiences, and that met standards of good filmmaking. We also considered how the film had been received by a wide range of audiences, from sophisticated museum-goers to those with a beginner's interest in art and art history. To be included a film had to meet the demands of at least some sector of the public, and so much the better if it was one of those rare films that reached a variety of audiences.

As we reviewed the material, we also came to realize what a difficult task the filmmaker had set for himself when he undertook to interpret on film a work of art, to translate one medium into another. Furthermore, as we examined the films, we became aware of the large number that had been made for television. These films, though often carefully researched and skillfully produced, usually had an entirely different esthetic from those films made primarily for theatrical and non-theatrical exhibition. Thus, the character of a large number of the films in this 1977 edition of *Films on Art* is quite different from those in the 1952 edition, few of which were produced for television.

William Sloan
Supervising Film Librarian
New York Public Library

Margareta Akermark
Associate Director, Department of Film
The Museum of Modern Art, New York

Acknowledgments

The American Federation of Arts is pleased to present this source book, *Films on Art*, for use wherever films on art are shown.

As is always the case with a project of this scope, there are numerous individuals who have aided in its preparation whose contributions can never be fully acknowledged. I would like to take this opportunity, though, to express our special appreciation to the central contributors and in particular the Canadian Centre for Films on Art—Dorothy Macpherson, Director; Jean Cleinge, Special Film Consultant; and Barbara Munro, Coordinator—for completing the book in spite of what, at times, seemed like insurmountable obstacles. Warm thanks are also extended to William Sloan, Supervising Film Librarian of the New York Public Library System, and Margareta Akermark, Associate Director, Department of Film, The Museum of Modern Art, who were special advisers on the project, and have painstakingly reviewed its preparation at critical stages. We are also grateful to Willard Van Dyke, Chairman of the AFA Film Advisory Committee and former Director of The Museum of Modern Art's Film Department, who was an instrumental supporter of the project from its inception.

In addition, I would like to thank Dr. Jean Sutherland Boggs, whose support on behalf of the National Gallery of Canada came at a crucial moment; Henri Moquin of the National Film Board of Canada for his supervision during the final stages of the book's preparation; Steven Aronson, Director of the AFA Film Program, who coordinated the numerous aspects of the project; Marilyn Singer, freelance writer, who assisted invaluably in the preparation of the Introduction; and Susan Dallas, the AFA Film Coordinator, who prepared the subject index.

Finally, I wish to thank Donald Holden of Watson-Guptill Publications, who has been the most patient and thorough of publishers, and without whose constant encouragement this book would never have been possible. Mrs. Macpherson has also indicated special acknowledgments in her Foreword to this book, and to these individuals, as well as to all those who remain unnamed, we extend our deepest thanks.

Wilder Green
Director
The American Federation of Arts

Introduction

In 1952, The American Federation of Arts published a reference text entitled *Films on Art, 1952* which, as Dorothy Macpherson points out in her Foreword to this volume, grew out of two AFA-sponsored film festivals and was one of the first publications in the United States to deal with the film on art. The text, now out of print and outdated in many respects, included several introductory essays which made important statements on the nature of the film on art. Perhaps Dr. H. W. Janson in his essay "College Use of Films on Art" summarized best:

> What, then, is the film on art? First of all, it is not, and never can be, the equivalent of an illustrated lecture. Those comparatively few pictures where the continuity is provided by the spoken commentary, rather than by the images themselves, invariably fail to hold the viewer's attention. . . In other words, the basic *sine qua non* of a good film on art is that it must be an effective motion picture in both conception and execution.

Since the art of filmmaking has greatly developed in the past twenty-five years, it follows that the film on art has developed with it. It was with this in mind that AFA requested the Canadian Centre for Films on Art to compile for the user of films on art—the film librarian, the art educator, the museum or organization programmer, the audio-visual specialist, and the interested layman—a new source book which lists and describes over 450 selected films currently available from sources in the United States and Canada. The films range from television series, curriculum films, and lectures to works by independent filmmakers, and documents of exhibitions as well as the lives and works of individual artists. They do not include "how-to," classroom films, nor, with a few notable exceptions, animation, avant-garde, or industrial films. What the selected films all have in common is quality and availability to English-speaking audiences.

Initial reference material that formed the basis for the present volume included the two editions of the *Répertoire général international* (see Foreword) and the ten catalogs prepared over as many years by the Canadian Centre for Films on Art for the National Gallery of Canada. To supplement and bring the information up-to-date, Jean Cleinge, film producer (*VAN EYCK: FATHER OF FLEMISH PAINTING, MEMLING, RUBENS*) and cinéaste, was engaged by the Centre to research the whole field of films on art, including every available index from the Library of Congress listings to periodicals and distributors' catalogs. Over 2,000 titles were provisionally assembled and brief descriptions written at the Centre. The selection was made in cooperation with William Sloan and Margareta Akermark, who discuss the selections in their Preface.

Although compromises were sometimes necessary, the basis for all selections remained "quality." At the heart of the evaluation, as is the case in any evaluation process, was strong personal response. As Iris Barry, in her essay "Pioneering in Films on Art," put it:

> It is true, I think, that almost all films of any real quality of this kind seem to furnish a particular sensation of delight in seeing something with a new depth and penetration, as if for the first time: which is, again, the particular property of the motion picture. It exhibits. It also discovers. This sense of discovery, very like that of an astigmatic person who suddenly sees a new and richer world when he first puts on his new spectacles, even persists to a greater or less degree through subsequent viewings of the same film.

Does the film delight? Does it evoke a sense of discovery? Will it endure? These are important questions—questions of quality based on personal response—which governed the careful selection of the entries.

13

The book consists of alphabetical entries for the films, three indexes, and a list of sources and their addresses. The information in the entries was assembled by Jean Cleinge and is explained by him as follows:

NOTES ON ENTRIES

1. *Title*: This is normally listed as it appears on the print, but in rare cases where another title is given in distributors' catalogs, the second is also mentioned. The original title of a foreign film is given in brackets unless it is more commonly used than its translation; in such circumstances it is retained as the main title. Individual films from series are generally listed under the name of the series: for example, *GRANDEUR AND OBEDIENCE* is located under the entry for Sir Kenneth Clark's series *Civilisation*.

2. *Duration*: The nearest number of minutes of running time for the actual release print. When the running time is different from that of the original version, the credits denote this by "initially _____ minutes."

3. *Color*: The entry indicates whether the film is in color or black and white (B&W).

4. *Gauge*: All entries refer to available 16mm prints. When the original negative is 35mm, this is noted as it may have an influence on the quality of the print and it also indicates the possibility of obtaining a 35mm print for theatrical presentation.

5. *Sound*: All films have an optical sound track except for the very few indicated as silent. No films with magnetic sound tracks are listed.

6. *Country of Origin*: This generally refers to the country of the main production company. In some cases of international co-production, and with some multi-national film companies, two or more countries are mentioned.

7. *Date*: This generally refers to the first showing of the original version, often quite different from the date given in distributors' catalogs. There are many dates in the life of a film: the start of production, the copyright, the general release, the English version of foreign productions, the revised version, and the acquisition by the last distributor. Accurate information is important in order to differentiate between several films made on the same subject. In addition, dating is important because it reflects color changes in stock and print quality.

8. *Producer*: The producer is the individual, group, or company responsible for the making of the film. The name of the producer is occasionally followed by that of a sponsoring individual or organization.

9. *Credits*: These include all those who made important personal contributions: the director, the writer (who is sometimes narrator and participant), the photographer and the chief consultants. From these names, specialists can derive a good idea of the film's style and approach to its subject. When an original score has been composed for the film, the composer's name is also listed.

10. *Summary*: A brief description is followed by a more detailed account of what is shown and discussed, with an indication of how the film could be used.

11. *Distribution*: Rights to the films are held by distributors whose names and addresses are essential information. When demand for a film is insufficient, rights are not always renewed when agreements terminate, and it may be withdrawn from distribution or passed on to another company. Therefore, while every effort has been made to supply up-to-date information on sources, frequent changes do occur. We regret any inconvenience this may cause. We also hope that the information in this book will increase demand and thus prevent valuable films from disappearing from circulation.

Following the entries in this volume are three indexes and an alphabetical listing of the Canadian and American distributors for the films.

NOTES ON INDEXES

1. *Subject Index*: This index has been developed for the general film user. The films are divided into a wide variety of subject areas as well as the more obvious headings of art mediums, historical periods, and artist's nationality or chosen country of residence. Each film is given several entries whenever possible. Individual artists are not listed in this index.

2. *Artist Index*: Artists' names are listed with birth and death dates wherever possible. Survey films in which a particular artist is one among others of a period, movement, etc. are listed along with films devoted solely to the artist in question.

3. *Alphabetical Index*: All the films in this volume are listed here alphabetically, including individual films that are part of series and alternate film titles.

HOW TO ORDER FILMS USING THIS BOOK

The sources listed in this publication include commercial educational film distributors, university film libraries, museums, independent film producers, textbook publishers, galleries, public relations departments of corporations, governmental agencies, embassies, and filmmakers' cooperatives. These all differ greatly in services and policies. Some sources charge per individual screening of a film, while others bill for an entire week's screenings; still others charge only a small handling fee, while some have a free loan program. Some sources maintain large stocks of circulating prints and can therefore fill virtually all requests, while others have only one print that is in constant use. There are distributors who have established high standards for print quality and others who supply prints that may be worn. Some assess film users for damage to prints; others do not. Some accept telephone orders; others require pre-payment. There are sources that restrict film use to classrooms and others that permit public presentations for which admission may be charged, just as there are some who will not rent films to individuals, and others who will not rent to commercial cinemas. Some distributors have catalogs available on request and extra material on the films, such as program notes, stills, bibliographies, and study guides. Many will provide a free preview of a film being considered for purchase, but few will do the same for a film being considered for rental. The point is that to acquire information on prices, policies, services, and available films, the best—indeed the only—means is to write or telephone the distributor.

Once a programmer has selected a particular film for rental and located the address of the distributor in the back of the book, he or she should write stating the nature of the presentation (classroom, restricted screening, commercial presentation, etc.), whether admission is to be charged, the date desired (and an alternate, if possible), and, according to his or her understanding, the rental fee. If the distributor requires additional information, the user will be contacted. If no further information is needed, a confirmation of the order will be sent. If pre-payment is not expected the user will be billed at the time of the showing. The film should arrive a day or two before the screening date; if it is not received, the user should contact the source immediately. Cancellations are generally accepted if the film has not been shipped.

Anyone who considers purchasing a film with which he or she is not completely familiar is advised to ask for a preview. If this is the policy of the distributor, a confirmation and a preview print will be sent at the earliest possible date. Preview prints are in constant use, therefore their condition should not be taken as a guide to the quality of the purchase print. Anyone deciding to buy the film should send an order, which the distributor will fill as promptly as possible.

OTHER SOURCES

Some listed films may be in the collections of local university and college film libraries, public libraries, and museums which are not given here because they do not serve a national audience. These sources often have free loan or rental programs for groups and individuals. They are well worth investigating. For a partial list of film libraries send $5.00 to the Educational Film Library Association, 43 West 61st Street, New York, New York 10023, requesting a copy of their directory to university and college film collections.

A SPECIAL NOTE FOR FILM DISTRIBUTORS AND PRODUCERS

Please let the following organizations know of any new films on art completed or released which should be included in future editions of this book, together with changes of address and other relevant information.

The American Federation of Arts
41 East 65th Street
New York, New York 10021
U.S.A.

Canadian Centre for Films on Art
150 Kent Street
Ottawa, Ontario   K1A 0M9
Canada

Films on art

The Films

A PROPOS DES GOBELINS
27 mins. Color. France. 1970.

Producer: Agence française d'images.

Credits: Daniel Creusot, director.

Summary: Various aspects of French contemporary tapestry are shown in a visit to the Gobelins State Manufactory. Jean Lurçat, Mario Prassinos, and Victor Vasarely are among the well-known artist-designers who appear in the film.

U.S. distributor: FACSEA (rental, English version).

Canadian Distributor: Embassy of France (loan, French version).

ABDUCTION OF THE EMPEROR OF JAPAN
10 mins. Color. U.S.A. 1963.

Producer: Daniel Stempler for Gemini.

Credits: Bradley Smith, director and writer; Wango Weng, animation; Joseph Julian, narrator.

Summary: A lively and touching description of an historical event—the near-successful attempt to kidnap the Emperor of Japan. Photographed directly from the original Heiji-Monogatari-Emaki twelfth-century Japanese hand-painted scroll in the Boston Museum of Fine Arts. Details show violence and disorder between the fighting factions, chaotic court life, and colorful costumes and decor.

U.S. distributor: Film Images (sales and rental).

ABOUT A TAPESTRY
9 mins. Color. Switzerland. 1972.

Producer: Isa Hesse.

Credits: Ernst Bertschi and Isa Hesse, directors; Hermann Hesse, writer; Fred Haines, translator and narrator.

Summary: Ten years after Hermann Hesse's death, his daughter pays tribute to him by using his own comments to analyze a tapestry in his studio. This colorful piece, woven by Maria Gerö, is composed of birds, beasts, trees, and flowers; the writer discovers in it a universe of harmony, the celebration of life, designed by dedicated hands. Following the text of the novelist, the filmmakers give new dimension to a modest work of art.

U.S. distributor: New Yorker Films (sales and rental).

Canadian distributor: International Tele-Film Enterprises (rental).

THE ACROPOLIS OF ATHENS
30 mins. Color. Greece. 1960.

Producer: Argo Film Production.

Credits: R. Manthoulis and H. Papadakis, directors; Yannis A. Papayoannoy, music.

Summary: The film discusses the Sacred Rock from archaic times until the end of the classical period, and gives an analysis of its three main structures, the Parthenon, the Erechtheum, and the Temple of Nike. Original score is from ancient Greek melodies.

Canadian distributor: Embassy of Greece (loan).

AN ACT OF FAITH (*Look Up and Live* series)
20 mins. Initially 38 mins. Color. Britain. 1967.

Producer: BBC-TV.

Credits: John Read, director; Robin Whitworth, writer; Leo Genn, narrator; Kenneth Pakeman, music.

Summary: Covers all the stages of the rebuilding of the new Coventry Cathedral, which replaces the Medieval building destroyed by aerial bombardment. BBC cameramen followed the workers over a period of six years and visited the studios of the artists involved. Graham Sutherland designed the largest tapestry in the world, specially woven at Felletin in France; Sir Jacob Epstein conceived *St. Michael and the Devil,* one of his last sculptures; John Piper and three artists of the Royal College of Art created the immense stained glass windows. The architect was Sir Basil Spence.

Canadian distributor: BBC-TV Enterprises (sales and rental).

THE ADORATION OF THE MAGI
7 mins. Color. U.S.A. 1973.

Producers: David W. Powell and Cherrill Anson for the National Gallery of Art and Visual Images in cooperation with WETA-TV.

Credits: David W. Powell, director; Cherrill Anson, writer; Richard McLanathan, consultant; Daniel C. Diggles, Peter Vogt, and Stanley Wojewodski, narrators; Camerata Chorus of Washington and Point Branch Pro Musica, music.

Summary: A study in close-up of a single painting from the Samuel H. Kress collection: *The Adoration of the Magi* by Fra Angelico and Fra Filippo Lippi. The treatment brings the viewer into close contact with this fifteenth-century Florentine panel, with appropriate accompaniment of Medieval carols and Renaissance dance music.

U.S. distributor: National Gallery of Art (loan).

ADVENTURES IN PERCEPTION (*Living Arts in the Netherlands* series)
22 mins. Color. Netherlands. 1970.

Producer: Han van Gelder, Filmproduktie for the Ministry of Foreign Affairs.

Credits: Han van Gelder, director; Hans Locher and Jonne Severijn, writers; Felix Visser, narrator.

Summary: A good introduction to the work of the Dutch graphic artist Maurits Escher, filmed two years before his death. His drawings are specially suitable for camera work and animation: they are based on scientific principles, perspective, and visual illusions and metamorphosis (distortion of space). A concise commentary is enriched by Escher's comments about himself and his fascinating work.

U.S. distributor: BFA (sales and rental).

Canadian distributor: Holt, Rinehart and Winston (sales and rental); Canadian Film Institute for the Royal Netherlands Embassy (service charge).

AFRICAN ART AND SCULPTURE (*Tell It Like It Was* series)
21 mins. Color. U.S.A. 1971.

Producer: WCAU-TV, Philadelphia.

Credits: Michael Babatunde Olatunji, Dallie, narrators.

Summary: Ceremonial masks, sculptured animals and birds, bronze jewelry, and other art objects reveal the African's ancient reverence for beauty and living things, and his intellectual curiosity as he sought to understand the mysteries of fertility, life, and death. The film was made in Rhodesia, Nigeria, Gambia, and Mali.

U.S. distributor: Carousel Films (sales and rental); Association Films, Inc. (rental).

Canadian distributor: Marlin Motion Pictures (sales and rental).

AFRICAN CRAFTSMEN: THE ASHANTI
11 mins. Color. U.S.A. 1970.

Producer: Frank Gardonyi and Clifford Janoff.

Summary: The Ashanti tribesmen of Ghana in West Africa are skilled in many arts and crafts, including weaving and wood carving. Meticulous construction and decoration of their ceremonial wooden stools are part of the Ashanti tradition.

U.S. distributor: BFA (sales and rental).

Canadian distributor: Holt, Rinehart and Winston (sales and rental).

THE AGE OF ROCOCO (*Europäisches Rokoko*)
23 mins. Color. Originally 35mm. Federal Republic of Germany. 1958.

Producer: Walter Leckebusch, Munich.

Credits: Walter Leckebusch, director; Arno Schoenberger, Halldor Soehner, writers: Ludwig Kusche, music.

Summary: Made on the occasion of an exhibition organized in 1958 in Munich by the Council of Europe. The film presents a comprehensive review of the art and decoration of the eighteenth century, with paintings by Boucher, Nattier, Lancret, Moreau, Watteau, Gainsborough, and Canaletto. The ideas of the period are expressed by sculptured heads of the philosophers associated with them. Porcelain figures by Bustelli represent the characters of the Italian comedy at a period which can be considered the golden age of theater and opera. China, gold, silverware, and sumptuous religious art complete the description of the period.
(It should be mentioned that the colors of the print are somewhat faded.)

U.S. distributor: AV-ED Films (sales).

Canadian distributor: Canadian Film Institute for the National Gallery of Canada (loan).

THE AGE OF THE ROCOCO—FROM DIVINE RIGHT TO EQUALITY
(*History Through Art* series)
17 mins. Color. U.S.A. 1961.

Producer: Alemann Films.

Credits: Johanna Alemann, director; period music (Mozart).

Summary: The Rococo style is examined in the perspective of the period from the reign of Louis XIV in Versailles to the French Revolution and the declaration of American independence. Paintings by Watteau and others, architecture in Germany and Austria, and exquisite domestic interiors enriched with china and porcelain are studied in detail. (Study guide available.)

U.S. distributor: Alemann Films (sales).

Canadian distributor: International Tele-Film Enterprises (sales and rental).

ALBERT GLEIZES
16 mins. Color. Originally 35mm. France. 1967.

Producer: Les Films du Cyprès.

Credits: Pierre Alibert, director and writer; Bernard Dorival, consultant; Philip Gaunt, narrator; Perotin-le-Grand, music.

Summary: An analysis of the works and theories of Albert Gleizes, whose experiments in the rediscovery of form led eventually to the development of Cubism. A comparison of his successive treatments of the same object demonstrates the evolution of modern painting from Impressionism onwards.

U.S. distributor: International Film Bureau (sales and rental).

Canadian distributor: Educational Film Distributors (rental).

ALBERTO BURRI

13 mins. Color. Originally 35mm. Italy. 1960.

Producer: G. Martello, Corona Cinematografica, Rome.

Credits: Giovanni Carandente, director and writer; Franco Potenza, music.

Summary: Burri's abstract art studied through the development of his various techniques. After a brief account of his life, he is seen working on sacking, heated plastic, wood, and iron. His research with "combustions" is stressed. Many of his more significant works are reviewed.

U.S. distributor: Istituto Italiano di Cultura (loan).

ALBERTO GIACOMETTI

28 mins. Color. Switzerland. 1966.

Producer: Studio Scheidegger Productions, Zurich.

Credits: Ernst Scheidegger and Peter Münger, directors; Jacques Dupin, writer; Lance Tschannen, narrator; Armin Schibler, music.

Summary: More than a film on Giacometti, this is a film made in collaboration with Giacometti. In his Montparnasse studio—which he occupied from 1927—he draws and paints the portrait of Jacques Dupin, who gives his impressions both as model and friend of the artist. This sequence leads to a frank conversation on Giacometti's life and his conception of art. Childhood memories are evoked from views of his village in the Grisons district of the Swiss mountains. A selection of his sculpture includes the gigantic statues in the garden of the Maeght Foundation in the south of France. The last sequence of the film, made shortly before his death in 1966, shows Giacometti working on a small head in his Paris studio.

U.S. distributors: Film Images (sales and rental); Embassy of Switzerland, Washington, D.C. (loan).

Canadian distributor: Embassy of Switzerland (loan).

ALBERTO GIACOMETTI, 1901-1966

12 mins. Color. U.S.A. 1965.

Producer: Sumner Glimcher for C.M.C. Productions, Columbia University, New York.

Credits: Stuart Chasmar, director; Professor James H. Beck, Columbia University, consultant; Philip Sterling, narrator; Arnold Gamson, music.

Summary: A presentation of the works exhibited at the Museum of Modern Art in the last major retrospective just before the artist's death. The narration is a distillation of Giacometti's own writings, emphasizing his concern with reality and the relationship of man to man. Fifty years of his work are represented in drawings, paintings, and sculpture.

U.S. distributor: The Museum of Modern Art (rental); New York University Film Library (rental).

Canadian distributor: International Tele-Film Enterprises (sales and rental); Canadian Film Institute for the National Gallery of Canada (loan).

ALBRECHT DÜRER
10 mins. B&W. Britain. 1961.

Producer: BBC-TV.

Credits: Nicholas Selby, narrator; Sir Huw Weldon, television program editor.

Summary: The story of Albrecht Dürer, his life, his works, and most important of all, his philosophy. His masterpieces of woodcutting and engraving are shown, and the narration used is Dürer's own, taken directly from his writings.

U.S. distributor: Time-Life (sales only).

Canadian distributor: BBC-TV Enterprises (sales and rental).

ALBRECHT DÜRER (*Albrecht Dürer 1471-1528*)
12 mins. Color. Federal Republic of Germany. 1954.

Producer: Walter Leckebusch Film Studio, Munich.

Credits: Walter Leckebusch, director; Dorothée Randorf, writer.

Summary: A straightforward account of the life and work of the great German painter and engraver. With the city of Nuremberg as background, the film illuminates the Medieval ambience from which Dürer almost singlehandedly launched the Northern Renaissance.

U.S. distributor: Visual Resources (sales and rental).

Canadian distributor: Canadian Film Institute for the Embassy of the Federal Republic of Germany (rental).

ALECHINSKY (*Alechinsky d'après nature*)
21 mins. Color. Belgium. 1972.

Producer: Luc de Heusch for Belgian Ministry of Culture and Albina Productions, Paris.

Credits: Luc de Heusch, director and writer; Michel Portal, Jean-Pierre Drouet and Barre Philips, music.

Summary: Made with close cooperation between the artist and the director, the film is a document not only on Alechinsky's work, but also on his inner world and his memories. Old personal and family photographs, an animated sequence conceived and made by the artist, and shots from the Carnival of Binche, Belgium, are all interspersed with scenes of Alechinsky painting with acrylics, drawing with ink, and throwing water on his drawing to change its shape. A few paintings are shown that illustrate the personal signs he used as the handwriting of an imaginary language.

U.S. distributor: International Film Bureau (sales and rental).

Canadian distributor: Educational Film Distributors (sales and rental).

ALEX KATZ, ONE FLIGHT UP
8 mins. B&W. U.S.A. 1971.

Producer: Rudy Burckhardt

Credits: Rudy Burckhardt, director.

Summary: The entire film consists of different views of painted cut-out heads accompanied by the spoken lyrics of "Sergeant Pepper's Lonely Hearts Club Band." Alex Katz asked some thirty-five friends to pose for him. He painted them on aluminum and cut out the shapes they made. Mounted on a fifteen-foot table or standing on the floor, they were all brought together for an imaginary party. John Giorno made a tape of the people reciting a few lines of the Beatles' song.

U.S. distributor: Rudy Burckhardt (sales).

ALEXANDER CALDER: FROM THE CIRCUS TO THE MOON
15 mins. Color. U.S.A. 1963.

Producer: Hans Richter.

Credits: Hans Richter, director; Arnold Eagle, photographer; David Diamond, music.

Summary: Alexander Calder, world-famous for his mobiles, creates in his studio a personal world of animals and circus figures. Hans Richter touches them with moonbeams.

U.S. distributor: The Museum of Modern Art (rental).

Canadian distributor: Canadian Film Institute for the National Gallery of Canada (loan).

ALFRED WALLIS—ARTIST AND MARINER
23 mins. Color. Britain. 1973.

Producer: Mason Bruce Film Associates for the Arts Council of Great Britain.

Credits: Christopher Mason, director; Ben Nance, harmonium.

Summary: The works of this primitive artist are juxtaposed with past and present views of St. Ives in Cornwall, England, his hometown. Friends and relatives of the painter-fisherman provide the commentary.

U.S. distributor: The American Federation of Arts (rental); Films Incorporated (sales).

ALTAR MASTERPIECE (*The Work of Veit Stoss*) (*Dzielo Mistrza Stwosza*)
20 mins. B&W. Poland. 1952.

Producer: Film Polski.

Credits: Stanislaw Modzenski, director; Waldo Sait, English text; M. Carnovsky, narrator; Andrzej Panufnik, music.

Summary: The restoration after the war of the famous high altar created between 1477 and 1489 by Veit Stoss, master wood-carver and sculptor. The altar was located in St. Mary's Church, Krakow, from 1849 until World War II when the Nazis moved it to Nuremberg. "Gothic Concerto," composed for this film, is based on traditional Polish music of the sixteenth and seventeenth centuries.

U.S. distributor: Macmillan (sales and rental).

Canadian distributor: Canadian Film Institute for the National Gallery of Canada (loan).

AMEDEO MODIGLIANI
12 mins. B&W. Britain. 1962.

Producer: BBC-TV.

Credits: Nancy Thomas, director; Paulette Preney, narrator.

Summary: An interview with Modigliani's daughter Jeanne, in which she traces his artistic development. Many examples of his sculpture and painting illustrate her assessment of the artist's work.

U.S. distributor: Time-Life (sales only).

Canadian distributor: BBC-TV Enterprises (sales and rental).

AMERICA: THE ARTIST'S EYE (John Trumbull, Edwin Forbes, lithographs of Currier and Ives, Thomas Eakins)
14 mins. B&W. U.S.A. 1963.

Producer: Westinghouse Broadcasting Company.

Credits: Howard C. Jensen, director.

Summary: A brief survey of over one hundred years of history. The film includes: Trumbull's paintings of the Revolution; the Civil War etchings of Forbes; lithographs by Currier and Ives of mid- and late-nineteenth-century life; Eakins' paintings of late-nineteenth and early-twentieth-century social life.

U.S. distributor: Films Incorporated (sales and rental).

AMERICA TROPICAL
30 mins. Color. U.S.A. 1972.

Producer: KCET, Los Angeles, for NET.

Credits: Barry Nye, director.

Summary: The story of the struggle surrounding the mural *America Tropical*, which shows a man crucified upon a double cross under the eagle of U.S. currency, painted by Mexican political artist David Alfaro Siqueiros in 1932 in Los Angeles. After its appearance the government refused to renew Siqueiros' visa and within two years the entire mural was covered with whitewash. Siqueiros was painting the plight of the Mexican-American at a time when over 200,000 Mexican and Mexican-American citizens were being deported to Mexico on buses chartered by the Los Angeles County Welfare Department. The mural has recently been restored and preserved and the film shows the delicate process involved.

U.S. distributor: Indiana University (sales and rental).

Canadian distributor: Canadian Film Institute (sales); International Tele-Film Enterprises (sales and rental).

AMERICAN ART IN THE SIXTIES
58 mins. Color. U.S.A. 1973.

Producer: Blackwood Productions.

Credits: Michael Blackwood, director; Barbara Rose, writer and narrator.

Summary: A survey of the revolutionary trends of the 1960s—Pop art, Minimal art, Happenings, Post-Painterly Abstraction—made as a follow-up to Blackwood's *The New York School*. Painting and sculpture are presented by the following artists and experts: Carl André, Ron Davis, Dan Flavin, Sam Francis, Helen Frankenthaler, Ed Kienholz, Robert Irwin, Jasper Johns, Donald Judd, Ellsworth Kelly, Roy Lichtenstein, Morris Louis, Robert Morris, Kenneth Noland, Claes Oldenburg, Jules Olitski, Robert Rauschenberg, Larry Rivers, Ed Ruscha, George Segal, Frank Stella, Andy Warhol, Jack Youngerman, John Cage, Leo Castelli, and Clement Greenberg.

U.S. distributor: Blackwood Productions (sales and rental).

AMERICAN FOLK ART
13 mins. B&W. Britain. 1967.

Producer: BBC-TV.

Credits: Nancy Thomas, director.

Summary: An introduction to American folk art, only recently considered to be an authentic art form. Folk art was produced in the late eighteenth and early nineteenth centuries by itinerant painters, who were unknown and untrained. This primitive and charming style has had a marked influence on American painters of this century.

Canadian distributor: BBC-TV Enterprises (sales and rental).

AMERICAN FOLK ART (*Smithsonian* series)
24 mins. Color. U.S.A. 1966.

Producer: Craig Fisher, NBC News.

Credits: Craig Fisher, director and writer; Dr. Gerald S. Lesser, Harvard University, consultant.

Summary: Spontaneous creations of untrained craftsmen, produced in the United States during the eighteenth and nineteenth centuries and now preserved in the Smithsonian Institution. The narration contributes to an understanding of the effects of industrial, economic, historical, and social influences on art forms new and old.

U.S. distributor: McGraw-Hill Films (sales and rental).

THE AMERICAN IMAGE
54 mins. Color. U.S.A. 1967.

Producer: Frank De Felitta for NBC News.

Credits: Frank De Felitta, director; Aline Saarinen and John Lord, writers; E. G. Marshall, narrator; Glenn Paxton, music.

Summary: The United States of America, as seen through the eyes of its artists from Colonial days to the present. The survey is based on the resources of the Whitney Museum of American Art and the exhibition that opened its new building in New York City, "Art of the United States, 1670-1966"—one of the most comprehensive collections of American painting and sculpture ever assembled. Outstanding American artists, including Andrew Wyeth, Edward Hopper, Jack Levine, Robert Rauschenberg, and the late Stuart Davis, are interviewed in their studios and discuss their work.

U.S. distributor: McGraw-Hill Films (sales and rental).

Canadian distributor: McGraw-Hill Ryerson (sales and rental).

AMERICAN REALISTS
Part 1 (Eighteenth-Nineteenth Centuries)
23 mins. Color. U.S.A. 1965.

Part 2 (Twentieth Century)
14 mins. Color. U.S.A. 1965.

Producer: Harry Atwood, University of Arizona Radio-TV Bureau.

Credits: Harry Atwood, director; Robert M. Quinn, writer and narrator; Robert Muczynski, music.

Summary: A lively survey of American painters who remained essentially realist despite classical, romantic, and modern European influences. Both parts are based on a retrospective exhibition of paintings at the University of Arizona Museum of Art.

Part 1. Covers the period from colonial times to the Armory Show of 1913. Many artists are represented: Copley, Stuart, the Peales, Homer, Eakins, Ryder, Inness, the Hudson River School, Western scene painters, the Impressionists, and the New York Realists.

Part 2. Provides an analysis and historical perspective of realist paintings and painters from 1913 to the present. Included in the group are Stuart Davis, Walt Kuhn, Ben Shahn, Andrew Wyeth, John Marin, Ivan Albright, Milton Avery, Charles Demuth, and Reginald Marsh.

U.S. distributor: McGraw-Hill Films (sales and rental).

Canadian distributor: Canadian Film Institute for the National Gallery of Canada (loan).

AMERICAN SCULPTURE OF THE SIXTIES
19 mins. Color. U.S.A. 1967.

Producer: Harvey Flax for the Los Angeles County Museum of Art.

Credits: Jules Engel, director.

Summary: Major works of thirty-three prominent American sculptors filmed at the exhibition at the Los Angeles County Museum of Art. Artists represented include: Rauschenberg, Nakian, Noguchi, Judd, Kienholz, Nevelson, Cornell, Chamberlain, Conner, Harris, David Smith, Oldenburg, Calder, and Westerman.

U.S. distributor: Visual Resources (sales and rental).

THE AMERICAN VISION
35 mins. Color. Originally 35mm. U.S.A. 1965.

Producer: Francis C. Thayer, United States Productions for the National Gallery of Art.

Credits: J. Carter Brown, director and writer; Burgess Meredith, narrator; Frank Ledle Moore, music.

Summary: J. Carter Brown, now director of the National Gallery of Art, describes in chronological order American works from the late eighteenth to the early twentieth century displayed in the National Gallery of Art, Washington, D.C. The paintings reflect the national traits and interests of the time. They show people, landscapes, and scenes from everyday life painted in native and European traditions.

U.S. distributor: EBEC (sales and rental); National Gallery of Art (loan).

Canadian distributor: Canadian Film Institute (rental).

THE AMERICANS: THREE EAST COAST ARTISTS AT WORK
19 mins. Color. U.S.A. 1962.

Producer: Warren Forma, Forma Art Associates.

Credits: Warren Forma, director and photographer.

Summary: Three artists, Milton Avery, Hans Hofmann, and Jack Tworkov, painted for many years in Provincetown, Massachusetts. Hofmann and Tworkov are shown working and talking in their studios there. Avery, who spent many years in the same Cape Cod village, is seen in his New York apartment-studio in the last film ever shot of him.

U.S. distributor: Forma Art Associates (sales and rental).

Canadian distributor: Canadian Film Institute for the National Gallery of Canada (loan).

ANACOSTIA: MUSEUM IN THE GHETTO
18 mins. B&W. U.S.A. 1968.

Producer: John O'Toole, Carol Oughton for NET and Radio Center.

Credits: Garth Dietrick, director.

Summary: Shows how a neighborhood museum, a branch of the Smithsonian Institution located in a Washington ghetto, is bringing beauty, creativity, and joy to the children living there. Candid scenes show the museum's policy of involving children in its activities. The Smithsonian's secretary and patrons of the local museum present the rationale for the project. A youth explains why there is no vandalism of the exhibits. Scenes of the museum's surroundings emphasize a plea for more institutions to enter the ghettos.

U.S. distributor: Indiana University (sales and rental).

ANCIENT ART IN NORWAY
20 mins. Color. Norway. 1968.

Producer: Norsk Film A/S for the Ministry of Foreign Affairs.

Summary: The animal motif in ancient Norwegian art. Richly carved stave churches, engravings on stone, ornamentation of Viking ships, and objects discovered in Viking graves repeat the same theme.

U.S. distributor: Modern Talking Picture Services for the Norwegian Information Service in the United States (loan).

Canadian distributor: The Canadian Film Institute for the Embassy of Norway (rental).

ANCIENT ART OF PERU
15 mins. Color. U.S.A. 1960.

Producer: Penelope Strouth and François Piraud.

Credits: Penelope Strouth and François Piraud, directors and writers; Karl Lunde, narrator.

Summary: A survey of the art of the main civilizations of pre-Columbian Peru, which extended over a period of three thousand years. Ceramics, carvings, and textiles representing the Chavin, Mochica, Chimu, Tiahuanaco, and Inca cultures are shown principally by a succession of still photographs, some in close-up. The beauty of the film is due to the quality and colors of the works which have been selected. Ethnic music played on native instruments provides the accompaniment.

U.S. distributor: Film Images (sales and rental).

Canadian distributor: Canadian Film Institute for the National Gallery of Canada (loan).

THE ANCIENT CHINESE
24 mins. Color. U.S.A. 1974.

Producer: Julien Bryan, International Film Foundation.

Credits: Philip Stapp, designer.

Summary: In today's China, ancient customs and rituals are more a part of everyday life than in any other civilization. Examples are taken from Peking's Forbidden City, from a silk farm, and from an artist practicing calligraphy. Animation and actual photography based on early Chinese representations in works of art from outstanding museums and private collections, combined with views of China today, give life to the ancient traditions of China.

U.S. distributor: International Film Foundation (sales and rental).

Canadian distributor: Educational Film Distributors (sales and rental).

THE ANCIENT NEW WORLD
16 mins. Color. U.S.A. 1964.

Producer: Churchill Films with Ginn and Co.

Credits: David Hilberman, director.

Summary: The rise and fall of early civilizations in Mexico and Central America are described through animation and the use of pre-Columbian art objects. The film traces man's development from his migration from Asia during the ice ages to the period of high culture—the splendor of the Mayan civilization and the rise of the magnificent Aztec city-state.

U.S. distributor: Churchill Films (sales and rental).

Canadian distributor: Gordon Watt Films (sales and rental).

THE ANCIENT PERUVIAN
27 mins. Color. U.S.A. 1968.

Producer: Julien Bryan for International Film Foundation.

Credits: James D. Sage, director and writer; Sam Bryan, photographer; Gerald McDermott, animation; Thomas Wagner, music.

Summary: Live-action and animation inspired by Indian motifs trace the rise and fall of the Inca empire. The art, architecture, religions, and society of the pre-Columbian Peruvian are contrasted with scenes of contemporary life.

U.S. distributor: International Film Foundation (sales and rental).

Canadian distributor: Educational Film Distributors (sales and rental).

ANCIENT SARDIS
28 mins. Color. U.S.A. 1969.

Producer: Charles Lyman, Columbia College, Institute of Design and Cameras International.

Credits: Charles Lyman, director, writer, photographer, and editor.

Summary: Reconstruction by the Harvard-Cornell Expedition of the 2,500-year-old Turkish city of Sardis, the capital of Croesus and richest city of the ancient world. Tools similar to the originals are used to restore and repair sections of the city and its artifacts. Maps and drawings illustrate the importance of this archeological research on which the expedition spent over ten years.

U.S. distributor: Vision Quest (sales and rental).

ANCIENT WORLD: EGYPT (*The Ancient World* series)
66 mins. Color. U.S.A. 1955.

Producer: Ray Garner, Harmon Foundation, Egyptian Government, Archaeological Institute of America, Metropolitan Museum of Art.

Credits: Ray Garner, director; Michael Kane, narrator; Menelaos Pallandios, music.

Summary: A comprehensive, intelligent survey of the art and civilization of Egypt from the prehistoric period to the time of the Ptolemies. The historic role of the Nile is emphasized. Sakkara, the step pyramid, temples, the sphinx, and the pyramids at Giza are among the monuments visited.

U.S. distributor: New York University Film Library (sales and rental).

Canadian distributor: Canadian Film Institute (sales and rental).

ANCIENT WORLD: GREECE (*The Ancient World* series)
66 mins. Color. U.S.A. 1955.

Producer: Ray Garner, Archaeological Institute of America; Metropolitan Museum of Art.

Credits: Ray Garner, director; Menelaos Pallandios, music.

Summary: A scholarly attempt to recreate the civilization of Greece during the fifth century B.C. Extant art and literature of this golden age serve as the basis of the interpretation. The narration is composed of excerpts from religious, philosophic, and historical writings of the period.

U.S. distributor: New York University Film Library (sales and rental).

Canadian distributor: Canadian Film Institute (sales and rental).

ANDY WARHOL
53 mins. Color. U.S.A. 1973.

Producer: Michael Blackwood, Blackwood Productions.

Credits: Lana Yokel, director.

Summary: Andy Warhol is briefly encountered at the Factory, the Cannes Festival, and the Old Masters Room in the Brooklyn Museum. All Warhol's major graphic works are shown, as well as clips from many of his films. Other art world figures discuss Warhol and his career, among them, Clement Greenberg, Henry Geldzahler, Barbara Rose, David Bourdon, Mario Amaya, Harold Rosenberg, Emile de Antonio, and Philip Johnson.

U.S. distributor: Blackwood Productions (sales and rental).

ANEMIC CINEMA
7 mins. B&W. Originally 35mm. Silent. U.S.A. 1926.

Credits: Marcel Duchamp, director.

Summary: The title of this significant Dada film is a pun—anemic is an anagram of cinema. Nonsense phrases are inscribed around rotating spiral patterns related to Duchamp's "roto-reliefs," or optical discs, the predecessors of kinetic art.

U.S. distributor: The Museum of Modern Art (rental).

ANGKOR: THE LOST CITY (*Angkor—parole d'un empire qui fut*)
12 mins. B&W. Originally 35mm. Canada. 1961.

Producer: Roger Blais, National Film Board of Canada.

Credits: Morton Parker, director; Noel Stone, narrator.

Summary: Angkor Wat, a vast metropolis recovered from the jungle, is a sandstone temple almost a mile square with six hundred carved stone monuments. It reveals the glories of the past empire of the Khmers, ancestors of the Cambodians.

Canadian distributor: National Film Board of Canada (sales and loan).

ANSEL ADAMS
20 mins. B&W. U.S.A. 1958.

Producer: Larry Dawson.

Credits: David Myers, director; Nancy Newhall, writer; Beaumont Newhall, narrator.

Summary: Ansel Adams, accomplished creative photographer, is also a writer, teacher, musician, and mountaineer. His work includes landscapes, portraits, and industrial photography. The film shows his equipment, his home, and reveals his attitudes toward photography, art, and life in general.

U.S. distributor: International Film Bureau (sales and rental).

Canadian distributor: Educational Film Distributors (sales and rental).

ANTELAMI, THE BAPTISTRY OF PARMA (*Antelami, battistero di Parma*)
17 mins. Color. Originally 35mm. Italy. 1962.

Producer: Romor Film, Milan.

Credits: Carlo L. Ragghianti, director and writer; Daniele Paris, music.

Summary: A rare example of the virtuoso treatment of one monument only. The camera work dramatically conveys the Baptistry's massive, octagonal exterior and spacious interior. A detailed discussion of Antelami's sculpture and the seventeenth-century frescoes of the interior offers a lucid analysis of their stylistic precedents.

U.S. distributor: The Roland Collection (sales and rental).

ANTONI GAUDI
22 mins. Color. Britain. 1971.

Producer: Scottish Educational Film Association.

Credits: N. Thomson, director.

Summary: Shows the major architectural achievements of Antonio Gaudi, starting with the works that influenced his strange and personal Art Nouveau style. Some of his theories are explained with the help of architectural drawings. The film analyzes the Casa Vicens, the Palacio and Park Güell, the Casa Batlló, the Casa Milá, and the famous Sagrada Familia.

U.S. distributor: International Film Bureau (sales and rental).

Canadian distributor: Educational Film Distributors (sales and rental).

ANTONIO GAUDI
29 mins. Color. U.S.A. 1964.

Producer: International Media Films.

Credits: Ira Latour, director; George Collins, technical adviser and writer of commentary.

Summary: A study of the work of one of architecture's greatest innovators. Using Gaudí's credo, "originality is a return to the origin," as a guideline, the film shows how the architect's highly personal sense of space evolved from the Mediterranean forms he knew so well. Major developments in his career are presented and discussed: the Casa Vicens, Palacio Güell, Finca Güell, Parque Güell, Casa Batlló, Casa Milá, Santa Coloma de Cervelló, and the Sagrada Familia.

U.S. distributor: The Museum of Modern Art (rental); New York University Film Library (rental).

Canadian distributor: International Tele-Film Enterprises (sales and rental).

AN ARCHITECT FOR TODAY (*Essays: I. M. Pei* series)
9 mins. Color. U.S.A. 1969.

Producer: Rick Hauser for WGBH Educational Foundation with a grant from the Massachusetts Council for the Humanities.

Credits: Rick Hauser, Joyce Chopra, directors; Peter Hoving, photographer; Rick Hauser, narrator.

Summary: This is the fourth of five film essays on architecture by I. M. Pei. He studies the job of the architect in the 1970s, the spaces we live in, and the people who shape them. He considers that our age has no refinement, and our cities are incredibly dull. Ours, he says, are successful architects without any artistic talent; yet to be a great architect one must also be a great artist.

U.S. distributor: Museum at Large (sales and rental, singly or as a series).

THE ARCHITECTURE OF JAPAN
20 mins. Color. Japan. 1962.

Producer: International Motion Picture Company for the Ministry of Foreign Affairs of Japan.

Credits: Fumio Kamei, director.

Summary: A survey of public and domestic architecture in Japan from the traditional wooden structure to the steel, glass, and concrete seen in Tokyo today. The beauty of the patterns, the flow from one room to the other through sliding partitions, and the harmony with nature are clearly shown. Examples include the Horyuji Temple, the Tadaiji Temple in Nara, and the Katsura Villa in Kyoto. (See also the film HORYUJI TEMPLE.)

U.S. distributor: Embassy of Japan (loan).

Canadian distributor: Embassy of Japan (loan); Association Films (loan, in Ontario only).

AROUND AND ABOUT JOAN MIRO
63 mins. Color. U.S.A. 1956.

Producer: Thomas Bouchard.

Credits: Thomas and Diane Bouchard, directors: Edgard Varèse, music.

Summary: Joan Miró's work and development as an artist between 1915 and 1959; a glimpse into his enchanted world and the sources of his fantasies. Things Miró loves—folk dances, toys, the wild countryside, Medieval relics—undergo poetic mutations to win reincarnation in his canvases. Much of the film was photographed with Miró in Barcelona and other parts of his native Catalonia, and he is also shown in New York working on two large murals and several paintings. Varèse, father of "concrete music," composed and arranged the music for one sequence of the film.

U.S. distributor: Thomas Bouchard (rental).

AROUND THE WORLD IN EIGHTY FEET
24 mins. Color. U.S.A.

Producer: Arthur L. Smith, Richard B. Tisdale, and Mary C. Black for Colonial Williamsburg Incorporated.

Credits: Arthur L. Smith, director; Howard Scammon, narrator; Eddie Weaver, music.

Summary: This unusual film centers on a painting by an unknown New England folk artist, possibly Erastus Salisbury Field. It is a sweeping panorama—eighty feet long and one foot high—depicting an imaginary trip around the world. The delightful sketches are set off by sprightly nineteenth-century tunes played on a Wurlitzer organ.

U.S. distributor: Colonial Williamsburg Foundation (sales and rental).

THE ART CONSERVATOR (*Museum Without Walls* collection)
20 mins. Color. Originally 35mm. U.S.A. 1971.

Producer: Bruce Seth Green for Universal Education and Visual Arts.

Credits: Bruce Seth Green, director and photographer; Ben Johnson, Conservator of the Los Angeles County Museum of Art, consultant; Basil Polidouris, music.

Summary: A demonstration of the examination, treatment, and restoration of damaged art objects in the conservation laboratory of a museum: the Los Angeles County Museum of Art. The equipment is interesting and the photography excellent, but some of the methods used may be considered controversial.

U.S. distributor: Universal Education and Visual Arts (sales and rental).

Canadian distributor: Universal Education and Visual Arts (sales and rental).

ART FOR TOMORROW (*The 21st Century* series)
25 mins. Color. U.S.A. 1969.

Producer: Isaac Kleinerman, CBS News.

Credits: Peter Poor, director; Roy McMullen, writer of commentary; Walter Cronkite, narrator.

Summary: The evolution of science and technology has led to the development of new art forms which include the use of colored lights, new materials, and various combinations of shapes, motions, and sounds by cybernetics and computer programming. In its exploration of some of the more important trends, the film visits the studios of Nicholas Schoffer, Victor Vasarely, and Yaacov Agam in Paris, Bridget Riley in London, Takis in Greece, Wen-Ying Tsai and Tinguely in New York.

U.S. distributor: CBS Publishing Group (sales).

ART IN EXHIBITION
28 mins. Color. U.S.A. 1964.

Producer: Yale University Audio-Visual Center for the Yale Alumni Board.

Credits: David Anderson, director and writer; Robert Strone, narrator; Ron Riddle, music.

Summary: Andrew C. Ritchie, director of the Yale University Art Gallery, demonstrates the mounting of a major exhibition, from the selection of the pictures to their final placement in the gallery. He searches for balance, harmony, points of rest and focus to maintain interest, and a sense of progression within the limitations of the gallery's exhibition space. Over 250 works are included. Artists represented include Picasso, Rembrandt, Pollock, Léger, Renoir, Gauguin, Degas, El Greco, Holbein, Hals, and Tintoretto.

U.S. distributor: Macmillan (sales); Association Films, Inc. (rental).

Canadian distributor: Canadian Film Institute for the National Gallery of Canada (loan).

ART IN REVOLUTION
50 mins. Color. Britain. 1972.

Producer: Plus International Productions for the Arts Council of Great Britain.

Credits: Lutz Becker, director; Edward Braun, writer; Camilla Gray, research; Chris Stanley, narrator.

Summary: A synthesis of politics and art in the U.S.S.R. between 1917 and the death of Lenin, based on a unique exhibition held in 1972 at London's Hayward Gallery. Posters, architectural models, graphic design, decorative arts, and theatrical sets show the influence of revolutionary forms of art—Cubism, Futurism, Suprematism, and Constructivism. Documentary footage by Dziga Vertov completes the evocation of the period.

U.S. distributor: The American Federation of Arts (rental); Films Incorporated (sales).

ART NOUVEAU

28 mins. Color. Czechoslovakia. 1973.

Producer: William L. Snyder.

Credits: Kube Jurecek, director and writer; Jiri Mucha, writer.

Summary: Alfons Mucha, Czech painter and friend of Gauguin, Rodin, and Toulouse-Lautrec, was an important creator of Art Nouveau, although more than half a century passed before his work was appreciated. This is a faithful statement about Mucha, and about many aspects of Art Nouveau and the period at the turn of the century during which it flourished.

U.S. distributor: Macmillan (sales and rental).

THE ART OF CLAUDE LORRAIN

25 mins. Color. Britain. 1970.

Producer: Balfour Films, London, for the Arts Council of Great Britain.

Credits: Dudley Shaw Ashton, director; Sir Anthony Blunt, director of the Courtauld Institute of Art, writer and narrator; Don Smithers, music.

Summary: This careful and beautiful study explores how the classicist and pre-impressionist tendencies developed in Lorrain's landscapes. Focus is on the drawings and paintings, their light, intensity, serenity, and feeling of the eternal "now."

U.S. distributor: The American Federation of Arts (rental); Films Incorporated (sales).

Canadian distributor: Canadian Film Institute for the National Gallery of Canada (loan).

THE ART OF HERMANN ZAPF

17 mins. Color. U.S.A. 1968.

Producer: Noel Gordon.

Credits: Harold Peter, director; Peter Seymour, writer.

Summary: A description of the purposes, uses, and styles of calligraphy, tracing the history of various lettering forms. Hermann Zapf, an internationally known calligrapher, discusses the materials he uses and demonstrates his techniques.

U.S. distributor: Hallmark Films and Recordings (sales and rental).

THE ART OF SEEING
9 films, 10 mins. each (except FIGURES, 14 mins.). Color. U.S.A. 1969.

Producer: ACI for the American Federation of Arts under a grant from the Ford Foundation.

Credits: Stelios Roccos, director; Rudolf Arnheim, project adviser; Alice M. Kaplan, Roy Moyer, consultants.

Summary: Intended to develop and train visual perception, mainly among children, and to link everyday experiences with the world of museum paintings and statues. The series forms a nine-part curriculum in visual education, but each film can be used independently. (Teaching guides available.)

THE ART OF SEEING. An introduction; shows the ways of seeing a farmer's journey to market.

LIGHT. Considered as a device for emphasizing or concealing objects.

COLOR. Discusses the emotional effects of color.

SHAPE. Explains the arrangements of shapes.

MOVEMENT. Shows movement as it occurs everywhere and how it can be reproduced.

ABSTRACTION. From numbers and symbols to the representation of three-dimensional living objects.

SPACE. Shows how different kinds of spatial organization affect us.

FIGURES. Their interpretation reflects the temperament of the artist; from them we learn much about other people and ourselves.

SAME SUBJECT-DIFFERENT TREATMENT. The same object is seen in many different ways; forms are not absolute in our changing world.

U.S. distributor: Films Incorporated (sales and rental).

Canadian distributor: Visual Education Centre (sales and rental).

ART OF THE SIXTIES
30 mins. Color. U.S.A. 1967.

Producer: Leonard Harris for WCBS-TV News.

Credits: Merril Brockway, director and writer; Leonard Harris, narrator.

Summary: Documentation of the major directions in modern American art during the first seven years of the 1960s. The artists themselves explain their works; included are Claes Oldenburg's monumental Pop works, Donald Judd's hard-edge two- and three-dimensional paintings, and Robert Rauschenberg's three-dimensional objects in motion. Also appearing in the film are George Segal, Jackson Pollock (stock-shot), Willem de Kooning, Franz Kline, Adolph Gottlieb, Barnett Newman, Tony Smith, Jackie Casson, Rudy Stern, Len Lye, and Les Levine. (Guide available.)

U.S. distributor: BFA (sales and rental).

Canadian distributor: Holt, Rinehart and Winston (sales and rental).

ART, PEOPLE, FEELINGS
15 mins. Color. U.S.A. 1971.

Producer: Paul Burnford Films.

Credits: Paul Burnford, Michael Lyon, directors.

Summary: Visual arts are considered as a medium to communicate feelings. The film briefly reviews a large number of works of art from various media and all periods, including the present. Their basic principles are stated; their intentions are suggested. A quick tempo gives life, color, and brilliance to the film, which provides an introduction to art appreciation and stimulates discussion.

U.S. distributor: Pyramid (sales and rental).

Canadian distributor: International Tele-Film Enterprises (sales and rental).

THE ART SHOW THAT SHOCKED AMERICA (*Eye-Witness* series)
28 mins. B&W. U.S.A. 1963.

Producer: CBS.

Credits: Camera 3, Sir Kenneth Clark, participant.

Summary: The Armory Show of 1913 as re-created in New York. Some of the 1,300 paintings and sculpture originally exhibited are reproduced here, including works by American and European artists—Duchamp, Matisse, Brancusi, Ryder, and Van Gogh. In an interview Lord Clark emphasizes the enormous impact of the Armory Show on the art world of sixty years ago.

U.S. distributor: CBS Publishing Group (sales).

THE ARTIST AT WORK—JACQUES LIPCHITZ, MASTER SCULPTOR
12 mins. Color. U.S.A. 1968.

Producer: Encyclopedia Britannica Educational Corporation.

Credits: Bert Van Bork, director; James D. Breckenridge, Northwestern University, collaborator.

Summary: A study of the artist working in his studio, commenting on several of his creations displayed there, and demonstrating how he strives to reflect present-day standards in his sculpture. His remarks give added meaning to his works, which range from a statue of Prometheus to a bronze portrait of John F. Kennedy.

U.S. distributor: EBEC (sales and rental).

ARTIST IN MANHATTAN–JEROME MYERS
10 mins. Color. U.S.A. 1969.

Producer: Barry Downes Productions.

Credits: Barry Downes, Linda Marmelstein, directors; David Wayne, narrator; Jerome Myers' *Artist in Manhattan,* source of narration; Yoel Dan, music.

Summary: A tribute to Jerome Myers, a key figure in the famous Ashcan School of American art and one of the founders of the historic Armory Show of 1913. His drawings and paintings provide a portrait of a city the artist saw fast disappearing–New York at the beginning of the twentieth century, with its colorful immigrant street life, the band concerts in Central Park, the bustling street markets with their pushcart vendors, and the East River parks on hot summer evenings.

U.S. distributor: Barry Downes Productions (sales and rental).

ARTIST'S PROOF
25 mins. Color. Originally 35mm. Britain. 1957.

Producer: The Honourable Robert Erskine, St. George's Gallery Prints, London.

Credits: John Gibbon, director; The Honourable Robert Erskine, John Gibbon and Julian Cooper, writers of commentary; Ian Wallace, narrator; Gerald Gover, music.

Summary: Six British artists demonstrate the various techniques of printmaking. Roland Jarvis makes a woodcut, Alistair Grant a lithograph, Anthony Gross an etching, Merlyn Evans an aquatint, Anthony Harrison an engraving, and John Coplins a silk screen. The painstaking and intricate processes are a revelation to the layman and a stimulus to the practicing artist.

U.S. distributor: Macmillan (sales and rental).

Canadian distributor: Canadian Film Institute for the National Gallery of Canada (loan).

ARTS OF VILLAGE INDIA
26 mins. Color. Britain. 1970.

Producer: British Film Institute for the Arts Council of Great Britain.

Credits: Bruce Beresford, director and photographer; Hallam Tennyson, writer; authentic Indian village music.

Summary: A study of Indian folk art. Outstanding examples of everyday objects, such as toys, religious paintings, tools, clothes, blankets, and musical instruments, are reviewed. Some are isolated on display, while others are shown as they are being used in the village.

U.S. distributor: Films Incorporated (sales and rental).

AT THE TURN OF THE AGE—HANS HOLBEIN (*Im Zwielicht de Zeiten*)
15 mins. Color. Originally 35mm. Federal Republic of Germany. 1964.

Producer: Walter Leckebusch Film Studio, Munich.

Credits: Herbert E. Meyer, director and writer; Jakob Trommer, music.

Summary: The paintings, drawings, and prints of Hans Holbein are shown in the context of events in his life. Contrasting Bosch's Medieval visions with the ideals of the Italian Renaissance, the film establishes Holbein's intermediate position. His English portraits and, briefly, his drawings illustrating Erasmus' *Praise of Folly* are shown. Close-ups of objects in the paintings and animation of certain prints enliven the production.

U.S. distributor: The Roland Collection (sales and rental); Embassy of Switzerland (loan); Modern Talking Pictures for the Embassy of the Federal Republic of Germany (loan).

Canadian distributor: Canadian Film Institute for the National Gallery of Canada (loan); Embassy of Switzerland (loan).

UN AUTRE REGARD (*Another Look*)
19 mins. Color. Originally 35mm. France. 1966.

Producer: Occident, Paris.

Credits: Philippe Brunet, director and writer; Gil Dayvis and André Kerr, music.

Summary: The discovery of African art by early-twentieth-century artists. Its esthetic value was recognized by revolutionary painters, first with the Fauves—Matisse, Vlaminck, and Derain. A few years later its influence was more positive on the work of the Cubists—Braque, Picasso, Modigliani—and on the sculpture of Zadkine, González, Gaudier-Brzeska, and Duchamp-Villon. Masterpieces of African art on exhibit in Dakar and in Paris lead to the conclusion that the revelation of primitive art and the revolution of modern art are two interdependent events which reintroduced an element of daring into the over-disciplined Western tradition.

U.S. distributor: FACSEA (rental).

Canadian distributor: Embassy of France (loan).

AVATI AND THE MEZZOTINT
19 mins. Color. U.S.A. 1973.

Producer: Tee Bosustow.

Credits: Tee Bosustow, director, writer, and editor.

Summary: A rare opportunity to see the many stages in the creation of a mezzotint (from the Italian *mezzo tinto*—middle tone), a graphic art form which originated in the seventeenth century and was used in general as a means of reproducing works of art. Mario Avati, using this ancient method in the creation of original works, is seen sketching, preparing copper plates, and with his printer, inking the plates for the actual printing process.

U.S. distributor: Illumination Film (sales and rental).

AVEC CLAUDE MONET

22 mins. Color. France. 1966.

Producer: Skira Flag Films.

Credits: Dominique Delouche, director and writer; Maurice Thiriet, music.

Summary: The great French Impressionist painter was inevitably influenced by the surroundings in which he worked. This film re-creates his life by showing the places where he lived and painted, and the evolution of his painting at the various stages of his career.

U.S. distributor: FACSEA (rental).

Canadian distributor: Embassy of France (loan).

BALLET MECANIQUE

14 mins. B&W. Originally 35mm. Silent. France. 1924.

Producer: Fernand Léger.

Credits: Fernand Léger, director and writer; Dudley Murphy, photographer.

Summary: Often cited as the first film on art, this is also the first made by a prominent painter and the first to be called an "abstract film." It employs a minimum of drawn or painted geometrical forms. Most of its components are concrete: kitchen implements, close-ups of faces, and the famous repeated scenes of a woman climbing a staircase. The elements are used as objects in motion in a rhythmical composition. The music composed for the film by Georges Antheil is only available on pianola-roll.

U.S. distributor: The Museum of Modern Art (rental).

BARBARA HEPWORTH

29 mins. B&W. Britain. 1961.

Producer: John Read for BBC-TV.

Credits: John Read, director and writer; Dame Barbara Hepworth and Bernard Miles, narrators.

Summary: An interview with Barbara Hepworth, in which she shows how the magnificent setting of her home in Cornwall is inspiration for much of her work. She is seen in and around her studio, with a wide selection of her sculpture in wood, metal, and stone placed in natural surroundings, demonstrating how nature and art merge in her work.

U.S. distributor: Time-Life (sales and rental).

Canadian distributor: BBC-TV Enterprises (sales and rental).

BARBARA HEPWORTH AT THE TATE
12 mins. Color. Britain. 1968.

Producer: British Film Institute for the Arts Council of Great Britain.

Credits: Bruce Beresford, director and photographer; Dame Barbara Hepworth, narrator; Hugh Evans, artistic adviser.

Summary: In April and May, 1968, a major retrospective exhibition of Dame Barbara Hepworth's sculpture was held at the Tate Gallery, London. This is a straightforward record of that event, giving a broad view of her work and showing the general setting of the sculptures and their scale in relation to people.

U.S. distributor: The American Federation of Arts (rental); Films Incorporated (sales).

BARNETT NEWMAN (*Artists*—or *U.S.A. Artists*—series)
30 mins. B&W. U.S.A. 1966.

Producer: Lane Slate, NET and Radio Center.

Credits: Lane Slate, director and photographer; Alan Solomon, consultant.

Summary: Made on the occasion of an exhibition of *The Fourteen Stations of the Cross* (1958-1966) at the Guggenheim Museum in New York. Each painting consists of one or more vertical bands of black or white. The artist states "they are not in a conventional sense 'church' art. They can exist without a church." They concern the Passion as he feels and understands it. The camera work was done at Barnett Newman's home, the Guggenheim exhibition, his studio, and the docks of Lower East Side New York.

U.S. distributor: Indiana University (sales and rental).

Canadian distributor: The Canadian Film Institute for the National Gallery of Canada (sales and loan).

BARRY BRICKELL, POTTER
9 mins. Color. New Zealand. 1970.

Producer: Geoffrey Scott and Ronald Bowie for New Zealand Film Unit.

Credits: Lynton Diggle, director.

Summary: Every stage in the preparation of his pottery is handled by Barry Brickell, a recluse living on the remote Coromandel Peninsula of New Zealand, including digging the clay, transporting it to his workshop on a homemade railway, and mixing it to the consistency he needs to fashion his large, beautifully shaped jars.

U.S. distributor: Film Classic Exchange (rental).

Canadian distributor: Modern Talking Pictures for the New Zealand High Commission (rental).

BATIK (*Textile Design* series)
10 mins. Color. U.S.A. 1972.

Producer: State University College of New York, Buffalo.

Credits: Nancy Belfer, demonstrator.

Summary: The history of the Indian and Indonesian art of batik is a prelude for a demonstration by a leading artist, Nancy Belfer. She demonstrates the techniques involved in creating both the traditional and current pieces. Work done with heated wax and the tjanting tool is shown, as is printing with the copper headstamp, called a tjap.

U.S. distributor: ACI Films (sales).

Canadian distributor: Marlin Motion Pictures (sales and rental).

THE BAUHAUS: ITS IMPACT ON THE WORLD OF DESIGN (*Das Bauhaus: sein Beitrag zur Gestaltung unserer Umwelt*)
19 mins. Color. Federal Republic of Germany. 1968.

Producer: Art Film.

Credits: Detten Schleiermacher, director; Hans Eckstein, writer; Hans Posegga, music.

Summary: A rather brief look at an important landmark in the history of twentieth-century art—the founding of the Bauhaus in Weimar, Germany by Walter Gropius, with the aim of integrating artistic disciplines with constructional techniques. Through the use of archive film, interviews with the school's ex-students and former teachers (including Gropius, Josef Albers, and Mies van der Rohe) throw light on the methods and principles that have profoundly influenced subsequent thinking on architecture and design.

U.S. distributor: Modern Talking Pictures for the Embassy of the Federal Republic of Germany (loan).

Canadian distributor: Canadian Film Institute for the Embassy of the Federal Republic of Germany (rental).

BAZILLE, THE FIRST IMPRESSIONIST (*Le Maître de Montpellier*)
15 mins. Color. Originally 35mm. France. 1960.

Producer: Films Roger Leenhardt.

Credits: Roger Leenhardt, director and writer; Guy Bernard, music.

Summary: A sensitive approach to the paintings of Jean-Frédéric Bazille, friend of Renoir, Monet, Sisley, and Manet. Besides painting in Paris, Bazille liked to return and work at Montpellier, his hometown in the south of France. His promising career was very brief: he was killed at the age of twenty-nine during the Franco-Prussian War. Several of his canvases are preserved in the Louvre.

U.S. distributor: Film Images (sales and rental).

BERNARD BERENSON

50 mins. Color. Britain. 1971.

Producer: BBC-TV, Bavarian Television Service and NET.

Credits: Stephen Hearst, director; Ann Turner, director of Boston and stills sequences; Sir Kenneth Clark, writer, narrator and participant; Iris Origo and Alda Anrep, participants.

Summary: A portrait of the renowned art critic and historian. Memories of Sir Kenneth Clark, now Lord Clark of Saltwood, are complemented by interviews with two of Berenson's friends, the author Iris Origo and his former librarian. A visit to the villa, I Tatti, where he lived so many years and which he left to Harvard University after his death, reveals the splendor of Berenson's home, its setting, and the art treasures within. Paintings of landscapes and Renaissance houses viewed alongside actual scenes of the Italian countryside tantalize the senses with a mingling of art and reality.

Canadian distributor: BBC-TV Enterprises (sales and rental).

BERNARD LEACH: A POTTER'S WORLD

29 mins. B&W. Britain. 1961.

Producer: BBC-TV.

Credits: John Read, director; Bernard Leach, narrator.

Summary: The famous British potter, Bernard Leach, at his studio in St. Ives, Cornwall, discusses the craftsman's philosophy and the relation of his own work to Japanese tradition with its roots in the concepts of Zen Buddhism. The camera follows the master potter through the designing, throwing, decoration, and firing of a large pot, while his relaxed but profound comments compel sustained interest.

U.S. distributor: Time-Life (sales and rental).

Canadian distributor: BBC-TV Enterprises (sales and rental); Canadian Film Institute for the National Gallery of Canada (loan).

BLACK HAS ALWAYS BEEN BEAUTIFUL

17 mins. B&W. U.S.A. 1971.

Producer: NET.

Credits: Philip Burton, Jr., director; William L. Gaddis, editor.

Summary: The black photographer James Van Der Zee, who worked for six decades in relative obscurity, is now acclaimed as a master. This self-taught artist has documented the black experience in Harlem. He is shown at work and explains how he tries to record each subject as he sees it. His stills include Harlem schoolchildren, the Black Yankees, Marcus Garvey, and Bill "Bojangles" Robinson.

U.S. distributor: Indiana University (sales and rental).

Canadian distributor: Canadian Film Institute (sales and rental).

THE BOOK OF KELLS
20 mins. Color. Ireland.

Producer: Ulster Television.

Credits: Andrew Grogkarg, director; John Keyes, narrator.

Summary: G.O. Simms, Archbishop of Armagh, introduces this presentation of the famous ninth-century illuminated manuscript of the Gospels, preserved in Trinity College, Dublin. A printed facsimile is used for the film. With the aid of close-up photography and careful examination of the colorful illuminated pages, the film reveals superb portraits, beautifully monogrammed passages, and graceful decoration showing Oriental, Scandinavian, and Egyptian influences.

U.S. distributor: Pictura (sales and rental).

Canadian distributor: International Tele-Film Enterprises (sales and rental).

BORROMINI
14 mins. Color. Originally 35mm. Italy. 1959.

Producer: Documento Film, Rome.

Credits: Primo Zeglio, director; Alfredo Mezio, writer; Domenico Gauccero, music.

Summary: The most important achievements of the great Roman architect, Francesco Borromini, one of the three most celebrated masters of Baroque, are compared with those of Bernini. Among the works shown are his masterpiece, the tiny San Carlo alle Quattro Fontane, Sant' Ivo della Sapienza (its plan based on a six-pointed star), the Palazzo Barberini, Collegio della Propaganda Fide, Oratory of San Filippo Neri, Sant' Agnese, and Sant' Andrea delle Fratte.

U.S. distributor: Istituto Italiano di Cultura (loan).

BOURDELLE, or ANTOINE BOURDELLE
22 mins. B&W. Originally 35mm. France. 1950.

Producer: André Robert, Marcelle Goetze.

Credits: René Lucot, director; A. Honegger, music.

Summary: Although made in 1950 this is a valuable documentary, especially in view of the lack of a more recent film in America on this celebrated French sculptor. We follow Bourdelle making furniture with his father, studying at an art school, arriving in Paris at the age of twenty-three, and working with Rodin, who influenced him greatly. Rodin's sculptures and some of Bourdelle's are compared. A visit is made to his former house, now Musée Bourdelle.

U.S. distributor: FACSEA (rental).

Canadian distributor: Embassy of France (loan).

THE BRANCUSI RETROSPECTIVE AT THE GUGGENHEIM
(*Constantin Brancusi*)
23 mins. Color. U.S.A. 1971.

Producer: Paul Falkenberg and Hans Namuth.

Credits: Paul Falkenberg and Hans Namuth, directors; Sidney Geist, writer of commentary and narrator; Gheorghe Zamfir, music (Rumanian flute).

Summary: The retrospective exhibition held in New York from November, 1969, through February, 1970, displayed seventy-nine sculptures and twenty-four drawings in what was the most comprehensive Brancusi show ever assembled. Following a brief tour of the sculptor's Paris studio (reconstructed at the Musée National d'Art Moderne) the film shifts to the Guggenheim Museum, alternating the presentation of the actual exhibition with imaginative turntable shots of selected pieces. Excellent camera work and narration, combined with sensitive handling of the artist's work, provide a record worthy of its subject.

U.S. distributor: Museum at Large (sales and rental).

BRASILIA
13 mins. Color. U.S.A. 1961.

Producer: G. Tamarski, International Film Bureau.

Credits: G. Tamarski, director.

Summary: A documentary on the building of Brazil's new capital, recording the steps in its development from Lucio Costa's master plan to the emerging life and growth of the futuristic city. The film shows the Plaza of Three Powers from various angles, Oscar Niemeyer's concrete-ribbed glass cathedral, government buildings, residential areas, and the President's Palace, as well as outstanding sculpture, an integral part of the initial project. The building of new roads and airports is also recorded.

U.S. distributor: International Film Bureau (sales and rental).

Canadian distributor: Educational Film Distributors (sales and rental).

BREAKING IT UP AT THE MUSEUM
8 mins. B&W. U.S.A. 1960.

Producer: D. A. Pennebaker.

Credits: D. A. Pennebaker, director.

Summary: A record of a unique event: in the Sculpture Garden of the Museum of Modern Art, on March 17, 1960, Jean Tinguely's *Homage to New York,* the "self-constructing and self-destructing" machine, destroyed itself more or less as planned. John Canaday wrote in the *New York Times,* "Mr. Tinguely makes fools of the machines, while the rest of mankind supinely permits machines to make fools of them." (See also HOMAGE TO JEAN TINGUELY.)

U.S. distributor: Pennebaker, Inc. (sales and rental).

BRONZE

13 mins. Color. Originally 35mm. Canada. 1969.

Producer: François Séguillon for the National Film Board of Canada.

Credits: Pierre Moretti, director; Maurice Blackburn, music; no narration.

Summary: The viewer shares with the sculptor, Charles Daudelin of Montreal, the conception and execution of the monumental bronze outside the National Arts Centre in Ottawa. The work begins with a model shaped in Styrofoam with knife, saw, and blowtorch in the exact form the finished bronze will take. The film is without words but with music to evoke mood.

U.S. distributor: Learning Corporation of America (sales and rental).

Canadian distributor: The National Film Board of Canada (sales and rental).

BRONZE CASTING: VINCENT KOFI (*The Lost-Wax Method of Bronze Casting*)

18 mins. B&W. U.S.A. 1972.

Producer: Fotosonic and the Harmon Foundation.

Credits: Leo Steiner, director; Harold Castor, adviser; Charlotte Nelson, writer of commentary; Dwight Waist, narrator.

Summary: A step-by-step demonstration of the lost-wax method of bronze casting, from clay model to finished bronze sculpture. In the New York workshop of Vincent Kofi and Harold Castor, Kofi, sculptor and teacher from Ghana, employs a method discovered centuries ago.

U.S. distributor: Pictura (sales and rental).

Canadian distributor: International Tele-Film Enterprises (sales and rental).

THE BRONZE ZOO

16 mins. Color. U.S.A. 1973.

Producer: Sonya Friedman.

Credits: Sonya Friedman, director.

Summary: The sculptor Shay Rieger is known for her bronze animals (hippo, aardvark, baboon, crane) and for her books, a natural extension of her work. We follow here the birth of one of her bronzes: a yak. The artist looks at her subject, makes sketches, builds an armature, casts in the lost-wax process, fixes the color of the patina, and finally the yak takes its place in a city library.

U.S. distributor: Texture Films (sales and rental).

Canadian distributor: International Tele-Film Enterprises (sales and rental).

BRUEGEL AND THE FOLLIES OF MEN: BABEL
(*Bruegel et la folie des hommes: Babel*)
18 mins. Color. Originally 35mm. Belgium/France. 1966.

Producer: Jean Cleinge for the Belgian Ministry of Education and Specta Films, France.

Credits: Jean Cleinge, director, writer, and editor; André Souris, music.

Summary: This is the first part of a diptych on Bruegel's paintings. It is an attempt to penetrate the inner universe of the artist and discover his attitude to the world around him. Proverbs and popular turns of speech form the basis of the commentary, and the music is inspired by the period. The ambiguity of human relations and the vanity of men who disrupt the natural harmony of life are the main themes of this film.

U.S. distributor: International Film Bureau (sales and rental).

Canadian distributor: Canadian Film Institute for the National Gallery of Canada (French version—loan).

BRUEGEL AND THE FOLLIES OF MEN: DULLE GRIET
(*Bruegel et la folie des hommes: Dulle Griet*)
18 mins. Color. Originally 35mm. Belgium/France. 1966.

Producer: Jean Cleinge for the Belgian Ministry of Education and Specta Films, France.

Credits: Jean Cleinge, director, writer, and editor; André Souris, music.

Summary: The fantastic is the main theme of this second part of the exploration of Bruegel's paintings. It is a result of man's conflict with society and nature, of the terrible confrontation between death and the will to live. The work of Bruegel represents disasters, war, massacres, hell, the wanderings of the "Dulle Griet" (Mad Meg), and "The Triumph of Death."

U.S. distributor: International Film Bureau (sales and rental).

Canadian distributor: Canadian Film Institute for the National Gallery of Canada (French version—loan).

BUMA—AFRICAN SCULPTURE SPEAKS
9 mins. Color. U.S.A. 1952.

Producer: Encyclopaedia Britannica Educational Corporation.

Credits: Henry R. Cassirer, director; Ladislas Segy, writer; Lewis Jacobs, editor; authentic tribal music.

Summary: A sensitive approach to Central and West African sculpture. The ancient carved wooden statues and masks shown were considered as a protection against the dangers of everyday living and fear of the unknown.

U.S. distributor: EBEC (sales and rental).

THE CALDER MAN
14 mins. Color. Britain. 1967.

Producer: The London Film Unit of the International Nickel Co.

Credits: D. G. Hannaford, director.

Summary: Alexander Calder, famous for his mobiles, was commissioned by the International Nickel Company to create a giant "stabile" for Montreal's Expo '67. The artist is seen throughout the entire process—from the first sketches in his studio, to casting in the factory and final supervision on the site of the erection of the 67-foot (20 meters), 50-ton sculpture. By a juxtaposition of silhouettes and the play of light and shade, the sculpture is given life and a very real movement.

U.S. distributor: The Museum of Modern Art (rental).

Canadian distributor: Canadian Film Institute for the National Gallery of Canada (loan).

CALDER'S CIRCUS (*Cirque Calder*)
19 mins. Color. France. 1961.

Producer: Société nouvelle Pathé-Cinéma.

Credits: Carlos Vilardebo, director; Alexander Calder, participant and narrator.

Summary: Shows Alexander Calder and the miniature circus which he built in 1929. This toy was a foretaste of what was to become the essential characteristic of the art of his mobiles: a taste for fantasy and color, combined with a mastery of craftsmanship in steel wire. Apart from the ingenuity of the artist, the film reveals his warmth, humor, and tenderness.

U.S. distributor: Pathé Cinema Corporation.

CARVED IN IVORY
30 mins. Color. Britain. 1974.

Produced with a grant from the Arts Council of Great Britain.

Credits: Michael Gill, director; Lord Clark, writer and narrator; Walter Lassaly, photographer.

Summary: Derived from the exhibition "Ivory Carvings in Early Medieval England" held at the Victoria and Albert Museum in 1974. Lord Clark's commentary locates in their historical and artistic context the small ivory sculptures created by the anonymous masters of the years A.D. 700-1200. Most of these beautiful little works are devotional objects and represent scenes of the life of Christ or the lives of the saints. They come from various British, European, and American collections.

U.S. distributor: The American Federation of Arts (rental); Films Incorporated (sales).

CHAIM SOUTINE
28 mins. Color. U.S.A. 1970.

Producer: Rita Morrison.

Credits: Jack Lieberman, director and writer.

Summary: The life and work of Chaim Soutine, beginning with his youth and flight from Nazi persecution, are recorded by means of documentary techniques (dramatization and interviews). Some of his first work is analyzed; his painting styles and his character are intimately explored through interviews with his friends, including sculptor Jacques Lipchitz and several collectors.

U.S. distributor: RJM Productions (sales and rental).

Canadian distributor: Canadian Film Institute for the National Gallery of Canada (loan).

THE CHAPEL OF RONCHAMP (*La chapelle de Ronchamp*)
11 mins. Color. Originally 35mm. France. 1967.

Producer: Artis Film and Procinebel.

Credits: Jacques de Casembroot, director; Dany Gérard, writer; Jacques de Casembroot, Le Corbusier, writers of commentary; Dom Clément Jacobi, music.

Summary: A study of LeCorbusier's country church, superbly adapted to its location on the top of a mountain in southern France. A chapel of white concrete, distinguished by the architect's use of light and shade and the interplay of proportions, it is one of the most revolutionary buildings of the twentieth century.

U.S. distributor: Visual Resources (sales and rental).

Canadian distributor: International Educational Films (sales, French version only); Embassy of France (loan).

CHARLES BURCHFIELD: FIFTY YEARS OF HIS ART
14 mins. Color. U.S.A. 1966.

Producer: Radio-TV Bureau, University of Arizona.

Credits: Harry Atwood, photographer and editor; Sheldon Reich, writer; Robert Keyworth, narrator; Robert Muczynski, music.

Summary: A presentation of the major works of the artist, based on a 1965 retrospective exhibition at the University of Arizona Museum of Art. These include his early paintings (1915-1919), in which a note of fantasy expresses his love for calligraphy and Chinese painting; his well-known realist watercolors (1920-1942), penetrating portrayals of American life in small towns; his works from the last period (1943-1965) expressing his personal vision of nature. Burchfield's draftsmanship and his mastery of watercolors are sensitively shown.

U.S. distributor: International Film Bureau (sales and rental).

THE CHARM OF LIFE (*Les charmes de l'existence*)
17 mins. Originally 25 mins. B&W. France. 1950.

Producer: From St.-Germain-des-Prés.

Credits: Jean Grémillon and Pierre Kast, directors; Rex Harrison, narrator.

Summary: The French Academy painters (1860-1910). A lighthearted satire on "official art" and a portrait of the social history of France at the turn of the century. Bouguereau, Bonnat, Carolus-Duran, Garnier, J.-P. Laurens were acclaimed by their contemporaries who laughed at the Impressionists and refused their works for the Salon. In fact, the effect of this parody has always been ambiguous: the charm of the out-of-date paintings often outweighs their absurdity, and there is a constantly increasing interest in the period.

U.S. distributor: Pictura (sales and rental).

Canadian distributor: International Tele-Film Enterprises (sales and rental).

THE CHICAGO PICASSO
60 mins. Color. U.S.A. 1967.

Producer: Lane Slate, NET.

Credits: Mallory Slate, director; Manny Albam, music.

Summary: A record of the history of Pablo Picasso's largest sculpture, the controversial steel figure unveiled at the Civic Center Plaza in Chicago on August 15, 1967. The story begins with the first contact with the artist and his original conception. A detailed account of its construction by the U.S. Steel Company follows, including the eighteen months required to build a preliminary ten-and-a-half-foot (3.2 meters) scale model in wood. Sir Roland Penrose, friend and biographer of the artist, guides us on a brief visit to the first major exhibit of Picasso's sculpture in the United States. (Some fading in the color was noted.)

U.S. distributor: Indiana University (sales and rental).

Canadian distributor: International Tele-Film Enterprises (sales); Canadian Film Institute (sales).

CHINA—TIMES OF JADE AND BRONZE
CHINA—TIMES OF SILK AND GOLD
2 films, 50 mins. each. Color. Britain. 1974.

Producer: Michael Gill for BBC-TV.

Credits: Michael Gill, director; Professor William Watson and Magnus Magnusson, participants and narrators.

Summary: This long documentary has been produced to place the famous touring exhibition of 400 recent archeological finds in the context of China, past and present. The first film, *Times of Jade and Bronze*, relates the long journey of the filmmakers across the vast country. It shows the sites where the treasures were discovered; it describes everyday life and also deals with prehistoric and early historical treasures. The second film, *Times of Silk and Gold,* is almost entirely devoted to art. The horse, an object of veneration for 2,000 years, is a frequent subject of painting and sculpture (particularly in ceramics and metal). One of the world's greatest Buddhist shrines is visited. For the first time Europeans descend into the recently excavated tomb of a T'ang princess who committed suicide. A visit to Sian, the ancient capital, reveals its precious silverware, its gardens, and its traditional palaces and buildings.

Canadian distributor: BBC-TV Enterprises (sales and rental).

CHRISTO: FOUR WORKS IN PROGRESS
28 mins. Color. U.S.A. 1971.

Producer: Blackwood Productions.

Credits: Michael and Christian Blackwood, directors; David Bourdon, narrator.

Summary: Sequences from the preparatory stages to completion of four projects:
1) *Wrapped Girl,* London, 1963; 2) *5,600 Cubic Meters Package* for the international exhibition Documenta 4 in Kassel, Germany, 1968; 3) *Wrap-In, Wrap-Out,* the wrapping of the Museum of Contemporary Art in Chicago, 1969; and 4) *Wrapped Coast,* Little Bay, Sydney, Australia, 1971.

U.S. distributor: Blackwood Productions (sales and rental).

CHRISTO'S VALLEY CURTAIN
27 mins. Color. U.S.A. 1973.

Producer: Maysles Films.

Credits: David and Albert Maysles, directors; Ellen Giffard, writer.

Summary: Artist Christo, with the help of engineers, ironworkers, and students, hangs an immense orange curtain, a quarter of a mile long, across a valley in Colorado—a tremendous feat of art and engineering. Scenes of the planning and execution are interwoven to make the viewer aware of the dimensions of the artistic experience.

U.S. distributor: Maysles Films (sales and rental).

CHRISTO: WRAPPED COAST
28 mins. Color. U.S.A. 1970.

Producer: Blackwood Productions.

Credits: Michael Blackwood, director.

Summary: Christo and his army of helpers wrap one mile of the coastline at Little Bay, Sydney, Australia, with one million square feet of woven polypropylene banded by thirty-five miles of rope. As the project progresses, the coastline takes on an eerie glacial appearance, changes to a wrapped bundle and is finally ripped apart by the force of the wind.

U.S. distributor: Blackwood Productions (sales and rental).

CIVILISATION series
13 films, 50 mins. each. Color. Originally 35mm. Britain. 1969.

Producer: Michael Gill and Peter Montagnon for BBC-TV.

Credits: Sir Kenneth Clark (Lord Clark of Saltwood), writer, narrator, and participant; Michael Gill, director of numbers 1, 3, 5, 8, 10, 12, and 13; Peter Montagnon, director of numbers 2, 6, 7, 9, and 11; Ann Turner, director of number 4.

Summary: One man's "personal view" of Western civilization from the decline of the Greco-Roman empire to the modern industrial state, epitomized in the city of New York. Reference is constantly made to architecture, painting, sculpture, music, philosophy, and literature. The shooting took place in 11 countries, 117 locations, 18 libraries, and 118 museums. The series has been extremely successful, both as television and film programs; it has stimulated warm discussions and controversy. Though closely integrated, each part stands firmly on its own merits.

1. THE FROZEN WORLD (The Skin of Our Teeth). The Dark Ages, the six centuries following the collapse of the Roman Empire.

2. THE GREAT THAW. The twelfth century from the Abbey of Cluny to the Cathedral of Chartres.

3. ROMANCE AND REALITY. The later Middle Ages in France and Italy.

4. MAN—THE MEASURE OF ALL THINGS. The Renaissance in Florence, Urbino, and Mantua.

5. THE HERO AS ARTIST. Papal Rome in the early sixteenth century; Michelangelo, Raphael, and Leonardo.

6. PROTEST AND COMMUNICATION. The Reformation: from Dürer, Luther, and Erasmus to Montaigne and Shakespeare.

7. GRANDEUR AND OBEDIENCE. The Counter-Reformation in Rome, St. Peter's splendor.

8. THE LIGHT OF EXPERIENCE. From the telescope and microscope to the realism of Dutch painting.

9. THE PURSUIT OF HAPPINESS. The Rococo churches and palaces of Bavaria and their relation to the music of Bach, Handel, Haydn, and Mozart.

10. THE SMILE OF REASON. The eighteenth century from elegant salons to revolution; the palaces of Blenheim and Versailles; Edinburgh and Thomas Jefferson's home in Virginia.

11. THE WORSHIP OF NATURE. Landscapes: from Tintern Abbey, the Lake District, and the Swiss Alps to Turner and Constable.

12. THE FALLACIES OF HOPE. The Romantic Movement: Beethoven, Byron, Géricault, Turner, Delacroix, and Rodin.

13. HEROIC MATERIALISM. The world in which we live: industrial England, skyscrapers of New York, radio telescope, and the exploration of space.

U.S. distributor: Time-Life (sales and rental).

Canadian distributor: BBC-TV Enterprises (sales and rental); Canadian Film Institute for the National Gallery of Canada (loan).

CIVILISATION (Compilation Film)
50 mins. Partly B&W, Partly Color. Originally 35mm. Britain. 1972.

Producer: Michael Gill and Peter Montagnon for BBC-TV.

Credits: Michael Gill and Peter Montagnon, directors; Sir Kenneth Clark (Lord Clark of Saltwood), writer, narrator, and participant.

Summary: More an anthology than a digest. Sections of the famous television series have been selected to serve as an outline of the history of Western civilization as described by Sir Kenneth Clark.

U.S. distributor: Time-Life (sales and rental).

Canadian distributor: BBC-TV Enterprises (sales and rental).

CLAES OLDENBURG
52 mins. Color. U.S.A. 1975.

Producer: Blackwood Productions.

Credits: Michael Blackwood, director.

Summary: A comprehensive record of Oldenburg's itinerary and achievements: memories of childhood in Chicago, where he arrived from Sweden at the age of seven; his five-story house on the West Side of Manhattan and his studio in New Haven. Using the vernacular of commercialism, he projects disturbingly distorted images of reality—giant hamburgers, ice bags and pool balls, a soft bathtub and an immense soft drum set (for Aspen College). His way of expression ranges from drawings on paper or sand to monuments in metal and plastic, and composite "happenings."

U.S. distributor: Blackwood Productions (sales and rental).

CLAES OLDENBURG (*Artists*–or *U.S.A. Artists*–series)
30 mins. B&W. U.S.A. 1966.

Producer: Lane Slate for NET.

Credits: Mallory Slate, director; Alan Solomon, writer; Jim Dine, narrator; Manny Albam, music.

Summary: An introduction to Claes Oldenburg, originator of "happenings" and an early Pop artist. He is shown preparing for his 1966 show at the Sidney Janis Gallery in New York City and working on his "soft sculpture" (kapok-stuffed vinyl on canvas) at his East Side studio.

U.S. distributor: Indiana University (sales and rental).

Canadian distributor: Canadian Film Institute for the National Gallery of Canada (sales and loan).

CLARENCE SCHMIDT–THE WOODSTOCK ENVIRONMENT
23 mins. Color. U.S.A. 1967.

Producer: Cornell University Archive Production.

Credits: W. C. Lipke, director; Clarence Schmidt, participant.

Summary: A valuable record of the impermanent work of a naive artist. Clarence Schmidt built his living quarters into the crest of Ohayo Mountain and worked to shape the environment to his dream, using natural and junk objects of every type. (The central structure was destroyed by fire in 1968.) The film differentiates between the obsessive artist without an audience–a creator who has no wish to sell–and today's consumer-oriented society.

Canadian distributor: Canadian Film Institute for the National Gallery of Canada (loan).

CLAUDE MONET–The Man Who Gave Birth to the Impressionist School
(*Pioneers of Modern Painting* series, no. 3)
40 mins. Color. Britain. 1972.

Producer: Colin Clark for Independent Television Corporation.

Credits: Colin Clark, director; Lord Clark, writer and narrator.

Summary: Born by the sea, Claude Monet is renowned as a painter of water and as one of the originators of Impressionism, a name derived from one of his paintings. Lord Clark believes that Monet, "determined to rely solely on his direct response to nature" with no reference to the art of the past, "simply anticipated the ordinary, natural vision . . . and people were not yet prepared to admit that they saw things in this way." His life was marked by struggle and bitter attacks, and he received recognition only in his old age. Twenty years after his death, interest in his work was revived by admiring New York artists striving to go on, from where Monet left off, into formal abstraction.

U.S. distributor: Independent Television Corporation (sales); National Gallery of Art (loan).

Canadian distributor: ITC of Canada (sales); Canadian Film Institute for the National Gallery of Canada (loan).

COLLECTOR'S PIECES (British Museum)
15 mins. Color. Britain. 1973.

Producer: John King, BBC-TV.

Credits: Robin Drake, director; Derek Jones, writer of commentary.

Summary: A demonstration of book restoration in the British Museum, this film, introduced by Hugh Scully, is of special interest to art conservators. A department of experts is responsible for the care of those volumes among the Museum's eight million manuscripts and books that have become worn and torn. Bindings are restored and new gold leaf applied to leather backs.

Canadian distributor: Canadian Film Institute for the British High Commission (rental).

COLOSSAL KEEPSAKE NO. 1
12 mins. B&W and Color. U.S.A. 1969.

Producer: Hentschel-Richardson.

Summary: An immense and excited crowd gathered on the Yale campus for the final stages of construction and the installation of Claes Oldenburg's first monumental sculpture— a twenty-nine-foot-tall (8.8 meters) red lipstick mounted on a base with caterpillar treads. Oldenburg himself climbed a stepladder to insert the tube which inflated the red vinyl lipstick with a sudden burst of color.

U.S. distributor: Castelli-Sonnabend Tapes and Films, Inc. (sales and rental).

CONTEMPORARY AMERICAN SCULPTURE IN THE COLLECTION OF THE ART INSTITUTE OF CHICAGO
21 mins. Color. U.S.A. 1971.

Producer: The Art Institute of Chicago.

Credits: Celia Marriott, director.

Summary: A review of ten pieces of sculpture from the 1950s and 1960s in the collection of the Art Institute of Chicago. Among the works included are David Smith's *Cubi VII,* Louise Nevelson's *America Dawn*, John Chamberlain's *Toy*, José de Rivera's *Brussels Construction*, Alexander Calder's *Clouds Over Mountains*, and George Segal's *Couple*. The sound track consists mainly of quotations from artists and critics.

U.S. distributor: The Art Institute of Chicago (sales).

Canadian distributor: Canadian Film Institute for the National Gallery of Canada (loan).

THE CORBIT-SHARP HOUSE
14 mins. Color. U.S.A. 1965.

Producer: Willard Van Dyke.

Credits: Wheaton Galentine, director; Howard Enders, writer (based on John A. H. Sweeney's book "Grandeur on the Appoquinimink"); Irwin Bazelon, music.

Summary: The Georgian style house at Cantwell's Bridge (now Odessa), Delaware, built in 1772 by a Quaker tanner, William Corbit. This jewel of eighteenth-century architecture went unnoticed until H. Rodney Sharp restored it in the 1930s and presented it to the community of Winterthur. Scenes of the Philadelphia and Odessa of Corbit's time precede the visit to this richly furnished house, where the impression of life is given by sound effects and details such as lighted fires and fresh flowers.

U.S. distributor: Film Images (sales and rental).

LE CORBUSIER (*Museum Without Walls* collection)
55 mins. Color. Originally 35mm. France. 1973.

Producer: Condor Films.

Credits: Carlos Vilardebo, director; Douglas Cooper, narrator.

Summary: Carlos Vilardebo, one of the great architect's collaborators, deals with the life and works of Le Corbusier. The film explains Le Corbusier's revolutionary ideas on architecture and urban renewal, and shows their practical application in his most important buildings in Europe and Asia.

U.S. distributor: Universal Education and Visual Arts (sales and rental).

Canadian distributor: Universal Education and Visual Arts (sales and rental).

COROT
18 mins. Color. France. 1965.

Producer: Roger Leenhardt.

Credits: Roger Leenhardt, director and writer; Guy Bernard, music.

Summary: The film emphasizes Jean-Baptiste Corot's contribution to the development of French Impressionism, a lifetime spent in trying to define on canvas the varying patterns of light and shadow in nature. His paintings are juxtaposed here with those of his contemporaries John Constable, Theodore Rousseau, Jean-François Millet, and Claude Monet, to create a feeling for the entire period.

U.S. distributor: The Roland Collection (sales and rental).

Canadian distributor: Canadian Film Institute for the National Gallery of Canada (loan).

CUBA: ART AND REVOLUTION
46 mins. Color. Britain. 1970.

Producer: Peter Adams, BBC-TV.

Credits: Peter Adams, director and writer; James Mossman, participant; John Stockbridge, narrator.

Summary: A survey, made from a Western point of view, on all aspects of the arts in Cuba ten years after Castro's rise to power. Artists (with special emphasis on poster designers), writers and poets, film directors, actors, and dancers are interviewed about the interrelation of creation and the revolution and the political and esthetic role of the artist. The viewer is made aware of the great effect the revolution has had on shaping the progress of the arts in Cuba.

U.S. distributor: Time-Life (sales and rental).

Canadian distributor: BBC-TV Enterprises (sales and rental).

CUBISM (*Le cubisme*)
17 mins. Color. Originally 35mm. France. 1953.

Producer: Spartacus Films, Paris.

Credits: Pierre Alibert, director; Francis Seyrig, music.

Summary: A comprehensive survey of Cubism as a philosophy of art. The film states that Cubism corresponds to a period of renewal, research, and sometimes of exaggerations. It analyzes outstanding paintings by Braque, Léger, Delaunay, La Fresnaye, Gleizes, Picasso, Gris, Villon, and Metzinger.

U.S. distributor: FACSEA (rental).

Canadian distributor: Embassy of France (loan).

DADA
31 mins. B&W. Belgium. 1969.

Producer: Prociné for the Ministry of National Education of Belgium.

Credits: Greta Deses, director; Marcel Jance, consultant.

Summary: The history of this brief and audacious movement in modern art and literature is presented in interviews with Max Ernst, Hans Richter, Marcel Duchamp, Man Ray, and Gabriele Picabia Buffet. The film includes an authentically re-created stage presentation from the Cabaret Voltaire, Zurich, whence Dada emerged in 1916.

U.S. distributor: International Film Bureau (sales and rental).

Canadian distributor: Educational Film Distributors (sales and rental); Canadian Film Institute for the National Gallery of Canada (loan).

DAPHNI: VIRGIN OF THE GOLDEN LAURELS
17 mins. B&W. Greece. 1951.

Producer: Spiro Harocopos.

Credits: George Hoyningen-Huene, director; Angelo Procopiou, writer; Aldous Huxley, writer of English commentary; Ethel Barrymore and Maurice Evans, narrators; Howard Brubeck, music.

Summary: Eleventh-century mosaics in the Church of Daphni, in Attica, Greece. This early black-and-white film remains one of the most valuable and sensitive records of Byzantine art. The camera follows the scenes of the two cycles represented: the Passion of Christ and the Legend of Mary. The commentary is of special interest both because of its writer and narrators.

U.S. distributor: Film Images (sales and rental).

Canadian distributor: Canadian Film Institute for the National Gallery of Canada (loan).

DAUMIER, EYE-WITNESS OF AN EPOCH (*Daumier, témoin d'une époque*)
11 mins. B&W. Originally 35mm. Netherlands. 1972.

Producer: Nico Crama.

Credits: Nico Crama, director; Mart Ambry and Nico Crama, writers; David Brierley, narrator; period music (Jacques Offenbach).

Summary: The lithographs of Honoré Daumier express his political views; they also reflect the important events of the period 1832-1872. Without reference to his paintings or sculpture, the film shows clearly the extent to which a caricaturist can become identified with the life of his time.

U.S. distributor: Visual Resources (sales and rental).

Canadian distributor: Faroun Films (sales and rental).

DAVID HOCKNEY'S DIARIES
28 mins. Color. U.S.A. 1971.

Producer: Blackwood Productions.

Credits: Michael and Christian Blackwood, directors.

Summary: David Hockney, British Pop artist of the 1960s, shares his snapshot albums and explains how his paintings derive from the photos and from many drawings. He is shown working on a portrait of London fashion designer Ossie Clark and his wife Celia. He reminisces about his trips to America and discusses his early paintings and drawings.

U.S. distributor: Blackwood Productions (sales and rental).

DEGAS
7 mins. Color. U.S.A. 1973.

Producer: David W. Powell and Cherrill Anson, National Gallery of Art, Visual Images.

Credits: David W. Powell, director; Cherrill Anson, Evelyn Anderson, writers; Peter Vogt, narrator; Richard McLanathan, consultant.

Summary: Paintings and graphics by Edgar Degas shown parallel to frames from pioneer motion pictures by Eadweard Muybridge. The film attempts to prove that Degas' art was influenced by his interest in photography.

U.S. distributor: National Gallery of Art (rental).

DINA IN THE KING'S GARDEN (*Dina chez les rois*) (*Maillol Sculpture*)
10 mins. Color. Originally 35mm. France. 1966.

Producer: Les Films du Prieuré.

Credits: Dominique Delouche, director; Richard Strauss (Francis Poulenc in original French version), music.

Summary: Robust and with a compelling earth-mother quality, Dina was the perfect model for Aristide Maillol to use for the adaptation of classical elegance in his sculpture. She embodied the idealism of ancient Greece and the sensuality of the early twentieth century. This is a filmic ballad based on the bronze nymphs standing in the snow-covered Tuileries gardens in Paris.

U.S. distributor: The Roland Collection (sales and rental).

Canadian distributor: Embassy of France (loan).

DOCUMENT OF A PAINTING
24 mins. Color. U.S.A. 1974.

Producer: Elizabeth Wiener.

Credits: Elizabeth Wiener, director and photographer; John Cage, music.

Summary: The step-by-step creation of a three-dimensional painting by a young New York painter, George Peck. The painting is formed by the repetition of an original shape which depicts a particular line moving through space at its own speed. The artist discusses his theories of motion, repetition, and color in relation to contemporary thought. The latter part of the film is devoted to an "event" on a beach, as further illustration of the artist's intention.

U.S. distributor: Elizabeth Wiener (sales and rental).

DOCUMENTA 68 or ART BETWEEN TODAY AND TOMORROW (*Kunst zwischen heute und morgen*)
27 mins. Color. Federal Republic of Germany. 1968.

Producer: Cinecentrum grumbh.

Credits: Kurt Zimmermann, director.

Summary: The exhibition Documenta, Kassel, takes its name from the desire of the German people at the end of the war to "document" the art of their lost years and to make new creative contacts with the art world. This film of Documenta 4 presents the fourth in a continuing survey of contemporary trends.

U.S. distributor: Modern Talking Pictures for the Embassy of the Federal Republic of Germany (loan under first title).

Canadian distributor: Canadian Film Institute for the Embassy of the Federal Republic of Germany (rental under second title).

DONG KINGMAN
15 mins. Color. U.S.A. 1954.

Producer: James Wong Howe for the Harmon Foundation.

Credits: James Wong Howe, director and photographer; Tom Prideaux, writer; Edmund Ryan, narrator; authentic Chinese music.

Summary: Shows the development of a single painting in connection with the life of the artist. We follow Dong Kingman from his sketches in New York's Chinatown to the final touches in his apartment. His sensibility to his environment is expressed by a number of quick glimpses of signs, weapons, facades, his cat and his home.

U.S. distributor: Living Artists Productions (sales and rental).

THE DRAWINGS OF LEONARDO DA VINCI
28 mins. Color. Britain. 1953.

Producer: Basil Wright for the British Film Institute Experimental Production Fund and the Arts Council of Great Britain.

Credits: Adrian de Potier, director; Michael Ayrton, writer; A. E. Popham, adviser; Sir Laurence Olivier and C. Day Lewis, narrators: Alan Rawsthorne, music.

Summary: The genius of Leonardo da Vinci revealed through his drawings, the only remaining evidence for many of his artistic and scientific projects. The drawings, the largest collection ever made, were assembled by the Royal Academy of London for the quincentenary celebration of his birth. The film, a permanent record of this important exhibition, was made from these original drawings on a photographic bench specially installed at the Royal Academy. The commentary emphasizes Leonardo's insatiable curiosity and evokes a sense of wonder and reverence.

U.S. distributor: Films Incorporated (sales and rental).

Canadian distributor: Visual Education Centre (sales and rental).

DUNCAN GRANT AT CHARLESTON
33 mins. Color. Originally 35mm. Britain. 1970.

Producer: Christopher Mason, Mason-Bruce Productions.

Credits: Christopher Mason, director; Duncan Grant, Quentin Bell, Angelica Garnett, participants; Brian Harvey Garret, music.

Summary: Duncan Grant, at 86, is interviewed at Charleston, his country home in Sussex, by Quentin Bell, the son of Clive and Vanessa Bell and nephew of Virginia Woolf. The house, where he has lived since 1916, has been subtly decorated by Vanessa Bell and himself: walls, doors, folding screens, curtains, carpets, tables, mirrors, tapestries, pottery, and paintings are, for the most part, their own work. Against this evocative background, Duncan Grant recalls his memories of Roger Fry and his Omega Workshop, the Bloomsbury Group, and the French painters he met at Gertrude Stein's Paris apartment.

U.S. distributor: Monument Film Corporation (sales and rental).

Canadian distributor: New Cinema Enterprises (sales and rental); Canadian Film Institute for the National Gallery of Canada (loan).

DUTCH MASTERPIECES OF THE EIGHTEENTH CENTURY
16 mins. Color. U.S.A. 1973.

Producer: Woelm-Polister.

Credits: Jim Woelm, director and writer; Dick Polister, photographer and editor.

Summary: Based on a Minneapolis exhibition, "Dutch Paintings and Drawings, 1700-1799." The introduction recalls, by means of works of art, the flourishing situation of Holland at this period while the rest of Europe was at war. The paintings are surveyed by subject: still lifes, interiors, street scenes, architecture, portraits, seascapes, and landscapes. A large number of artists and their work are shown very briefly. The music is occasionally obtrusive.

U.S. distributor: Woelm-Polister (sales).

DWELLINGS (by Charles Simonds)
13 mins. Color. U.S.A. 1974.

Producer: Rudy Burckhardt.

Credits: Rudy Burckhardt, director; Charles Simonds, participant.

Summary: A poetic approach to the small constructions of Charles Simonds. Since 1970, he has spent most of his time going around the streets of New York building clay dwellings for an imaginary civilization of Little People who are migrating through the city. While Charles Simonds creates according to his fantasy, he pays no attention to the life of the city—even when a car is burning close to him.

U.S. distributor: Museum at Large (sales and rental).

EASTER ISLAND
10 mins. Color. U.S.A. 1969.

Producer: Coleman Film Enterprises.

Credits: Dr. J. Donald McIntyre, Kansas City Museum, director, writer and photographer.

Summary: Mystery still surrounds the ancient people who carved the gigantic statues on Easter Island and placed them in position without the use of poles or logs. This document, filmed entirely on location, tells the story of the island, its early inhabitants, and the giant stone figures that stand for miles like an army at attention.

U.S. distributor: RMI Film Productions (sales and rental).

Canadian distributor: Viking Films (sales and rental).

EASTER ISLAND: PUZZLE OF THE PACIFIC
28 mins. Color. U.S.A. 1970.

Producer: Arnold Eagle, ABC News.

Credits: Arnold Eagle, director; James Giggans, writer; Peter Jennings, narrator.

Summary: A presentation of the theories developed by Arnold Eagle and Dr. William Malloy, professor of Archaeology at the University of Wyoming, based on their research on Easter Island. They explore the culture and art of the island, the mystery surrounding the people who created it, their disappearance, and the strange, undeciphered script and gigantic statues they left behind.

U.S. distributor: Macmillan (sales); Association Films, Inc. (rental).

EDOUARD MANET—The First Revolutionary Artist
(*Pioneers of Modern Painting* series, no. 1)
40 mins. Color. Britain. 1972.

Producer: Colin Clark for Independent Television Corporation.

Credits: Colin Clark, director; Lord Clark, writer and narrator.

Summary: Lord Clark affirms that Manet's *Olympia*, which "caused one of the loudest and fiercest outcries in the whole history of art," marked the real beginning of modern painting—an opinion he feels would have been shared by the other five artists in the series. Although Lord Clark describes the style of the painter as "straightforward naturalism, now out of fashion," Manet was considered the first revolutionary artist, "positively persecuted by the Establishment." The film contains comments on his personal life and some of his most beautiful canvases.

U.S. distributor: Independent Television Corporation (sales); National Gallery of Art (loan).

Canadian distributor: ITC of Canada (sales); Canadian Film Institute for the National Gallery of Canada (loan).

EDVARD MUNCH—The Norwegian Master of Expressionism
(*Pioneers of Modern Painting* series, no. 6)
40 mins. Color. Britain. 1972.

Producer: Colin Clark for Independent Television Corporation.

Credits: Colin Clark, director; Lord Clark, writer and narrator.

Summary: This study of Edvard Munch begins in the small Norwegian town of Aagardstrand, which had so great an influence on his work. Lord Clark suggests that people subjected to the violent contrasts of a northern climate feel more intensely than others the opposition of life and death, good and evil. He discusses Munch's changing styles—his progression through Impressionism to Expressionism and his simplified technique to convey a state of mind, using the painting *Jealousy* as an example. In the last sequence Lord Clark guides the viewer through the museum specially designed for the large collection of paintings the artist left to the city of Oslo.

U.S. distributor: Independent Television Corporation (sales); National Gallery of Art (loan).

Canadian distributor: ITC of Canada (sales); Canadian Film Institute for the National Gallery of Canada (loan).

EDVARD MUNCH: PAINTINGS
39 mins. Color. U.S.A. and Norway. 1967.

Producer: Clifford B. West, OIP Films.

Credits: Clifford B. West, director and photographer; Robert Jager, music.

Summary: A companion film to *Edvard Munch: Prints*. The artist's diary is used as a basis for the commentary. The paintings of Munch's *Frieze of Life*, following the themes of sickness, suffering, and the fear of life, are related to his own experiences and are for him a kind of confession. Self-portraits of different periods reveal the evolution of his style.

U.S. distributor: Film Images (sales and rental).

EDVARD MUNCH: PRINTS
(EDVARD MUNCH: GRAPHICS, WATERCOLORS, DRAWINGS, AND SCULPTURE)
27 mins. Color. U.S.A. and Norway. 1967.

Producer: Clifford B. West, OIP Films.

Credits: Clifford B. West, director and photographer; Bente E. Torjusen and Gillian Ford Shallcross, writers of commentary; E. G. Burrows, narrator; Robert Jager, music.

Summary: This is the first part of a diptych on Munch's work filmed in Norway. Although the approach is biographic, his technical contributions to printmaking are stressed, especially his segmented and separately inked color woodcuts which require only one impression to print. Munch's most famous graphics are studied in minute detail and special effects are used to focus on the texture and to pinpoint the centers of interest.

U.S. distributor: Film Images (sales and rental).

EDWARD BURRA

31 mins. Color. Britain. 1973.

Producer: Balfour Films, Carole K. Smith, for the Arts Council of Great Britain.

Credits: Peter K. Smith, director.

Summary: Portrait of a solitary, disillusioned artist, yet an actor able to conceal his feelings behind an evasive, charming facade. His painting seems to belong to the past, to the Surrealist and Expressionist period of the 1930s, the "interregnum" so well pictured by Grosz and now appearing as a tragic caricature. Burra's detached treatment of the sociological and political themes in his work heightens their impact, reflecting the cold impersonality of the twentieth century toward its atrocities.

U.S. distributor: The American Federation of Arts (rental); Films Incorporated (sales).

THE EGG AND THE EYE

25 mins. Color. U.S.A. 1967.

Producer: Jeffrey Brown and Edie Brown Eisenberg, The Egg And The Eye, Incorporated.

Credits: Jeffrey Brown and Edie Brown Eisenberg, directors; Staats Cotsworth, narrator.

Summary: An iconographical approach to the egg throughout the history of art and literature. The film discovers images of the egg in Saharan cave paintings; in the works of Hieronymus Bosch and Piero della Francesca; in the Surrealist paintings of Dali and De Chirico; in the sculpture of Brancusi and Nakanishi; in the Op and Pop movements; and finally in Kaprow's "happenings." The commentary supports the visual exploration of the egg with quotations from Plato, Ruskin, da Vinci, and Harold Rosenberg.

U.S. distributor: Carousel Films (sales and rental); Association Films, Inc. (sales and rental).

1848 or THE REVOLUTION OF 1848

22 mins. B&W. Originally 35mm. France. 1948.

Producers: A. F. Films (Coopérative Générale du Cinéma Français).

Credits: Victoria Spiri Mercanton, Marguerite de la Mure, Albert Saboul, directors; Pierre Courtade, writer; Michael Alexander, American adaptation; Guy Sorel, narrator; Guy Bernard, music.

Summary: Produced on the occasion of the centennial of the 1848 uprising in Paris, this documentary is still of interest today. By means of etchings, engravings, ink drawings, and paintings, it examines the conditions of life and the causes of discontent which led to the fierce street fighting, the fall of Louis-Philippe, and the rise of Louis Napoleon. Daumier, Decamps, Delacroix, and Gavarni are among the artists whose works preserve a lively record of this terrible year.

U.S. distributor: Film Images (sales and rental).

ELECTRIC GALLERY PLUS THREE (*Art and Music Education* series)
12 mins. Color. Canada. 1972.

Producer: Cyril Bursell, McCurdy-Bursell Films.

Credits: Jim McCurdy, director, writer, and editor.

Summary: A new form of art is born, neither painting nor sculpture, based on electronics and electric light. Three artists are interviewed: Norman White, who is "more interested in the process than in the result"; Martin Hirschberg and Zbigniew Blazye, who are shown preparing their magic experiences. The last part of the film reviews a series of their works in an art show.

U.S. distributor: Oxford Films (sales and rental).

Canadian distributor: Marlin Motion Pictures (sales and rental).

EMIL NOLDE
12 mins. Color. Federal Republic of Germany. 1965.

Producer: Th. N. Blomberg.

Credits: Th. N. Blomberg, director; Friedhelm Heyde, writer and photographer; Joachim Ludwig, music.

Summary: The art and life of one of the most representative of the German Expressionist painters. This documentary was made in Seebull, where Nolde spent the last years of his life and where many of his most significant works are exhibited. His paintings are shown in chronological order and the influence of the North Friesian landscape is emphasized. The commentary often draws upon his own statements.

U.S. distributor: The Roland Collection (sales and rental); Modern Talking Pictures for the Embassy of the Federal Republic of Germany (loan).

Canadian distributor: Canadian Film Institute for the Embassy of the Federal Republic of Germany (loan).

ENCRE (Ink)
20 mins. Color. Originally 35mm. Belgium. 1964.

Producer: Sofidoc, Brussels.

Credits: Jean Cleinge, director; André Souris, music; no narration.

Summary: Three painters, Alechinsky, Appel, and Ting, each create an original lithograph with the help of the printer Beaudet and his fellow craftsmen. They use early-twentieth-century machines and traditional tools. The whole process is followed, from the direct drawing on the stone down to the final printing.

U.S. distributor: International Film Bureau (sales and rental).

Canadian distributor: Educational Film Distributors (sales and rental); Canadian Film Institute for the National Gallery of Canada (loan).

EPSTEIN or EPSTEIN IN EDINBURGH
19 mins. B&W. Britain. 1962.

Producer: Campbell Harper Films for Educational Films of Scotland.

Credits: Henry Cooper, director and editor; Tom Fleming, narrator.

Summary: A comprehensive collection of the works of the great British sculptor, Sir Jacob Epstein, was assembled for the Memorial Exhibition presented as part of the Edinburgh Festival of 1961. The film, a unique record of this exhibition, reveals Epstein as a magnificent portraitist, the creator of a number of intensely controversial works of sculpture (*Rima, Adam*), and also as an exceptionally talented draftsman and colorist.

U.S. distributor: Carman Educational Associates (sales and rental).

Canadian distributor: Carman Educational Associates (sales and rental).

ERNST BARLACH (*Barlach Studien*)
15 mins. Color. Federal Republic of Germany. 1966.

Producer: Hart-Film.

Credits: Wolf Hart, director, writer and photographer; H. M. Majevski, music; no narration.

Summary: A fresh interpretation by means of camera, music, and montage of the work of a leading figure of early German Expressionism. The film concentrates on twelve wood carvings of single figures displayed in a museum. The camera explores the volume, texture, latent movement, and the emotions of these tragic figures.

U.S. distributor: Visual Resources (sales and rental).

ESKIMO ARTIST: KENOJUAK or KENOJUAK
20 mins. Color. Originally 35mm. Canada. 1964.

Producer: Tom Daly, National Film Board, and the Department of Northern Affairs and National Resources.

Credits: John Feeney, director, writer, and editor; James Houston, consultant; Eldon Rathburn, music.

Summary: A study of an Eskimo graphic artist showing the sources of her inspiration in the Canadian Arctic where twilight, snow, sky, and air throng with shadows. Her words, spoken as commentary, give further meaning to the images she creates. From her designs the Co-operative Art Centre of Cape Dorset produces a limited number of prints on fine rice paper.

U.S. distributor: National Film Board of Canada (U.S.A.) (sales and rental).

Canadian distributor: National Film Board of Canada (sales and loan); Canadian Film Institute for the National Gallery of Canada (loan).

EUGENE ATGET
10 mins. B&W. Originally 35mm. U.S.A. 1963.

Producer: Harold Becker Productions.

Credits: Harold Becker, director; Wardell Gaynor, animation; music by Erik Satie; no narration.

Summary: Paris at the turn of the century, seen in the rare photographs of Eugene Atget. Streets, cafés, shop windows, gardens with statues, chestnuts in bloom, a barrel organ, provide a beguiling and nostalgic exhibition of the work of this distinguished French photographer.

U.S. distributor: Harold Becker.

Canadian distributor: Canadian Film Institute for the National Gallery of Canada (loan).

EUGENE BOUDIN or BOUDIN
20 mins. Color. France. 1966.

Producer: Les Films Demeter, Paris.

Credits: Raphaël Motte, director and writer; Bruno Gillet, music.

Summary: The life and work of the artist whose investigations into the atmospheric effects of light paved the way for the experiments of the Impressionists. The Seine estuary and the beaches of Normandy with their particular light were a major source of inspiration for Boudin. His copious diary provided the material for the narration.

U.S. distributor: FACSEA (rental).

Canadian distributor: Embassy of France (loan).

EXCAVATIONS AT LA VENTA
29 mins. Color. U.S.A. 1963.

Producer: Aline Evans and the Department of Anthropology for the University of California Extension Media Center, Berkeley (with a grant from the National Science Foundation).

Credits: Aline Evans, director and editor; C. C. Macauley, photographer and editor; Robert F. Heizer, consultant; Anthony Ostroff, narrator.

Summary: A clear description through color still photographs, models, film, and detailed animation of the large-scale archeological diggings in 1955 at the Olmec site on the island of La Venta, Tabasco, Mexico. Dating from 800 B.C., La Venta is the earliest of the religious centers discovered in Central America. This film is intended mainly for specialists.

U.S. distributor: University of California (sales and rental).

Canadian distributor: International Tele-Film Enterprises (sales and rental).

EXETER
29 mins. Color. Canada. 1972.

Producer: Wolf Koenig, National Film Board of Canada for the National Gallery of Canada.

Credits: Gerald Budner, director; Michael Kane, narrator; The Dunstable Consort, music.

Summary: The cathedral at Exeter is considered the finest example of the Decorative period, 1250-1350. Its nave is the longest unbroken stretch of Gothic vaulting in the world. This intense film tells its story with the help of Medieval manuscripts, sculpture, and ornamentation, combined with scenes of present-day workers and townsfolk bartering their produce in the marketplace or participating in the cathedral's services and ceremonies.

U.S. distributor: International Film Bureau (sales and rental).

Canadian distributor: National Film Board (sales and loan).

EXPERIMENTS IN CUBISM or AN EXPERIMENT IN CUBISM
(*L'esperienza del cubismo*)
11 mins. B&W. Italy. 1949.

Producer: Geo Taparelli for Lux Film.

Credits: Glauco Pellegrini, director; Rodolfo Sonego, writer; Renato Guttuso, technical adviser; Luigi Dallapiccola, music.

Summary: An explanation of the technique of Cubist paintings, showing how the artist continues to draw on nature for the sources of his material but recomposes it for his own specific ends. The film relies on purely cinematic means to make its point, using animation, angle-shots, and superimpositions with originality and inventiveness.

U.S. distributor: Macmillan (sales and rental).

Canadian distributor: Canadian Film Institute for the National Gallery of Canada (loan).

EXPRESSIONISM
26 mins. Color. U.S.A. 1971.

Producer: Egons Tomsons for International Film Bureau.

Credits: George Barford, Professor of Art, Illinois State University, writer; Daumons Tomsons, animation.

Summary: A didactic account of the revolution in painting which exploded in Germany before World War I. After briefly acknowledging the influence of Van Gogh, Gauguin, and Munch, the formal beginnings of Expressionism in Dresden are studied through the works of the artists known as "Die Brücke" (The Bridge): Kirchner, Heckel, Schmidt-Rottluff, Nolde, and Pechstein. The closely related paintings by Kokoschka and Beckmann are also shown. The survey continues with the artists of the second major Expressionist group, "Die Blaue Reiter" (The Blue Rider) of Munich: Marc, Kandinsky, Klee, and others.

U.S. distributor: International Film Bureau (sales and rental).

Canadian distributor: Educational Film Distributors (sales and rental).

THE EXPRESSIONIST REVOLT
10 mins. Color. U.S.A. 1957.

Producer: Detroit Institute of Arts.

Credits: Virginia Harrison, director and writer; Edward Chudakoff, music.

Summary: A survey of the German Expressionist paintings housed in the Detroit Institute of Arts, a significant collection which includes works from the decade before World War I. Among those represented are Ernst Ludwig Kirchner, Karl Schmidt-Rottluff, Vassily Kandinsky, Oskar Kokoschka, Emil Nolde, Max Pechstein, Ernst Barlach, Franz Marc, Lyonel Feininger, and Paul Klee. Five of these artists shared a common studio and formed the group "Die Brücke" (The Bridge). They were largely instrumental in the development of the woodcut as an important medium, especially for posters.

U.S. distributor: Film Images (sales and rental).

Canadian distributor: Canadian Film Institute for the National Gallery of Canada (loan).

FAUVISM (*Fauvisme*)
(*Pathways of Modern Painting* series, no. 4)
17 mins. Color. Originally 35mm. France. 1971.

Producer: Jacqueline Jullien, Les Films du Cyprès and the International Film Bureau.

Credits: Pierre Alibert, director; Bernard Dorival, consultant; Philip Gaunt, narrator; Francis Seyrig, music.

Summary: Discusses the place of Fauvism in the history of painting. The Fauves were characterized by their use of color as applied to express form, light, and volume. Techniques used by the Fauves are compared with those of other schools, including the Impressionist and Neo-Impressionist painters and the Nabis. Examples of Fauvist work photographed in various French museums include paintings by Vlaminck, Matisse, Duchamp, Delaunay, Dufy, and Derain.

U.S. distributor: International Film Bureau (sales and rental).

Canadian distributor: Educational Film Distributors (sales and rental).

FERNAND LEGER IN AMERICA—HIS NEW REALISM
30 mins. Color. U.S.A. French with English translation. 1942.

Producer: Thomas Bouchard.

Credits: Thomas Bouchard, director; Fernand Léger, narrator; Edgard Varèse, music.

Summary: Léger by Léger, an intimate document on Léger's life and production in New York during World War II. We accompany him through the streets, in his apartment where he cooks, in the country where he paints. In his narration, he gives his views on a great variety of subjects.

U.S. distributor: Thomas Bouchard (rental).

FIGURES IN A LANDSCAPE
18 mins. Color. Britain. 1953.

Producer: British Film Institute for the Arts Council of Great Britain.

Credits: Dudley Shaw Ashton, director, writer, and photographer; Jacquetta Hawks, writer of commentary; Cecil Day Lewis, narrator; Priaulx Rainer, music.

Summary: Examples of Barbara Hepworth's sculpture, placed against the landscape of her native Cornwall, are seen both as an integral part and an outgrowth of the Cornish landscape. She is shown at work in her studio at St. Ives, where the creation of a new carving is followed from its first sketches to completion.

U.S. distributor: Films Incorporated (sales and rental).

A FILM FOR LUCEBERT (*Een film voor Lucebert*)
20 mins. Color. Netherlands. 1972.

Producer: Johan van der Keuken.

Credits: Johan van der Keuken, director, photographer, editor; Lucebert, writer; Willem Brecker, music.

Summary: The cry of revolt of a poet and painter, Lucebert who was impressed in his childhood by working class riots and then by World War II. The film shifts from shocking views of poverty, physical disabilities, and slaughter to soap bubbles, umbrellas, folk festivities, and details of Lucebert's paintings, mysteriously linked with these images of reality. The commentary takes the form of an intermittent recital of his poetry. The last sequence shows him creating a painting; by means of animation, the image constantly transforms itself, is destroyed and reinvented.

U.S. distributor: Royal Netherlands Embassy (loan).

FLANDERS IN THE 15TH CENTURY—THE FIRST OIL PAINTINGS
25 mins. Color. U.S.A. 1962.

Producer: Detroit Institute of Arts.

Credits: John D. Moore, director, writer, and narrator; period music by Guillaume Dufay.

Summary: A comparative study based on some of the finest Flemish oil paintings in the collection of the Detroit Institute of Arts. Painters include Jan van Eyck, Rogier van der Weyden, Gerard David, Master Michiel, and two other artists known only as The Master of the St. Lucy Legend and The Master of the St. Ursula Legend.

U.S. distributor: Film Images (sales and rental).

A FLOATING WORLD OF JAPANESE PAINTING (*Ukiyo-e*)
20 mins. Color. U.S.A.

Producer: American Educational Films.

Credits: Shin-ichi-Yuize, music.

Summary: A chronological presentation of 300 examples of the Ukiyo-e painters' favorite subject matter: the kimono-clad beauties of the day. Works by modern artists carrying on the Ukiyo-e tradition are also reviewed. Ukiyo-e woodblock prints, famous throughout the world, had a definite influence on European Impressionism. This film reveals an art form which has had little exposure; an art form which represents a new popular Japanese expression in reaction against the traditional samurai culture during the Tokugawa Era (1600-1868).

U.S. distributor: American Educational Films (sales and rental).

Canadian distributor: Bellevue Film Distributors (sales).

THE FORBIDDEN CITY
43 mins. Color. U.S.A. 1972.

Producer: Lucy Jarvis, NBC Educational Enterprises.

Credits: Tom Priestly, director.

Summary: A description of the imperial citadel, called Ku Kung or the Forbidden City, in the center of Peking, China. From 1421 to 1911 Ku Kung was the home of the emperors of China; today it is a splendid museum of Chinese history and culture. This visit to the Forbidden City recalls the period when the Mings and Manchus ruled China in isolated splendor, while the majority of the people lived in poverty.

U.S. distributor: Films Incorporated (sales and rental).

Canadian distributor: Visual Education Centre (sales and rental).

FRAGMENTS (*Toredek*)
16 mins. Color. Hungary. 1966.

Producer: Mafilm Studio, Budapest.

Credits: Agoston Kollanyi, director.

Summary: The Tartar invasion of Hungary left the country's major art monuments almost totally destroyed, but the fragments remaining form a magnificent collection that challenges comparison, in many respects, with the world's greatest. Many pieces are shown, with examples from Gothic and other periods.

U.S. distributor: Macmillan (sales and rental).

Canadian distributor: Canadian Film Institute for the National Gallery of Canada (loan).

FRANCIS BACON—PAINTINGS 1944-1962
11 mins. Color. Britain. 1963.

Producer: Dudley Shaw Ashton, Samaritan Films London, for the Arts Council of Great Britain and Marlborough Fine Art, Ltd.

Credits: Dudley Shaw Ashton, director; David Thompson, writer; Elisabeth Lutyens, music; John Hollingsworth, conductor; no commentary.

Summary: A free interpretation in film of the work of the painter, showing some of the material in which he found inspiration and how it has been used in his startling and arresting compositions. Velázquez's *Pope Innocent X*, Muybridge's *Animals in Motion*, and shots from the Odessa Steps sequence of *Potemkin* are juxtaposed with the paintings.

U.S. distributor: The American Federation of Arts (rental); Films Incorporated (sales).

Canadian distributor: Canadian Film Institute for the National Gallery of Canada (loan).

FRANKLIN WATKINS
32 mins. B&W with Color. U.S.A. 1950.

Producer: Philadelphia Museum of Art.

Credits: E. M. Benson, director, writer, and narrator.

Summary: The Philadelphia painter at work in his studio on *Death and Resurrection* and *The Fire Eater*, portraits of the late Justice Owen Roberts and I. Stogdall Stokes. Two related themes are studied: the development and meaning of a portrait and the explanation of two large murals painted over a period of several years. The narration and music somewhat detract from this document on the slow growth of an artist.

U.S. distributor: Film Images (sales and rental).

FROM DADA TO SURREALISM (*La clef des chants surréalistes*)
40 mins. B&W. Originally 35mm. Belgium. 1966.

Producer: Art et Cinéma, Belgium.

Credits: Paul Haesaerts, director and writer; Frédéric Devreese, music.

Summary: An introduction to the concepts and compositions of Surrealism, starting from its literary sources in André Breton and the nihilistic Dada school founded in Zurich during World War I. The artists reviewed include de Chirico, Magritte, Delvaux, Brauner (with his variations), Picasso (for his distortions), Ernst, Chagall, Dali, Klee, and Miró.

U.S. distributor: Macmillan (sales).

FROM DORIC TO GOTHIC (*Equilibre*)
20 mins. B&W. France. 1954.

Producer: Marcel de Huebsch for Atlantic Films, Paris.

Credits: André Gillet, director; Henri Séguy, consultant; Jacques Ibert, music; Arthur Knight, American adaptation.

Summary: The history and principles of architecture, presented with clarity and simplicity. The fundamentals of balance are illustrated in the development of the roof, from the pillar and beam construction of the Greek temple to the vaulted arch of the Gothic cathedral. Animation, diagrams, and scale models are used, as well as actual scenes including several French cathedrals.

U.S. distributor: Macmillan (sales).

Canadian distributor: International Educational Films (sales—French version only); Canadian Film Institute for the National Gallery of Canada (loan—English version).

THE FUNERAL OF STEF HALACEK (*Pogreb Štefa Halačeka*)
16 mins. Color. Originally 35mm. Yugoslavia. 1960.

Producer: Zora Film, Zagreb.

Credits: Branko Ranitovic, director; Ivo Lhotka-Kalinski, music.

Summary: Naive paintings by some of Yugoslavia's most famous primitive artists illustrate the good and bad times in the life of a typical peasant from a poor Croatian village in "grandfather's days." The painters include Ivan Generalic, Mirko Virius, and Dragan Gaza.

U.S. distributor: Yugoslav Information Center (loan).

Canadian distributor: Embassy of the S.F.R. of Yugoslavia (rental).

GAINSBOROUGH (*Canvas* series no. 1—*Personal Reflections on Great Paintings*)
20 mins. Color. Britain. 1966.

Producer: John Furness, BBC-TV.

Credits: Derek Trimby, director; William Thomson, participant, writer, and narrator.

Summary: An introduction to the art of Thomas Gainsborough by William Thomson, a Canadian artist, at Kenwood House, Hampstead. Using the portrait of Lady Howe as focal point and term of reference, he reviews and comments on this and many other Gainsborough paintings.

U.S. distributor: Time-Life (sales only).

Canadian distributor: BBC-TV Enterprises (sales and rental).

GALLERY: A VIEW OF TIME
14 mins. Color. Canada. 1969.

Producer: Don Owen Associates for the Albright-Knox Art Gallery, Buffalo, N.Y.

Credits: Don Owen, director.

Summary: A vivid impression of the Albright-Knox Art Gallery in Buffalo, New York, through a motion picture which is itself a work of art. Over a hundred great works from the Gallery's collections—paintings, sculpture, light and mirror shows, as well as the building's superb architecture—are seen in a brilliant montage of sound, motion, and color, giving the viewer a sense of time as well as place.

U.S. distributor: Macmillan (sales and rental).

Canadian distributor: Canadian Filmmakers' Distribution Centre (sales and rental).

THE GALLERY DOWN UNDER or THE GALLERY (*Outlook* series)
9 mins. Color. Australia. 1970.

Producer: Gil Brealey, the Commonwealth Film Unit.

Credits: Philip Mark Law, director and writer; L. Dempsey, music; no narration.

Summary: A glimpse of the National Gallery in Victoria, New South Wales, a building of outstanding features and attractions reflecting Australia's progressive architecture. Of special interest is the architect's use of water in pools, fountains, and falls, and the use of glass in walls, window arrangement, and the notable stained glass ceiling in the great hall.

U.S. distributor: Independent Film Producers Company; Australian Information Service (sales and rental).

Canadian distributor: Australian High Commission (loan).

GAUGUIN IN TAHITI: THE SEARCH FOR PARADISE
51 mins. (In two parts, 31 & 20 mins.) Color. U.S.A. 1967.

Producer: Martin Carr, CBS News.

Credits: Martin Carr, director and writer, using quotations from Gauguin; Charles Kuralt and Michael Redgrave, narrators; Gerald Fried, music.

Summary: An account of Gauguin's life and an insight into the personality of a great artist. The film explains many of the reasons why Gauguin went to the South Pacific, where as an artist he created the paradise he failed to find there as a man. How his life in Tahiti affected his work and the influences it had on his art are graphically presented. (Teacher's guide available.)

U.S. distributor: CBS Publishing Group (sales).

GENESIS OF AN IDEA: ABRAHAM RATTNER
16 mins. Color. U.S.A. 1960.

Producer: Allen Leepa.

Credits: Allen Leepa, director, writer, and photographer; A. V. Center, Michigan State University, technical assistance; Allen Leepa and Abraham Rattner, narrators; Robert Shinberg, music.

Summary: Gives an intimate view of the painter Abraham Rattner. The artist discusses what it means to be working today and the creative challenges of painting. He demonstrates his methods as he deals with the theme of Moses, showing how his idea develops in the numerous sketches and paintings which he prepares.

U.S. distributor: Film Images (sales and rental).

GEORGES BRAQUE
22 mins. B&W. Originally 35mm. France. 1950.

Producer: Stanislas Fumet, Paul Claudon, Film du Temps, CAPAC.

Credits: André Bureau, director; Stanislas Fumet, writer; Hurd Hatfield, narrator.

Summary: Shows a master of modern art at work revealing his technique and his philosophy of art. Braque's contributions to modern art influenced not only Cubism but also subsequent trends in painting and sculpture. The highlights of this documentary are the examination of many works, close-ups of the artist and, in particular, one sequence of Braque drawing on a piece of glass placed between him and the camera so that one can see the development of the lines.

U.S. distributor: Film Images (sales and rental).

Canadian distributor: Embassy of France (loan—French version).

GEORGES ROUAULT
30 mins. Color. Originally 35mm. France. 1971.

Producer: Cofilmdoc, Paris.

Credits: Pierre Courthion, Isabelle Rouault, Geneviève Nouaille-Rouault, directors and writers.

Summary: With meticulous care and devotion Rouault's daughters have composed this film biography of their famous father. Using rare photographs and live footage—historical and contemporary—the film re-creates Rouault's childhood, his apprenticeship in the atelier of Gustave Moreau, his Fauve period, his social protest, the *Miserere*, and the last glowing Biblical landscapes. (A longer version in four parts, 14 mins. each, is available from FACSEA on rental.)

U.S. distributor: Texture Films (sales and rental).

Canadian distributor: International Tele-film Enterprises (sales and rental).

GEORGES SEURAT—The Most French of Painters
(*Pioneers of Modern Painting* series, no. 4)
40 mins. Color. Britain. 1972.

Producer: Colin Clark for Independent Television Corporation.

Credits: Colin Clark, director; Lord Clark, writer and narrator.

Summary: "Silent and secretive, gentle and obstinate." Nothing is known of the short, private life of Georges Seurat, of whom Lord Clark says, "He concentrates in himself all the intellectual currents of the time: the interest in Primitive and Oriental art, the beginnings of Art Nouveau and Symbolism, above all the belief in Science." One of the painters who carried Impressionism into new directions, he developed the method of Pointillism in which tiny patches of color build up the composition.

U.S. distributor: Independent Television Corporation (sales); National Gallery of Art (loan).

Canadian distributor: ITC of Canada (sales); Canadian Film Institute for the National Gallery of Canada (loan).

GERMANY—DADA (*Museum Without Walls* collection)
55 mins. Color. Originally 35mm. U.S.A. 1968.

Producer: Helmut Herbst.

Credits: Helmut Herbst, director; Hans Richter and Richard Huelsenbeck, participants and narrators.

Summary: Shows the phenomenon of the Dada art movement, with actual photographs of its leaders and recordings of music and poetry. Dada is presented as a revolt against the slaughter of World War I. Its influence lasted longer than the movement itself, which had faded by 1923. The film shows how the Dadaist group affected cartoons, architecture, typography, advertising, theater, and even costume design.

U.S. distributor: Universal Education and Visual Arts (sales and rental).

Canadian distributor: Universal Education and Visual Arts (sales and rental).

GERTRUDE STEIN: WHEN THIS YOU SEE, REMEMBER ME
89 mins. Color. U.S.A. 1970.

Producer: Perry Miller Adato.

Credits: Perry Miller Adato, director; Marianna Norris, writer; Therese Bonney, stills photographer; Barbara Chase, Betty Henritze, William Redfield, narrators; Al Carmines, Virgil Thomson, music.

Summary: The film biography of a woman and a city who came together at a moment of revolutionary ferment in art and literature. It is the recaptured essence of Paris of the twenties and thirties and the remarkable woman whose circle embraced Picasso, T. S. Eliot, Hemingway, Matisse, Marie Laurencin, Lipchitz, Sherwood Anderson, Ezra Pound, and many other avant-garde writers and painters.

U.S. distributor: McGraw-Hill Films (sales and rental).

Canadian distributor: McGraw-Hill Ryerson (sales and rental); Canadian Film Institute for the National Gallery of Canada (loan).

GIACOMETTI

14 mins. B&W. Britain, 1965.

Producer: David Sylvester, the British Film Institute and the British Broadcasting Corporation for the Arts Council of Great Britain.

Credits: Michael Gill, director; David Sylvester, writer; Roger Smalley, music.

Summary: A unique record of Giacometti at work in the small room in Paris which remained his only studio from 1929 until his death. His intense concentration while drawing and modeling is paralleled by the stillness and silence of the works themselves. The commentary is sparse but includes a few comments by the artist.

U.S. distributor: The American Federation of Arts (rental); Films Incorporated (sales).

GIACOMETTI (*Canvas* series no. 2—*Personal Reflections on Great Paintings*)

20 mins. Color. Britain. 1966.

Producer: John Furness, BBC-TV.

Credits: Derek Trimby, director; Edwin Mullins, participant, writer, and narrator.

Summary: From the Tate Gallery in London, Edwin Mullins gives his views on Giacometti, not only as a sculptor but painter and draftsman as well. The film is built upon a portrait of Caroline, which is used as a leitmotiv throughout the survey. Mullins gives examples showing the influence of Egyptian art on Giacometti's work.

U.S. distributor: Time-Life (sales only).

Canadian distributor: BBC-TV Enterprises (sales and rental).

THE GIFT

30 mins. Color. Originally 35mm. U.S.A. 1975.

Producer: Chuck Olin Associates for the First National Bank of Chicago.

Credits: Chuck Olin, director and writer; Pierre Provoyeur, director of The Chagall Museum, Nice, narrator; Marc Chagall, participant.

Summary: How Marc Chagall created *The Four Seasons*, the seventy-foot-long mosaic for the city of Chicago. Chagall was filmed at Biot, in the South of France, and in Chicago, while he and his mosaicist worked on the three-year project. The artist explains in his own words (with English subtitles) certain changes in color, form, and composition. He follows the mounting and joining of 128 separate panels on the First National Plaza, Chicago.

U.S. distributor: Chuck Olin Associates (sales and rental).

GIORGIO MORANDI
16 mins. Color. Italy. 1974.

Producer: Libero Bizzarri.

Credits: Libero Bizzarri, director; Marie-Zoe Greene-Mercier, consultant for English version; Franco Potenza, music.

Summary: An analysis of more than forty paintings by this widely acclaimed Italian artist. Influenced by Cézanne and by Cubism, Morandi remained an independent who produced a series of single theme variations. Subtle discriminations in light and tone are the basis of his landscapes and still life paintings.

U.S. distributor: International Film Bureau (sales and rental).

Canadian distributor: Educational Film Distributors (sales and rental).

GIOTTO AND THE PRE-RENAISSANCE (*Museum Without Walls* collection)
47 mins. Color. U.S.A. and Italy. 1969.

Producer: Lionello Torossi for Universal Education and Visual Arts.

Credits: Luciano Emmer, director; Kenneth Donahue, English adaptation; Richard Basehart, narrator; Ennio Moricone, music.

Summary: Luciano Emmer, acknowledged master of films on art in the forties, presents his great subject in a new and experimental manner. He effectively combines a dramatic treatment of Giotto's paintings with very wide-angle shots of the buildings and old cities, and he also demonstrates the method of painting a fresco according to Cennini's *Libro dell'Arte*. Most of the film is devoted to Giotto's work in Assisi, Padua, and Florence, but Sienese and Florentine art of the fourteenth century is also discussed.

U.S. distributor: Universal Education and Visual Arts (sales and rental).

Canadian distributor: Universal Education and Visual Arts (sales and rental).

GLASS (*Glas*)
11 mins. Color. Originally 35mm. Netherlands. 1958.

Producer: Bert Haanstra, Filmproduction, Laren, with grants from the Netherlands Ministry of Education, Arts, and Sciences and the Koninklijke Glasfabrieken, Leerdam.

Credits: Bert Haanstra, director and writer; Pim Jacobs, music; no narration.

Summary: A colorful and lyrical treatment of the ancient art of glassblowing and the men who create this elegance and beauty. Their oneness with the molten glass through the control and the timing of their hands, body movements, and breath is contrasted with modern mechanical processes of mass production. A rhythmic jazz score counterpoints the images of men, glass, and machines.

U.S. distributor: Royal Netherlands Embassy (loan).

Canadian distributor: Canadian Film Institute for the National Gallery of Canada (loan).

THE GLORY OF GOYA
17 mins. B&W. U.S.A. 1953.

Producer: Pictura Film Distribution Corporation.

Credits: Luciano Emmer, director; music by Albéniz performed by Andrés Segovia.

Summary: Luciano Emmer here considers Goya not only as a great painter, but also as a keen observer and a kind of reporter. His work is the record of an era, with its joys and sufferings. A brilliant sequence re-creates a bullfight by the rapid editing of details taken from the series of Tauromaquia etchings.

U.S. distributor: Pictura (sales and rental).

GOD'S MONKEY: HIERONYMUS BOSCH
13 mins. Color. U.S.A. 1955.

Producer: Hugh Chisholm.

Credits: George Hoyningen-Huene, director; Hugh Chisholm, writer; Dave Ballard, narrator.

Summary: An exploration of the Prado triptych, *The Garden of Delights,* painted by Hieronymus Bosch some time in the early 1500s. The first panel represents the Garden of Eden before the Fall of Man; the second, the alluring pleasures of the flesh; and the third, the regions of hell where man is faced with the torments of expiation.

U.S. distributor: Film Images (sales and rental).

Canadian distributor: Canadian Film Institute for the National Gallery of Canada (loan).

GOYA
20 mins. B&W. Originally 35mm. U.S.A. 1955.

Producer: Ben Berg, Irving Block for Artemis Productions.

Credits: Ben Berg, director; Irving Block, writer; Victor Perrin, narrator; Vincente Gómez, music (guitar).

Summary: A skillful selection of details from the works of Francisco de Goya y Lucientes, stressing his graphic work. An intelligent commentary presents an engrossing narrative of the artist's life and art and the turbulent era in which he lived.

Canadian distributor: Canadian Film Institute for the National Gallery of Canada (loan).

GOYA
7 mins. Color. U.S.A. 1973.

Producer: David W. Powell, Cherrill Anson.

Credits: David W. Powell, director; Cherrill Anson, writer; Ed Hunter, narrator; Richard McLanathan, consultant.

Summary: Paintings and prints from the National Gallery of Art collections testify to the two-sided artistic legacy of Francisco de Goya—his satiric portraits of the dissolute court of Spain's Carlos IV, and his black-and-white prints showing the *Disasters of War,* his nightmarish fantasies, and the atmosphere of the bullfight.

U.S. distributor: National Gallery of Art (rental).

GOYA (*Museum Without Walls* collection)
54 mins. Color. Originally 35mm. U.S.A. 1973.

Producer: Universal Education and Visual Arts.

Credits: Allan Brown, director; Ricardo Montalban, narrator.

Summary: Based on Goya's work that is housed in Madrid's Prado Museum. The artist's life is traced through his creations: cartoons (actually oils on canvas) for the Royal Tapestry Manufactory, paintings of royalty and friends, frescoes, etchings (the *Caprichos*), the bull-fight series and the "black paintings" which once decorated the walls of his own house. The evolution of his style and his gradual involvement with social issues are both clearly expressed.

U.S. distributor: Universal Education and Visual Arts (sales and rental).

Canadian distributor: Universal Education and Visual Arts (sales and rental).

GOYA: DISASTERS OF WAR (*Les désastres de la guerre*)
20 mins. B&W. Originally 35mm. France. 1951.

Producer: Argos Films.

Credits: Pierre Kast, director; Jean Grémillon, writer of commentary and music.

Summary: Goya's famous series of aquatint engravings—an impassioned outcry against the inhumanity of war—was made following the Napoleonic invasion of Spain. This film was produced shortly after the end of World War II, when the filmmakers shared his rage against the futility and agony of war. The engravings are grouped under six main headings: the joie de vivre of a frivolous society, foreign invasion and war, the disasters of war, revolt of the people, its suppression by the invaders, and grief.

U.S. distributor: Film Images (sales and rental).

THE GRAIN IN THE STONE (*The Ascent of Man* series)
52 mins. Color. Britain.

Producer: BBC-TV.

Credits: Adrian Malone, director; Dr. Jacob Bronowski, writer and narrator.

Summary: Dr. Bronowski discusses architecture, the builder and the sculptor, from the first splitting of the stone to its eventual place in a wall, a cathedral, a city. From the Inca city Machu Picchu, Greek temples of Paestum, the Roman aqueduct at Segovia, and the Gothic cathedral at Rheims, to modern Los Angeles, the film expresses man's faith and genius as architect and builder.

U.S. distributor: Time-Life (sales and rental).

Canadian distributor: BBC-TV Enterprises (sales and rental).

GRANDMA MOSES

22 mins. Color. Originally 35mm. U.S.A. 1950.

Producer: Falcon Films.

Credits: Jerome Hill, director; Archibald MacLeish, writer and narrator; Hugh Martin, music.

Summary: A living portrait of Anna Mary Moses (1860-1961), famous primitive painter better known as Grandma Moses. We see her simple farm life in upper New York State; her albums of fading photographs that refreshed memories of things past; her personal way of painting, sitting perched on the family Bible; and the special preparation of her painting boards. The second half of the film is an exploration of her work.

U.S. distributor: Film Images (sales and rental).

GREEK SCULPTURE

25 mins. Color. Originally 35mm. Britain. 1959.

Producer: Gladys and Basil Wright, Marsden Film Production, London.

Credits: Basil Wright and Michael Ayrton, directors; Denys Haynes, adviser; Michael Ayrton, writer; Leo Genn, narrator; Humphrey Searle, music.

Summary: More than twenty-five years after its production, the colors of this film have faded and the camera work and editing may seem somewhat elementary by present-day standards. Nevertheless it is still one of the best films in this field because of the sensitivity of its directors to their subject, Greek sculpture between 3000 B.C. and 300 B.C. Examples in stone, bronze, and terracotta are shown, intercut with some brief close-ups of hands— Henry Moore's hands—working marble and bronze. Basil Wright, the producer, is one of the masters of the British documentary movement of the thirties and the director of the classic *Song of Ceylon.*

U.S. distributor: International Film Bureau.

Canadian distributor: Canadian Film Institute for the National Gallery of Canada (loan).

GUERNICA

15 mins. B&W. Originally 35mm. France. 1950.

Producer: Pierre Braunberger, les Films du Panthéon.

Credits: Alain Resnais, director; Paul Eluard, writer of narration; Eva Le Gallienne, narrator; Guy Bernard, music.

Summary: A famous documentary film inspired by the art of Picasso and especially by his masterpiece, *Guernica.* Drawings, sketches, paintings, and sculpture by the artist are mixed with newsreel footage, actual photography, and works of art by other artists in a protest against the world's forces of destruction and oppression.

U.S. distributor: Pictura (sales and rental); Grove Press Film Division (sales and rental).

GUSTAVE COURBET, THE FIRST REALIST (*L'homme à la pipe*)
20 mins. Color. France. 1965.

Producer: Films Roger Leenhardt.

Credits: Roger Leenhardt, director and writer; Jean Wiener, music (arranged from nineteenth-century themes).

Summary: The great French realist painter seen through forty of his canvases. His turbulent career is traced: his early manhood in Ornans and Paris, his scorn of tuition, rejection of Romantic subject matter, and arrogant response to criticism. His participation in the Paris Commune in 1871 resulted in heavy fines, imprisonment, and exile. He had continuing influence on the work of many artists, including Millet and Degas.

U.S. distributor: Film Images (sales and rental); FACSEA (loan).

Canadian distributor: Canadian Film Institute for the National Gallery of Canada (loan).

HAIDA CARVER (*Art et légende*)
12 mins. Color. 16 & 35mm. Canada. 1964.

Producer: Richard Gilbert, National Film Board of Canada.

Credits: Richard Gilbert, director and writer; William Weintraub, narrator; Eldon Rathburn, music.

Summary: A visit to the workshop of a young Indian artist from the village of Masset in the Queen Charlotte Islands, who carves miniature totems from argillite, a stone-like jet. The film follows the artist to the island where he finds the stone, and then shows how he works it in the manner of his grandfather, a famous carver, who taught him the craft.

U.S. distributor: International Film Bureau (sales and rental).

Canadian distributor: National Film Board of Canada (sales and loan).

HANDLING WORKS OF ART
20 mins. Color. U.S.A. 1975.

Producer: The Downtown Community Television Center, New York.

Credits: Eric B. Rowlinson and Elizabeth L. Burnham, directors and writers.

Summary: Shows the correct methods of packing and transporting various types of works of art. Among the procedures demonstrated are the handling and moving of sculpture and framed works, including oversize paintings. The film was produced as a visual supplement to Rowlinson's article "Rules for Handling Works of Art," *Museum News*, April 1975.

U.S. distributor: The Museum of Modern Art (lease and rental).

HARRY BERTOIA'S SCULPTURE
23 mins. Color. U.S.A. 1964.

Producer: Clifford B. West, OIP Films.

Credits: Clifford B. West, director; Harry Bertoia, music; no narration.

Summary: Presents Harry Bertoia, designer and sculptor, celebrated for personal works in metal. The film shows the creation of his shimmering structures, restating natural shapes: screens and panels with intricately constructed and interlacing designs reflect the artist's fantasies.

U.S. distributor: Film Images (sales and rental).

HARTUNG or HANS HARTUNG (*Peintres français d'aujourd'hui* series)
15 mins. Part B&W, Part Color. Originally 35mm. France. 1964.

Producer: Sorafilms, Paris.

Credits: Guy Suzuki, director and photographer; Camille Bourniquel, writer; Roland Douatte, music.

Summary: A study of Hans Hartung, German-born abstract painter now living in Paris. He is seen working on a canvas in the Paris house he built which has studios for himself and his wife, artist Anna Eva Bergmann (also shown in the film). The rapid development of the painting is intercut with flashbacks of his childhood in Germany, studies in Dresden, and his first years in Majorca and France.

U.S. distributor: FACSEA (rental).

HE IS RISEN (*Project 20* series)
29 mins. Color. U.S.A. 1962.

Producer: Donald B. Hyatt, NBC News.

Credits: Donald B. Hyatt, director; Richard Hanser, writer; Alexander Scourby, narrator; Russell Bennett, music.

Summary: The Passion of Christ as shown through great religious paintings from Munich, Rome, Paris, and other European cities, as well as from art museums in the United States. No reference is made to the name of the artists, who include Bosch, Van Dyck, Tintoretto, Velázquez, and Caravaggio. Many paintings from the late Middle Ages and the Renaissance are shown through the animation technique of "still-pictures-in-action."

U.S. distributor: Films Incorporated (sales and rental).

Canadian distributor: Visual Education Centre (sales and rental).

HENRI GAUDIER-BRZESKA
30 mins. B&W and Color. Britain. 1968.

Producer: Corinne Cantrill, Firebird Films, London and Sydney, Australia.

Credits: Arthur Cantrill, director, writer, photographer and editor; David Lumsdine, music; Daniel Monceau and Richard Bebb, narrators.

Summary: Killed early in World War I after only three years of work as a sculptor in London, Gaudier-Brzeska, at twenty-three, was marked for greatness. His drawings, carvings and contributions to *Blast*, the magazine of the Vorticist movement, have been drawn on for this intimate film study. The narration makes use of his letters.

U.S. distributor: Film Images (sales and rental); Canyon Cinema Cooperative (rental).

Canadian distributor: Canadian Film Institute for the National Gallery of Canada (loan).

HENRI MATISSE
16 mins. Initially 22 mins. Color. Originally 35mm. France. 1970.

Producer: Jacqueline Jullien, Les Films du Cyprès.

Credits: Pierre Alibert, director; Pierre Schneider, adviser; Philip Gaunt, narrator; André Chini, music.

Summary: Made on the occasion of the centennial exhibition (see also THE HENRI MATISSE CENTENNIAL AT THE GRAND PALAIS) this provides the opportunity for a coherent view of the evolution of the artist's style. Each step of his experience is explained in chronological order. Most of his paintings are shown in their entirety with a minimum of animation. The Chapel of Vence appears as the symbol of Matisse's great artistic accomplishment. (Music tends to become overemphasized in some sections of the film.)

U.S. distributor: International Film Bureau (sales and rental); FACSEA (loan).

Canadian distributor: Educational Film Distributors (sales and rental); Embassy of France (loan).

THE HENRI MATISSE CENTENNIAL AT THE GRAND PALAIS
50 mins. Color. U.S.A. 1972.

Producer: Museum at Large.

Credits: Paul Falkenberg and Hans Namuth, directors; Pierre Schneider, writer and narrator; Henri Alekan, Hans Namuth, photographers; Tom Glazer, music.

Summary: The comprehensive 1970 centennial exhibition of 250 works, including some 20 paintings on loan from the Soviet Union. The long and detailed visit covers the whole of Matisse's production as a painter, sculptor, designer, and architect. Black-and-white stills and live footage show Matisse at work in his studio and in the Dominican Convent Chapel at Vence.

U.S. distributor: Museum at Large (sales and rental).

Canadian distributor: Canadian Film Institute for the National Gallery of Canada (loan).

HENRI ROUSSEAU—The Only Great Artist With No Professional Training
(*Pioneers of Modern Painting* series, no. 5)
40 mins. Color. Britain. 1972.

Producer: Colin Clark for Independent Television Corporation.

Credits: Colin Clark, director; Lord Clark, writer and narrator.

Summary: Lord Clark describes Rousseau as "the only great artist who had no professional training." He did not begin to paint until he was over forty but was able "to retain the child's gift of bold design and naturally harmonious color." Lord Clark discusses the simplicity of form and poetic inventiveness shown in Rousseau's canvases, including *The Sleeping Gypsy* and the series of jungle pictures, painted from his imagination and study of tropical plants in the Paris Botanical Gardens.

U.S. distributor: Independent Television Corporation (sales); National Gallery of Art (loan).

Canadian distributor: ITC of Canada (sales); Canadian Film Institute for the National Gallery of Canada (loan).

HENRY MOORE
17 mins. Color. U.S.A. 1947.

Producer: Falcon Films

Credits: James Johnson Sweeney, director, writer, and narrator; Erica Anderson, photographer.

Summary: Starting with the glamorous opening of The Museum of Modern Art's exhibition of wartime "shelter sketches," the film shows that the artist's sensitive understanding of the experience of his fellow Londoners sheltering underground from the blitz is coupled with his ability to convey his sense of their simple dignity and heroism. It studies the emotional impact of the distortion in Moore's sculpture, and emphasizes his respect for the different qualities of wood, stone, and cast metal which he never falsifies to imitate human flesh.

U.S. distributor: Film Images (sales and rental).

HENRY MOORE AT THE TATE GALLERY
14 mins. Color. Britain. 1970.

Producer: British Film Institute for the Arts Council of Great Britain.

Credits: David Sylvester, director; Walter Lassally, photographer and co-director; no narration, no music.

Summary: The 1968 retrospective at the Tate Gallery was visited by 100,000 visitors, making it impossible to see the pieces in relation to one another. The film provides the illusion of viewing the exhibition alone. The camera of Walter Lassally guides the audience in a personal journey in, out, around, and through the sculpture, unobstructed by visitors, narration, music, or special effects. Without these familiar props, David Sylvester (who made the film GIACOMETTI for the Arts Council of Great Britain) creates tension and drama through the sheer skill and sympathy with which the forms are presented.

U.S. distributor: The American Federation of Arts (rental); Films Incorporated (sales).

HENRY STRATER, AMERICAN ARTIST (1896-   )
30 mins. Color. U.S.A. 1975.

Producer: Jane Morrison Productions.

Credits: Jane Morrison, director; Arnold Eagle, consultant; Ruth Breton, violin.

Summary: A portrait of the life and works of a prolific realist painter of Ogunquit, Maine. Narrating throughout, Strater reveals himself to be a friendly but independent character who paints the subjects he likes in his own style—rocks, landscapes, nudes, portraits, and flowers. The film shows the Whitney gallery crowd in New York, the portraits of Ernest Hemingway, and the artist painting. Interviews with friends, relatives, a writer and an art dealer complement Strater's comments.

U.S. distributor: Jane Morrison (sales and loan); Museum at Large (sales and loan).

HISTORICAL RELICS UNEARTHED IN NEW CHINA
60 mins. Color. People's Republic of China. 1971.

Producer: Documentary Films Studios, Peking.

Summary: Art treasures recently discovered in China are presented. Relics dating from prehistoric times to the fourteenth century have come to light through large-scale excavations undertaken by China's archaeologists over the past two decades. Considered as the major archaeological finds of the century, they formed the core of the Chinese Art exhibition which has been seen all over the world, including Washington and Toronto.

U.S. distributor: Grove Press Film Division (sales and rental).

HOMAGE TO JEAN TINGUELY
11 mins. B&W. U.S.A. 1961.

Producer: Robert Breer, Grove Press Film Division.

Credits: Robert Breer, director.

Summary: A document on the short life and drastic demise of Jean Tinguely's "self-creating and self-destroying machine," *Homage to New York*, set to commit suicide in the garden of New York's Museum of Modern Art in 1960 as a protest against mechanized society. Unpredictable willful twists in this film record distinguish it as art in its own right, as well as an historically valuable documentary of an event in contemporary art. (See also BREAKING IT UP AT THE MUSEUM.)

U.S. distributor: Film-makers' Cooperative (rental); Grove Press Film Division (sales and rental).

HOMAGE TO RODIN
19 mins. Color. U.S.A. 1968.

Producer: Herb Golden.

Credits: Herb Golden, director and writer; Hugh Douglas, narrator.

Summary: An analysis of the work of Auguste Rodin, illustrated by numerous close-ups lighted and filmed with sensitivity to form and material (principally bronze). The film was made at the Los Angeles County Museum using the collection of the B. G. Cantor Art Foundation, second in importance only to that of the Rodin Museum in Paris. It covers the full range of his work, from *The Man with the Broken Nose* (1864), through his most productive period, (1880-1890) represented by *The Thinker* and *The Kiss*, to *The Hand of Rodin with Torso #3*, completed only three weeks before his death in 1917. The commentary describes the sculptor's life, frustrations, and his later recognition.
Note: This film should not be confused with the French film *Hommage a Rodin* (same duration), directed by Marc de Gastyne at the same period.

U.S. distributor: Pyramid (sales and rental).

Canadian distributor: International Tele-Film Enterprises (sales and rental).

HORYUJI TEMPLE
23 mins. Color. Originally 35mm. Japan. 1957.

Producer: Iwanami Productions for the National Commission for the Preservation of Culture, Tokyo.

Credits: Susumi Hani, director and writer; Akio Yashiro, music.

Summary: Built in the seventh century, during the Nara period, Horyuji is the oldest existing temple in Japan and houses many priceless objects of art. Placing emphasis on mood and feeling rather than architectural scholarship, the film captures the unique atmosphere which is Horyuji's own.

U.S. distributor: Japan Foundation (loan).

Canadian distributor: Embassy of Japan (loan).

HOWARD JONES (*Artists*—or *U.S.A. Artists*—series)
30 mins. Color. U.S.A. 1971.

Producer: Don Jeffries for ETS program service, KETC-TV, St. Louis, by a grant from the Corporation for Public Broadcasting and the National Endowment for the Arts.

Credits: Elaine Millaire, director; Howard Jones, participant; Ralph T. Coe, additional commentary.

Summary: Howard Jones, an artist involved with sound, light, and ideas, is also a professor of art at Washington University in St. Louis. His creations have an electronic relay system which responds with sound variations to the viewer's presence and movement. In his studio, he explains how he works. The last sequence of the film is devoted to his exhibition *Three Sounds* at the Howard Wise Gallery, New York, in November 1970.

U.S. distributor: Indiana University (sales and rental).

Canadian distributor: Canadian Film Institute (sales); International Tele-Film Enterprises (sales and rental).

I THINK IN SHAPES—HENRY MOORE
30 mins. Color. Britain. 1968.

Producer: J. Gibson, BBC-TV.

Credits: J. Gibson, director; Henry Moore, narrator.

Summary: To celebrate Henry Moore's seventieth birthday, the Tate Gallery arranged a retrospective exhibition of his life's work. Some of the larger carvings were displayed on the lawn, and as the sculptor walks through, running his hands over them, he speaks simply and directly about each piece, and about his background, motivation, and conception of art and life.

Canadian distributor: BBC-TV Enterprises (sales and rental).

IAN HUGO: ENGRAVER AND FILMMAKER
7 mins. Color. U.S.A. 1972.
(Revised version from the 11 mins. 1968 production.)

Producer: Ian Hugo.

Credits: Ian Hugo, director, participant, narrator and editor; David Horowitz, music.

Summary: While engraving a copper plate, Ian Hugo explains the similarities in his approach to the two arts, engraving and filmmaking. The movement suggested in the plates is demonstrated through changing light patterns on a series of his engravings and etchings. Finally, there is a fusion of the two artistic disciplines.

U.S. distributor: Film Images (sales and rental).

ICONS (*Ikony*)
14 mins. Color. Czechoslovakia. 1968.

Producer: Ceskoslovensky Film, Bratislava.

Credits: Martin Slivka, director; Krzysztos Penderecki, music; Joshua C. Taylor, consultant for English version.

Summary: The development of the icon, the typical religious painting of the Eastern Christian church from the fifteenth to the nineteenth century. As Western influence increased, the subjects became less stylized and more human. Priests and other unskilled artists were responsible for the appearance of folk art in the ornamentation of the borders. The film also explains the conventions by which profound beliefs were expressed in the clearest and most economical way.

U.S. distributor: International Film Bureau (sales).

Canadian distributor: Educational Film Distributors (sales and rental); Embassy of the Czechoslovak Socialist Republic (loan).

IMAGES OF LEONARD BASKIN (*Artists at Work* series)
28 mins. Color. U.S.A. 1965.

Producer: Forma Art Associates for NET.

Credits: Warren Forma, director and photographer; Ernest Pintoff, music.

Summary: Leonard Baskin, sculptor, graphic artist, educator, admits to some profound disagreements with current art and cultural trends. Baskin is a humanist who has tried to communicate moral ideas at a time when the American art scene has been dominated by Abstract Expressionism. His sculpture is in the permanent collection of The Museum of Modern Art, and since the early sixties his prints and engravings have won almost every graphic prize in the United States.

U.S. distributor: Forma Art Associates (sales and rental).

IMAGES MEDIEVALES (*Medieval Art*)
18 mins. Color. Originally 35mm. France. 1948-49.

Producer: Coopérative générale du Cinéma Français.

Credits: William Novik, director: Guy Delécluse, photographer; Bernard Delapierre, musical arrangement; James Johnson Sweeney, writer of English commentary; William Chapman, narrator.

Summary: This film, a classic in the "film on art" genre, is a supreme achievement in the technology of its time. It gives an intimate picture of life in the Middle Ages as recorded in the miniature paintings and illuminated manuscripts of the period in the French National Library. Sequences include: the story of Adam and Eve, the peasant's life, the princely court, the hunt, the tournament, war, the arts of peace, courtly love, legend and folk tale, baptism and burial, the dance of death, and the Last Judgment.

U.S. distributor: Film Images (sales and rental); The Museum of Modern Art (rental).

Canadian distributor: Canadian Film Institute for the National Gallery of Canada (loan).

IMAGINERO
52 mins. Color. U.S.A. 1970.

Producer: Film Study Center, Harvard University for the National University of Tucuman and the "Fondo Nacional de las Artes."

Credits: Jorge Preloran and Robert Gardner, directors.

Summary: The story of Hermogenes Cayo, Indian folk artist whose paintings and carvings express his own beliefs and those of his people. At the foot of the Andes in the remote and barren country of northwest Argentina lives this amazing man whose mystical experiences have flowered into an act of universal interpretation of the human condition. It is a rare privilege to meet Hermogenes Cayo and the film will not be easily forgotten or dismissed.

U.S. distributor: Phoenix (sales and rental).

Canadian distributor: International Tele-Film Enterprises (sales and rental).

IMOGEN CUNNINGHAM, PHOTOGRAPHER
20 mins. Color. U.S.A. 1972.

Producer: The American Film Institute for Time-Life.

Credits: John Korty, director.

Summary: A documentary on the life and work of Imogen Cunningham, pioneer portrait photographer whose career, beginning in 1901 and continuing until her death in 1976, covered almost two-thirds the life span of photography itself. A comprehensive selection of her work is witness to her achievement as an artist. Interviews and candid footage reveal the personality and intelligence of a vital woman, in her late eighties when this film was made.

U.S. distributor: Time-Life (sales and rental).

Canadian distributor: Marlin Motion Pictures (sales and rental).

IMPRESSIONISM AND NEO-IMPRESSIONISM (*Impressionnisme et Néo-Impressionnisme*) (*Pathways of Modern Painting* series no. 1)
25 mins. Color. Originally 35mm. France, 1970.

Producer: Jacqueline Jullien, Les Films du Cyprès and International Film Bureau.

Credits: Pierre Alibert, director; Bernard Dorival, consultant; Francis Seyrig, music; Philip Gaunt, narrator.

Summary: The origins of the movement are traced from the beginning of the nineteenth century, when the works of Constable, Turner, Delacroix, and others signal the revolutionary changes to come. A comparison of Manet's *Déjeuner sur l'herbe* with Titian's *Country Concert* illustrates the departures from classical painting. Increasingly the subject is subordinated to the study of light, a fresh approach evidenced in the cavases of Monet, Degas, Cézanne, Guillaumin, Sisley, Morisot, Pissarro, and Renoir. Neo-Impressionism, with its growing emphasis on construction and strongly defined forms, is summed up primarily in the works of Seurat, Cross, Signac, and Angrand.

U.S. distributor: International Film Bureau (sales and rental); FACSEA (rental).

Canadian distributor: Educational Film Distributors (sales and rental).

THE IMPRESSIONISTS (*Les impressionnistes*)
26 mins. Color. Originally 35mm. France. 1966.

Producer: Albert Skira, Flag Films, Paris.

Credits: Jean Claude Sée, director and writer; Artie Shaw, writer of English version; Artie Shaw and Evelyn Keyes, narrators; Georges Van Parys, music.

Summary: Outstanding Impressionist painters are studied and their paintings compared and contrasted with the places where they lived and worked. Albert Skira, the famous art book publisher, presents masterpieces by Manet, Monet, Cézanne, Van Gogh, Renoir, Degas, Seurat, Toulouse-Lautrec—all innovators whose courage and originality changed the direction of European art.

U.S. distributor: FACSEA (rental); Macmillan (sales and rental).

Canadian distributor: Embassy of France (loan).

IN SEARCH OF REMBRANDT

28 mins. Color. U.S.A. 1969-72.

Producer: Milan Herzog, NET.

Credits: R. F. Siemanowski, director and writer; James Mason, narrator; George Kleinsinger, music.

Summary: Paintings and drawings alternate with actual scenes to illustrate and document Rembrandt's technical mastery, dramatic sense, and humane insight into his subjects. His superb portraiture is allied to a fastidious rendering of physical detail. His greatest works are included: *The Night Watch, The Anatomy Lesson of Doctor Tulp, The Hundred Guilder Print*, and *Supper at Emmaus*. (A longer version—50 mins.—is available from the National Gallery of Art, Washington, D.C.)

U.S. distributor: Films Incorporated (sales and rental).

Canadian distributor: Visual Education Centre (sales and rental).

THE INCISED IMAGE

23 mins. Partly B&W, Partly Color. Australia. 1966.

Producer: Firebird Films, Sydney.

Credits: Arthur Cantrill, director, photographer and editor; Charles Lloyd, narrator.

Summary: Australian etcher Charles Lloyd, at work in London at Goldsmith's College and Editions Alecto, illustrating in detail his approach to the techniques of drypoint and one-plate color printing, the latter learned at Hayter's Atelier 17 in Paris. The commentary, edited from his recorded discussion, explains the processes as he works, and he speaks of his introduction to etching and printmaking at the Royal College of Art in London, and of the great satisfaction he derives from it. The last sequence interprets in animation his statement: "Each print is an adventure, a little journey of discovery."

U.S. distributor: Canyon Cinema Cooperative (rental); New York University Film Library (rental).

Canadian distributor: Canadian Film Institute for the National Gallery of Canada (loan).

INSIDE THE WORLD OF JESSE ALLEN

30 mins. Color. Originally 35mm. U.S.A. 1973.

Producer: Muldoon Elder for Vorpal Gallery Productions.

Credits: Steve Grumette, director, photographer and editor; Jesse Allen, narrator; Jeffrey Bihr, music.

Summary: A visit to the artist's San Francisco studio, where he discusses the fascination the world of nature holds for him. An admirer of Beardsley and Blake, Jesse Allen remembers the exotic creatures of his native Kenya and, without a plan, guides his swirling fantasies in a spontaneous organic outburst. The camera, accompanied by guitars, flutes, and African instruments, covers the canvases carefully, catching the most minute detail, striving to convey the artist's intimate and sensual relation to life and nature.

U.S. distributor: Vorpal Reproductions (sales and rental).

ISAMU NOGUCHI

28 mins. Color. U.S.A. 1971.

Producer: Blackwood Productions.

Credits: Michael Blackwood, director.

Summary: An insight into the variety and scope of the work of Isamu Noguchi, an international artist whose interests and projects have no geographical bounds. His two great mentors were Constantin Brancusi and Buckminster Fuller. Filmed with the sculptor himself at the Unesco Garden, Paris; in Spoleto, Italy, with Buckminster Fuller and Ezra Pound; at Noguchi's studio and the marble works near Pietrasanta, Italy; at the IBM Garden in New York State; and his studio in New York City. The film reviews four decades of Noguchi's work, and closes with his recent retrospective at the Whitney Museum of American Art.

U.S. distributor: Blackwood Productions (sales and rental).

THE IVORY KNIFE

17 mins. Color. Originally 35mm. U.S.A. 1965.

Producer: Red Parrot Films.

Credits: Jules Engel, director; Irwin Bazelon, music; no narration.

Summary: A study of the American painter Paul Jenkins, as he guides and forms the flow of vibrant colors over his unstretched canvas with ivory knives. The camera follows his eye and hand as he creates the brilliant color compositions characteristic of his paintings.

U.S. distributor: Martha Jackson Gallery (rental).

JACK LEVINE

23 mins. Color. U.S.A. 1964.

Producer: Zina Voynow, Peter Robinson, Herman J. Engel.

Credits: Zina Voynow, Peter Robinson, and Herman J. Engel, directors; Lewis Jacobs, Jess Paley, and Al Maysles, assistants; Henry Brant, music.

Summary: Beginning with a review of some of Levine's more important works, the main part of this film is devoted to the creation of a large canvas, seven by eight feet (2.1 x 2.4 meters), entitled *Witches' Sabbath*. The work, which lasted several weeks, is followed step-by-step, from underpainting to gallery show, including comments by the artist. Very few films participate so closely in the hazards of improvisation in the painting process.

U.S. distributor: Texture Films (sales and rental).

Canadian distributor: International Tele-Film Enterprises (sales and rental); Canadian Film Institute for the National Gallery of Canada (loan).

JACKSON POLLOCK
10 mins. Color. U.S.A. 1951.

Producer: Paul Falkenberg and Hans Namuth.

Credits: Paul Falkenberg and Hans Namuth, directors: Jackson Pollock, narrator; Martin Feldman, music.

Summary: This film classic is the only existing footage on the artist at work. Pollock, America's best-known Abstract Expressionist, demonstrates his ability to balance intuition, chance, and discipline. In the final sequence, he paints on glass, enabling the camera to view him in action.

U.S. distributor: Museum at Large (sales and rental).

Canadian distributor: Canadian Film Institute for the National Gallery of Canada (loan).

JACQUES LIPCHITZ or A CONVERSATION WITH JACQUES LIPCHITZ
(***Wisdom*** series)
28 mins. B&W. U.S.A. 1958.

Producer: James Nelson, NBC News.

Summary: During an interview in his studio at Hastings, N.Y., Jacques Lipchitz, sculptor and painter, talks to art critic Cranston Jones about his early association with the French Cubist movement. Surrounded by examples representing all stages of his work, he discusses the ideas and the artists that influenced his development of new techniques and new forms of expression in sculpture. The creator of such well-known works as *Acrobat à Cheval, Homme à la Guitare,* and *Blossoming* sees his art as a continuing search for a universal language.

U.S. distributor: Films Incorporated (sales and rental).

JAPAN: THE NEW ART
28 mins. Color. U.S.A. 1972.

Producer: Blackwood Productions.

Credits: Christian and Michael Blackwood, directors; Edward Fry, narrator.

Summary: Avant-garde Japanese artists are shown at work on a variety of projects: Jiro Yoshihara and members of the Gutai group constructing a monumental kinetic sculpture at Expo 70 in Osaka; Nobuo Sekine using natural elements—clay and earth—as materials for his sculptures; Ree Woo Fon attempting to bring art in contact with the real world of places and materials; Katsuhiku Narita using sumi logs in his sculptural work; and Jiro Takamatzu constructing fabric sculptures.

U.S. distributor: Blackwood Productions (sales and rental).

JAPANESE CALLIGRAPHY (*Calligraphie Japonaise*)
16 mins. B&W. France. 1957.

Producer: Films de la Pléiade.

Credits: Pierre Alechinsky, director; Christian Dotremont, writer of commentary; André Souris, music.

Summary: Discusses the traditional approach to Japanese calligraphy, its origins, purposes, and characteristics. Teaching methods are demonstrated, and several noted calligraphers are shown at work. Practitioners of the new generation demonstrate the influence of Western "action painting" in their new approach to an ancient art.

U.S. distributor: Macmillan (sales and rental).

Canadian distributor: Canadian Film Institute for the National Gallery of Canada (loan).

JASPER JOHNS (*Artists*—or *U.S.A. Artists*—series)
30 mins. B&W. U.S.A. 1966.

Producer: Lane Slate, NET and Radio Center.

Credits: Lane Slate, director; Alan Solomon, writer; Norman Rose, narrator.

Summary: The growth from sketchbook to completed canvas of a painting by Jasper Johns, whose insistence on two-dimensionality of surface and the use of banal material for subject matter (targets, flags, coat hangers, numbers, letters) helped initiate an entire new school of painting—Pop Art. Johns is shown at his studios in New York and Edisto Beach, South Carolina, and at the New York workshop of Tatyana Grosman.

U.S. distributor: Indiana University (sales and rental).

Canadian distributor: Canadian Film Institute for the National Gallery of Canada (sales and loan).

JASPER JOHNS: DECOY
20 mins. Color. U.S.A. 1972.

Producer: Blackwood Productions.

Credits: Michael Blackwood, director; Barbara Rose, narrator.

Summary: The creation of a major new work by Jasper Johns, executed at Tatyana Grosman's Universal Limited Art Editions, Long Island. The print *Decoy* marks an important advance in printmaking techniques: by using the new lithographic proofing press it is possible to combine eighteen progressive proofs into a single image of unprecedented richness and complexity. The close understanding between Mrs. Grosman, the printers, and the artist provides an example of collective creation.

U.S. distributor: Blackwood Productions (sales and rental); Visual Resources (sales and rental).

JIM DINE (*Artists—*or *U.S.A. Artists—*series)
30 mins. B&W. U.S.A. 1966.

Producer: Lane Slate, NET and Radio Center.

Credits: Lane Slate, director; Alan Solomon, consultant; Manny Albam, music.

Summary: Jim Dine explains that his works represent his interaction with his environment. Examples are shown from his "tie," "tool," "bathroom," "child's room," and "palette" periods. He explains why he undertook sculpture such as the furniture made from aluminum castings of familiar objects. A short happening is presented. Jim Dine sees happenings as a result of the artist's need to speak directly with the viewer. Finally he discusses his works with sprayed enamel backgrounds on which real objects are arranged.

U.S. distributor: Indiana University (sales and rental).

Canadian distributor: Canadian Film Institute for the National Gallery of Canada (loan).

JOAN MIRO MAKES A COLOR PRINT
20 mins. Color. U.S.A. 1948.

Producer: Thomas Bouchard.

Credits: Thomas Bouchard, director; Stanley W. Hayter, Ruthven Todd, narrators.

Summary: Miró at work on an etched color print in Hayter's Atelier 17 in Paris. The complete process is shown, from the first work on the copper plate to the finished print. This is an older, but very worthwhile film.

U.S. distributor: Thomas Bouchard (rental).

JOHN MARIN
20 mins. Color. U.S.A. 1968.

Producer: Radio-TV Bureau, University of Arizona, Tucson.

Credits: Harry Atwood, photographer and editor; Sheldon Reich, writer; Robert Keyworth, narrator.

Summary: A survey of John Marin's art from the earliest watercolors in 1888 to the unfinished pictures at his death in 1953, including glimpses of rarely seen paintings. The film conveys Marin's acute sensitivity to the quality of movement. Footage of the artist at the piano is used, as well as little-known photographs, some by Alfred Stieglitz.

U.S. distributor: International Film Bureau (sales and rental).

JOSE DE CREEFT
28 mins. B&W. U.S.A. 1966.

Producer: Robert Hanson.

Credits: Robert Hanson, director, writer, and photographer.

Summary: The creation of a contemporary sculpture from rough stone to finished work of art, photographed over a seven-week period. The sculptor, Spanish-born José de Creeft, once a member of the Paris School, is now living in Rye and Hoosick Falls, N.Y. He is one of the few men still working directly on stone with hand tools, usually of his own making.

U.S. distributor: Macmillan (sales and rental).

JOSEF ALBERS: HOMAGE TO THE SQUARE
25 mins. Color. U.S.A. 1970.

Producer: Hans Namuth and Paul Falkenberg.

Credits: Hans Namuth and Paul Falkenberg, directors.

Summary: Equipped with ruler, silver pencil, paint tubes, and a palette knife "instead of a hundred brushes," Albers explains his art in lively, lucid terms. Two of his former students, Richard Anuszkiewicz and Robert Rauschenberg, discuss his theories and influence, stressing his importance as a teacher.

U.S. distributor: Museum at Large (sales and rental).

JOURNEY INTO A PAINTING
21 mins. Color. U.S.A. 1969.

Producer: Leo Hurwitz Productions for the Ford Foundation and The American Federation of Arts.

Credits: Leo Hurwitz, director; Rudolf Arnheim, Alice Kaplan, and Roy Mayer, consultants.

Summary: A detailed study of *Still Life with Apples* by Paul Cézanne in The Museum of Modern Art. From the first rough form of the composition to the completed painting, the film takes the viewer on a step-by-step examination of the creation of a work of art. It clearly defines how the artist uses shape, color, design, and contrast to achieve his purpose.

U.S. distributor: Films Incorporated (sales and rental).

KALEIDOSCOPE ORISSA
37 mins. Color. Britain. 1967.

Producer: Mary Kirby, Pilgrim Films, London.

Credits: Robert Steele, director; Mary Kirby, photographer and editor; Clive Cazes, writer and narrator; Haimanti Chakravarty, research; Elisabeth Lutyens, music.

Summary: A study of the popular culture of the Indian state of Orissa, renowned for its intricately beautiful art produced, for the most part, with very simple tools. The molding and baking of ceramic pottery is demonstrated. Weaving and fabric printing show a combination of extraordinary color and design in fabrics for garments, notably those prepared specially for religious rituals.

U.S. distributor: International Film Bureau (sales and rental).

Canadian distributor: Educational Film Distributors (sales and rental).

KIENHOLZ ON EXHIBIT
21 mins. B&W. U.S.A. 1969.

Producer: June Steel, U.C.L.A.

Credits: June Steel, director.

Summary: The reactions of the public to the exhibition of Kienholz's unorthodox sculpture at the Los Angeles County Museum of Art; visitors are fascinated or repulsed by what they see, which barely escapes being banned as pornographic trash. The show with crowds, armed guards, tape-recorded guides, and lecture tours appears as a microcosm of society. The film can be used to introduce a discussion of what is good and bad art, as well as the wider issues implied.

U.S. distributor: The American Federation of Arts (rental).

KINETICS
20 mins. Color. Britain. 1972.

Producer: Plus International Productions and the Slade School of Fine Arts (Film Department) for the Arts Council of Great Britain.

Credits: Lutz Becker, director; John Ardar, narrator.

Summary: Based on an exhibition of the work of more than sixty artists shown at the Hayward Gallery, London, in 1970. The film concentrates on its visual and filmic aspects, creating a dazzling impression of light and movement. The fascination of this show is graphically conveyed through the medium of motion pictures.

U.S. distributor: The American Federation of Arts (rental); Films Incorporated (sales).

Canadian distributor: Canadian Film Institute for the National Gallery of Canada (loan).

THE KREMLIN
54 mins. Color. U.S.A. 1963.

Producer: George Vicas, NBC News (European Production Unit).

Credits: George Vicas, director and narrator; Norman Borisoff, writer; J. Baxter Peters, photographer; Georges Auric, music.

Summary: The first American-filmed tour of the Kremlin in Moscow, with emphasis on the architecture of Red Square and points of interest inside and outside the Kremlin walls. The turbulent history of Czarist Russia is reflected in this ancient fortified center, which encloses three cathedrals and a museum. One of the post-revolution buildings shown is the multi-purpose Palace of Congresses.

U.S. distributor: McGraw-Hill Films (sales and rental).

Canadian distributor: McGraw-Hill Ryerson (sales and rental).

L. S. LOWRY, "THE INDUSTRIAL ARTIST"
18 mins. Color. Britain. 1974.

Producer: Thompson Brothers.

Credits: Philip Thompson, director; L. S. Lowry, participant; Colin E. Cowles, music.

Summary: Actual photography of Manchester and its industrial suburbs, and candid camera shots of crowds and of children playing are intercut with paintings and accompanied by a dynamic brass band. L. S. Lowry himself comments on his "loving simple visions." His work, for all its naive and casual air, is based on ten years of study and classical technique. More recently, he has found his subjects near the sea—the boats and sailors that are also a part of industrial Britain.

U.S. distributor: Visual Resources (sales and rental).

Canadian distributor: Canadian Film Institute (sales and rental).

LARRY RIVERS
28 mins. Color. U.S.A. 1971-72.

Producer: Blackwood Productions.

Credits: Michael Blackwood, director.

Summary: While working on current paintings, constructions, and videotapes in his New York City loft, Rivers discusses his career and some older works which are shown in detail. Rivers' energetic style creates interest among general audiences as well as those with a special interest in his work.

U.S. distributor: Blackwood Productions (sales and rental).

LEONARDO: TO KNOW HOW TO SEE
55 mins. Color. Originally 35mm. U.S.A. 1972.

Producer: Robert Cosner for the National Gallery of Art.

Credits: R.F. Siemanowski, director and writer; Sir John Gielgud, narrator; music, George Kleinsinger.

Summary: The life and work of Leonardo da Vinci, including both artistic and scientific achievements. He could "see clearly what others could only see mistily." Even as a young boy he was preoccupied with nature—an interest reflected in his drawings of leaves and landscapes, shown intercut with views of the Tuscany countryside. As well as analyzing his major works in the Louvre, the Uffizi Gallery in Florence, the *Ginevra de' Benci* in the National Gallery of Art in Washington (the only Leonardo painting in America), and *The Last Supper* in Santa Maria delle Grazie in Milan, the film provides an opportunity to see many of his little-known works: the *Benois Madonna* in the Hermitage in Leningrad (filmed by the Russians); and drawings in the private collection of Queen Elizabeth of England.

U.S. distributor: National Gallery of Art (loan).

LICHTENSTEIN IN LONDON
20 mins. Color. Britain. 1968.

Producer: British Film Institute for the Arts Council of Great Britain.

Credits: Bruce Beresford, director, photographer and editor; David Sylvester, BBC, Alan Solomon, NET, participants.

Summary: Roy Lichtenstein's comic-strip paintings have made him one of the most controversial and internationally known of contemporary artists. The film records the impact made by his work during a retrospective exhibition, "The American Dream," at the Tate Gallery, London. The commentary juxtaposes remarks by the public with extracts from recorded interviews with the artist.

U.S. distributor: The American Federation of Arts (rental); Films Incorporated (sales).

Canadian distributor: Canadian Film Institute for the National Gallery of Canada (loan).

LIGHT-PLAY: BLACK-WHITE-GRAY
6 mins. B&W. Silent. Germany. 1930.

Producer: László Moholy-Nagy.

Credits: László Moholy-Nagy, director.

Summary: The forms and relationships of the Constructivist art of Moholy-Nagy, leading exponent of modern design in architecture, painting, typography, and theater. Figures of glass, steel and wire, including the artist's light-space modulator, move, merge, and dissolve in interrelated shapes and patterns.

U.S. distributor: Film Images (sales and rental).

LITHO
14 mins. Color. U.S.A. 1961.

Producer: Electra Films for the Amalgamated Lithographers of America.

Credits: Cliff Roberts, director.

Summary: A short history of lithography—from early methods to stone and press, then to examples of Lautrec's posters, and finally, to the actual steps of mass color reproduction. Examples of the lithographic processes are creatively filmed, accompanied by a lively jazz score.

U.S. distributor: Laura Singer (sales and rental).

Canadian distributor: Canadian Film Institute for the National Gallery of Canada (loan).

THE LIVING STONE
31 mins. Color. 35 mm. & 16mm. Canada. 1958.

Producer: Tom Daly, National Film Board of Canada.

Credits: John Feeney, director and writer; Maurice Blackburn, music.

Summary: This film shows the inspiration—often the belief in the supernatural—behind much of the early Eskimo sculpture. It centers round the legend of the carving of the image of a sea spirit to bring food to a hungry camp. Master carver Niviaksiak and other Inuit artists explain the part played by stone sculpture in the past and present.

U.S. distributor: National Film Board of Canada (U.S.A.) (sales and rental); New York University Film Library (rental).

Canadian distributor: National Film Board of Canada (sales and loan).

THE LONDON OF WILLIAM HOGARTH
28 mins. B&W. Britain. 1956.

Producer: Barnard-Cornwell Films.

Credits: Phil Barnard, director and narrator; James Watrous, writer; Don Voegli, music.

Summary: The spirit of London in the mid-eighteenth century—the nobility, the people in the streets, the bourgeois, the beggars, the theaters, and the fairs—is captured through the engravings of Hogarth, sometimes bitterly ironic, sometimes warmly sympathetic.

U.S. distributor: International Film Bureau.

THE LOON'S NECKLACE
11 mins. Color. Canada. 1949.

Producer: Crawley Films for Imperial Oil.

Credits: Radford Crawley, director; Douglas Leechman, writer; George Gorman, narrator.

Summary: The film brings to life one of the most delightful of North American Indian legends—how the loon acquired its distinguishing neck band. Authentic ceremonial masks from the National Museums of Canada in Ottawa, carved by Indians of British Columbia, establish the characters of the story and clearly portray the Indian's sensitivity to mood in nature.

U.S. distributor: EBEC (sales and rental).

Canadian distributor: Association Films (sales and rental in Ontario only); Imperial Oil Divisional Offices (loan in Québec and Maritimes only); Canfilms (sales and rental in Manitoba, Saskatchewan and Alberta); West Coast Audio-Visual (sales and rental in British Columbia only); National Film Board of Canada (loan); Canadian Film Institute for the National Gallery of Canada (loan).

LOREN MACIVER
2 parts, 23 mins. each. Color. Silent. U.S.A. 1964.

Producer: Maryette Charlton.

Credits: Maryette Charlton, director.

Summary: The producer, a painter and art teacher, has chosen the silent film as the proper medium for "expressed interpretation." The result is a long, rather amateurish film in two parts, each self-contained. Loren MacIver is seen throughout the four seasons roaming purposefully or idly, observing and transposing onto canvas movement and color from the city and country. Fifty paintings appear in the film.

U.S. distributor: Film Images (sales and rental).

LOUISE NEVELSON
25 mins. Color. U.S.A. 1971.

Producer: Fred Pressburger for Spectra Films.

Credits: Fred Pressburger, director; Hilton Kramer, writer; David Ford, narrator; Robert Pozar, music.

Summary: Interviews with Louise Nevelson, "environmental sculptor," intercut with works in her 1970 exhibition at the Whitney Museum of American Art in New York. Several pieces are shown as the film opens, giving the viewer an opportunity to react to them before the narration outlines stages in the development of her art. The artist comments on her work—the period when her pieces were painted all black and she saw herself as "an architect of shadow," then the transition to white, to gold, and to the use of plexiglas. The film includes the erection of an open-air metal sculpture welded on the spot.

U.S. distributor: Connecticut Films (sales and rental).

THE LOUVRE—A GOLDEN PRISON (*Humanities* collection)
45 mins. Color. Originally 35mm. U.S.A. 1964. (Edited version.)

Producer: Lucy Jarvis, NBC News for the Xerox Corporation.

Credits: John J. Sughrue, Jr., director; Sidney Carroll, writer; Charles Boyer, participant and narrator; Norman Dello Joio, music; Germain Bazin and Milton S. Fox, consultants.

Summary: A prestige production made for television and slightly shortened for 16mm distribution. The producers obtained special permission from the French authorities to bring film cameras into their great national art sanctuary. Charles Boyer as host tells the history of the royal palace since its beginnings in the Middle Ages, and describes the evolution of the art collections accumulated there throughout the centuries. Treasures of various kinds are shown, both to introduce important groups of objets d'art to the Louvre's international visitors, and as an invitation to further exploration of these magnificent collections.

U.S. distributor: EBEC (sales and rental).

Canadian distributor: Visual Education Centre (sales and rental).

LOVIS CORINTH—A LIFE IN PICTURES
(*Lovis Corinth—Ein Leben in Bildern*)
12 mins. Color. Originally 35mm. Federal Republic of Germany. 1958.

Producer: Knoop-Filmproduktion, Hamburg.

Credits: Hans H. Hermann, director and writer; Peter Sandloff, music.

Summary: Based on a comprehensive exhibition organized in Wolfsburg by the Volkswagen Company. The development of the painter as a man and artist is traced through the medium of his self-portraits and works from different periods of his activity. As one of the leaders of German Impressionism, Corinth became a charter member of the German Secession group and in later days moved very close to Expressionism.

U.S. distributor: Modern Talking Pictures for the Embassy of the Federal Republic of Germany (loan).

Canadian distributor: Canadian Film Institute for the Embassy of the Federal Republic of Germany (rental).

LUKAS CRANACH: THE REFORMATION ARTIST
(*Lukas Cranach: der Maler der Reformation*)
30 mins. B&W. Originally 35mm. Federal Republic of Germany. 1966.

Producer: Curt Oertel Studiengesellschaft, Wiesbaden.

Credits: Franz Oertel, director; Walter Hotz and Franz Oertel, writers.

Summary: Paintings, engravings, and book illustrations by Lukas Cranach the Elder, a close friend of Martin Luther, are used to illustrate life in Germany in the first half of the sixteenth century, with special emphasis on the tumult caused by the Reformation. Despite its lack of color, this is an interesting contribution to an understanding of the important role played by one of the most original of German artists.

U.S. distributor: Modern Talking Pictures for the Embassy of the Federal Republic of Germany. German version only (loan).

Canadian distributor: The Canadian Film Institute for the Federal Republic of Germany. In English (rental).

MACKINTOSH
33 mins. Color. Originally 35mm. Britain. 1968.

Producer: International Film Associates Limited, Films of Scotland for the Scottish Arts Council.

Credits: Murray Grigor, director and writer; Michael Roeves, narrator; Frank Spedding, music.

Summary: The life and significance of architect Charles Rennie Mackintosh, the driving force behind the Scottish Art Nouveau movement. The camera explores in detail the Glasgow School of Art, one of the first great modern buildings, his proposed plan for the Liverpool Cathedral, and his beautiful and revolutionary Glasgow Elementary School with its glass stair-tower, black ceiling, and stark white angular furniture. His posters, furniture, and interiors are shown, including Miss Cranston's famous tearooms, and the watercolors he painted in later life. (Study guide available.)

U.S. distributor: American Educational Films (sales and rental).

Canadian distributor: Bellevue Film Distributors (sales); Canadian Film Institute for the National Gallery of Canada (loan).

MAGIC MIRROR OF ALOYSE
27 mins. Color. Switzerland. 1967.

Producer: Dr. Alfred Bader, Institute of Nervous Diseases for the Center for the Study of Plastic Expression.

Credits: Dr. Alfred Bader, director and writer.

Summary: An examination of the brilliantly colored drawings made over a period of fifty years by a 77-year-old schizophrenic patient in a Swiss hospital. Aloyse's work exhibits a close relationship to Fauvism, Surrealism, and Cubism.

U.S. distributor: New York University Film Library (rental).

Canadian distributor: International Tele-Film Enterprises (sales and rental).

MAGRITTE (*Canvas* series no. 5—*Personal Reflections on Great Paintings*)
20 mins. Color. Britain. 1966.

Producer: John Furness, BBC-TV.

Credits: Leslie Megahey, director; David Sylvester, participant, writer, and narrator.

Summary: David Sylvester speaks on Magritte from the Tate Gallery, London. His main theme is "Time Transfixed," the English title of the painting *La durée poignardée.* The speaker seems to find his way easily through the maze of the pictures created by the Belgian Surrealist. He refers to *Alice*, to the reversed world, to the absurd with a nameless terror, and to the denial of gravity.

U.S. distributor: Time-Life (sales only).

Canadian distributor: BBC-TV Enterprises (sales and rental).

MAGRITTE: THE FALSE MIRROR
22 mins. Color. Britain. 1970.

Producer: The British Film Institute for the Arts Council of Great Britain.

Credits: David Sylvester, director; E. L. T. Mesens, Andrew Forge, Robin Campbell, narrators; music by Brahms.

Summary: Made during a retrospective at the Tate Gallery in 1969, the film is an assemblage of Magritte's images. The spoken commentary is confined to Magritte's statements and anecdotes from his close friends, Mesens and Scutenaire. They explain why Magritte has become one of the most significant painters of the twentieth century.

U.S. distributor: The American Federation of Arts (rental); Films Incorporated (sales).

Canadian distributor: Canadian Film Institute for the National Gallery of Canada (loan).

MAGRITTE or THE OBJECT LESSON (*Magritte—ou la leçon de choses*)
15 mins. Color. Originally 35mm. Belgium. 1960.

Producer: Luc de Heusch, Brussels, for the Ministry of Education.

Credits: Luc de Heusch, director and writer; Jacques Delcorde, Jean Raine, writers; Célestin Deliege, music.

Summary: An insight into the poetic universe of Belgian painter René Magritte, whose work calls into question "objective reality" and evokes the mystery of ordinary things. The artist himself appears on camera, and in his home in Brussels, he discusses his work and his perceptions with old friends of the Belgian Surrealist group.

U.S. distributor: Grove Press Film Division (sales and rental).

Canadian distributor: Canadian Film Institute for the National Gallery of Canada (loan).

MAILLOL (*Aristide Maillol, sculpteur*)
22 mins. B&W. Originally 35mm. France. 1943.

Producer: I.D.H.E.C., Paris.

Credits: Jean Lods, director; Claude Roy, writer of commentary; Claude Renoir, photographer; Roger Desormière, music.

Summary: A retrospective of the work and a glimpse into the life of the great French sculptor, Aristide Maillol, filmed shortly before his death in 1944. He is seen in his Mediterranean studio near Banyuls working on marble and Pyrenean stone, strolling in the garden, sketching and talking with his friends, and painting in the vineyards and olive groves of his native countryside.

U.S. distributor: FACSEA (rental).

LA MAISON AUX IMAGES
17 mins. Color. Originally 35mm. France. 1955.

Producer: Christiane Grémillon, Les Films du Dauphin.

Credits: Jean Grémillon, director and writer; Louis Page, photographer; Jean Grémillon, music.

Summary: Lacourière's workshop in Montmartre, the favored printing house for many famous artists. The different types of print, the stages in engraving, and the tools and application of colors are shown. Some of the artists are seen at work with their chosen tools: Dunoyer de Segonzac (needle), Miró and André Masson (brush), Trémois (chisel), Jean Laboureur, Dali, and Derain.

U.S. distributor: FACSEA (rental).

Canadian distributor: Embassy of France (loan).

THE MAKING OF A RENAISSANCE BOOK
25 mins. B&W. U.S.A. 1969.

Producer: American Friends of the Plantin-Moretus Museum.

Credits: Professor Dana W. Atchley III, director, writer, and narrator.

Summary: A full record of the making of letters and the printing process in the sixteenth century, based on the account Christophe Plantin gave in a book he wrote and published in 1567. In this educational film, made by a scholar, experts carry on the old procedures in Plantin's actual printing office which has been preserved in his house, today known as the Plantin-Moretus Museum of Antwerp, Belgium.

U.S. distributor: American Friends of the Plantin-Moretus Museum (sales).

Canadian distributor: Canadian Film Institute for the National Gallery of Canada (loan).

MALEVITCH SUPREMATISM
13 mins. B&W. Britain. 1971.

Producer: Plus International Productions for the Arts Council of Great Britain.

Credits: Lutz Becker, director; Rodney Wilson, research.

Summary: Based on a scripted but unmade animation by Malevitch, Russian pioneer of modern art. Malevitch worked from 1913 onward to establish "the supremacy of pure sensibility" by a totally nonobjective art exploring combinations and permutations of flat, geometrical elements.

U.S. distributor: The American Federation of Arts (rental); Films Incorporated (sales).

MANESSIER
15 mins. Color. Originally 35mm. France. 1967.

Producer: Les Films K.

Credits: Robert Hessens, director.

Summary: Alfred Manessier, whose abstract works are inspired by sacred themes, defines his own conception of the creative life.

U.S. distributor: FACSEA (loan).

MANTEGNA–THE TRIUMPH OF CAESAR
24 mins. Color. Britain. 1973.

Producer: Balfour Films for the Arts Council of Great Britain.

Credits: Dudley Shaw Ashton, director; Sir Anthony Blunt, writer and narrator; Philip Pickett, music; Robin Campbell, narrator of quotations.

Summary: A descriptive and historical account of the eight extant canvases of Mantegna's series *The Triumph of Caesar*. Commissioned in 1484 by the Marquis of Mantua, they were in the possession of the Gonzagas of Mantua until sold to Charles I and transferred to Hampton Court, where they still remain. Sir Anthony Blunt, Surveyor of the Queen's Pictures and director of the Courtauld Institute of Art, comments on each painting emphasizing details–the realism of background scenes, the delicate metal work of the soldiers' armor–which had been obscured until a recent restoration. The musical score is played on early Renaissance instruments.

U.S. distributor: The American Federation of Arts (rental); Films Incorporated (sales).

MARINO MARINI
20 mins. Color. Italy. 1970.

Producer: Martello.

Credits: G. Martello, director.

Summary: In his constant search for traditional simplicity of form, Marino Marini, "the last paladin of Western sculpture," has maintained two continuing motifs, the female figure (Pomona) and the horse and rider. Each film sequence is a visual description of Marini fusing technical skills to characterize an indefinable quality of unity of mass, personal vision, and symbolism. The sculptor's acute sensitivity to the life process, the élan vital, is apparent in examples of his work and dialogue.

U.S. distributor: Istituto Italiano di Cultura (loan).

MARK TOBEY ABROAD
30 mins. Color. U.S.A. 1973.

Producer: Robert Gardner for Harvard University Film Study Center.

Credits: Robert Gardner and Karl Muller, directors.

Summary: Twenty years after his first film on Mark Tobey (no longer in distribution) Robert Gardner has again photographed the painter at home in Basel, Switzerland. He provides a revealing portrait, illustrating Tobey's vitality and spirit as he recites poetry, plays the piano, and visits the nearby Kunstmuseum, commenting on old masters and modern innovators. He discusses his own work and that of other artists, including Picasso, with candor and objectivity, his keen wit lending humor and bite to his comments.

U.S. distributor: Phoenix (sales and rental).

Canadian distributor: International Tele-Film Enterprises (sales and rental).

MARQUET or ALBERT MARQUET
18 mins. Color. France 1962.

Producer: Les Films de Saturne, Paris.

Credits: Frédéric Mégret, Arcady, directors; Frédéric Mégret, writer; Arcady, music.

Summary: Many important canvases are reviewed in this study of the life and work of Albert Marquet (1875-1947). Interesting cinematographic effects are achieved by skillful juxtaposition of his drawings.

U.S. distributor: FACSEA (rental).

Canadian distributor: Embassy of France (loan); Canadian Film Institute for the National Gallery of Canada (rental).

A MASTERPIECE OF SPANISH PAINTING
25 mins. Color. U.S.A. 1961.

Producer: Radio-TV Bureau, University of Arizona, Tucson.

Credits: Harry Atwood, director, writer, photographer, and editor; Rober Quinn, writer and narrator.

Summary: A careful analysis of the twenty-six panels of a sixteenth-century Hispano-Flemish retablo painted under the supervision of the Renaissance master Fernando Gallego. Made for the Cathedral of Ciudad Rodrigo near Salamanca in Spain, this remarkable altarpiece has been in the Samuel H. Kress collection at the University of Arizona since 1960. The whole ensemble is presented in sequence from *The Creation* to *The Last Judgment*, with reference to the different artists who made it.

U.S. distributor: University of Arizona (sales and rental).

MATISSE

22 mins. B&W. Originally 35mm. France. 1945.

Producer: Comptoir général cinématographique.

Credits: François Campaux, director and writer; Jean Cassou, writer of commentary.

Summary: The unique interest of this film is that one sees Matisse himself working and talking. A famous sequence follows in slow motion the subtle movements of Matisse's brush, and provides a rare opportunity to analyze the gestures of creation. By a series of dissolves the painting *La blouse paysanne* is shown in all its successive stages.

U.S. distributor: FACSEA (rental).

MATISSE–A SORT OF PARADISE

30 mins. Color. Originally 35mm. Britain. 1969.

Producer: Allan King Associates, London, for the Arts Council of Great Britain.

Credits: Lawrence Gowing, John Jones, directors; music by Erik Satie.

Summary: Recording pictures gathered from all over the world for the 1968 London Exhibition, the film reveals the idyllic quality of Matisse's work. The commentary is drawn from Matisse's own words. The result is a close and vivid view of the achievements of one of the great colorists, culminating in the vast cut-paper dance compositions of his later years.

U.S. distributor: The American Federation of Arts (rental); Films Incorporated (sales).

Canadian distributor: Visual Education Centre (sales and rental); Canadian Film Institute for the National Gallery of Canada (loan).

MAX BECKMANN

14 mins. Color. Federal Republic of Germany. 1961.

Producer: Giovanni Angelli.

Credits: Giovanni Angelli, director.

Summary: A brief biography, with the help of self-portraits and photographs, and a good survey of Beckmann's most important drawings and paintings. Influences of other artists, from Signorelli to Léger, are mentioned. Beckmann's contribution was his Expressionist portrait of modern man, which played an important part in the international movement.

U.S. distributor: Modern Talking Pictures for the Embassy of the Federal Republic of Germany (loan).

Canadian distributor: Canadian Film Institute for the Embassy of the Federal Republic of Germany (rental).

THE MAYA OF MYSTERIOUS ANCIENT MEXICO
30 mins. Color. U.S.A. 1969.

Producer: Joe Kelley Film Productions and Instituto Nacional de Anthropologia de Mexico.

Credits: Carlos R. Margain, consultant.

Summary: Introduction to the Maya culture by means of visits to the ruins of ancient cities, and artifacts from the National Museum of Anthropology in Mexico City. Included are giant Olmec heads at Villa Hermose, ruins of Monte Alban at Oaxaca, murals at Bonampak, and the Maya classic city of Palenque with its famous tombs. The Maya system of numbering is also explained.

U.S. distributor: Joe Kelley Film Productions (sales).

Canadian distributor: Canadian Film Institute (rental).

MAYAKOVSKY–THE POETRY OF ACTION (*Films for the Humanities* series)
22 mins. Color. U.S.A. 1972.

Producer: Harold Mantell, Incorporated.

Credits: John Cullum, adapter and narrator.

Summary: Shows Mayakovsky's creation of a new Russian poetic style in the twenties. Original footage and sound reveal Mayakovsky the platform spellbinder, the actor, the world traveler. Other sequences show him with poet-novelist Boris Pasternak, composer Dimitri Shostakovitch, and fellow poets of the Futurist movement. Mayakovsky's paintings, drawings, and poetry counterpoint each other dramatically in this film, which also explores his volcanic creativity and his foredoomed struggle to reconcile the demands of poetry and power.

U.S. distributor: Films for the Humanities (sales and rental).

MEMLING: PAINTER OF BRUGES (*Memling, peintre brugeois*)
(*The Flemish Renaissance* series).
27 mins. Color. Originally 35mm. Belgium. 1973.

Producer: Resobel, Brussels; International Film Bureau, Chicago.

Credits: Jean Cleinge,director, writer and editor.

Summary: The civilization of Bruges at the end of the Middle Ages seen through Memling's paintings. Not only the town itself and the portraits of its distinguished inhabitants are analyzed, but pilgrimages are glimpsed in various panels. The *Mystery of the Passion* is one of the most precise documents on the performing of a play. The final section is devoted to *The Last Judgment* of Gdansk, and bears all the Medieval anguish.

U.S. distributor: International Film Bureau (sales and rental).

Canadian distributor: Educational Film Distributors (sales and rental); Canadian Film Institute (loan).

MICHELANGELO: THE LAST GIANT
67 mins. Color. U.S.A. 1967.

Producer: NBC News.

Credits: Lou Hazam, director and writer; Peter Ustinov (as the voice of Michelangelo) and José Ferrer, narrators; Laurence Rosenthal, music.

Summary: Ninety years of Michelangelo's life and his greatest works in slightly more than one hour! The narration draws heavily on quotations from his biographers and excerpts from his writings. Photographed in Europe, the film shows relevant landscapes, building interiors, monuments, and works of art establishing the artist in his time and place. Sculpture, paintings, and architecture by the great artist are studied in chronological order. (Teacher's guide available.)

U.S. distributor: McGraw-Hill Films (sales and rental).

Canadian distributor: McGraw-Hill Ryerson (sales and rental).

MISERERE (*Le "Miserere" de Georges Rouault*)
14 mins. B&W. Originally 35mm. France. 1950.

Producer: Les Films du Temps and Comptoir des Techniciens du Film.

Credits: Frédéric Durand and Abbé Morel, directors; Abbé Morel, writer; ancient music (Josquin des Prés).

Summary: A detailed study of the series of fifty-eight black-and-white prints conceived by Rouault during World War I, though not completed and printed until 1948. They reflect the artist's intense moral indignation at the horror and futility of war and also at the callous inhumanity of man to man.

U.S. distributor: Pictura (sales and rental); FACSEA (rental).

Canadian distributor: Embassy of France (loan, French version only).

MONET IN LONDON
18 mins. Color. Originally 35mm. Britain. 1974.

Producer: Balfour Films for the Arts Council of Great Britain.

Credits: David Thompson, director; Michael Gough, narrator.

Summary: During the winter months of 1899 and 1901, three main motifs were painted by Monet from a fifth-floor room in London's Savoy Hotel under different conditions of light and permutations of color. These were Charing Cross Bridge, Waterloo Bridge, and the Houses of Parliament. He returned to France with about one hundred canvases and worked on them for another three years. The film uses many of these paintings belonging to public and private collections throughout the world; they are slowly dissolved one into the other, and are combined with actual views of the Thames and contemporary photographs of London. The commentary is drawn from Monet's diaries and letters.

U.S. distributor: The American Federation of Arts (rental); Films Incorporated (sales).

Canadian distributor: Canadian Film Institute for the National Gallery of Canada (loan).

MONSIEUR INGRES

25 mins. B&W and Color. Originally 35mm. France. 1968.

Producer: Les Films Roger Leenhardt.

Credits: Roger Leenhardt, director and writer; Guy Bernard, music.

Summary: A valuable study of Jean-Auguste-Dominique Ingres, nineteenth-century leader of the classical tradition in painting. The film tells of his arrival in Paris at the age of sixteen to study under Jacques-Louis David, the eventual break with David, and his extended stay in Rome, where he began to paint many of his famous nudes. *La Grande Baigneuse, La Grande Odalisque*, and *Le Bain Turc* are analyzed, emphasizing Ingres' purity of line and perfection of craftsmanship.

U.S. distributor: Film Images (sales and rental); FACSEA (rental).

MOSES SOYER–PAINTINGS IN A LOW VOICE

28 mins. Color. U.S.A. 1963.

Producer: Clifford Evans.

Credits: Sidney Meyers, director; David Martin, music.

Summary: The ideals and ideas of the renowned American representational painter Moses Soyer, who is followed by the camera from the time he leaves his home in the morning to walk to his Greenwich Village studio, through an entire day of painting. He first looks, in a spirit of critical self-examination, at the drawings and sketches of the previous day. Many of his paintings are shown as he expresses his views on art and artists, the Depression years, and his apprehensions regarding the world around him.

U.S. distributor: Film Images (sales and rental).

Canadian distributor: Canadian Film Institute for the United States Embassy (rental).

A NATION OF PAINTERS

7 mins. Color. U.S.A. 1973.

Producer: National Gallery of Art.

Credits: David W. Powell, director; Cherrill Anson, Evelyn Anderson, writers; Daniel C. Diggles, narrator; Richard McLanathan, consultant; Fred Cherney, music.

Summary: The Garbisch Collection of naive paintings in the National Gallery of Art is shown. The folk tradition in the United States is presented as an indication of optimism and exuberant energy, especially remarkable during the post-Revolution and pre-Civil War period.

U.S. distributor: National Gallery of Art (loan).

THE NATIONAL GALLERY OF ART
48 mins. Color. U.S.A. 1967.

Producer: Lou Hazam, NBC News.

Credits: Tom Priestley, director; Lou Hazam, writer; H. Lester Cooke, consultant; Leroy Anderson, photographer; Robert Culp, narrator; George Kleinsinger, music.

Summary: A visit to the National Gallery of Art in Washington, D.C. and a lively presentation of many paintings from its collections of over 30,000 works of art. The architecture of the building is glimpsed, the various activities of the gallery outlined, and short interviews are given by the (then) director, John Walker, and restorer Francis Sullivan. Numerous canvases by outstanding artists are shown and discussed—paintings range from a twelfth-century Byzantine Madonna to those of Picasso and representatives of practically all American and European schools and periods.

Canadian distributor: Canadian Film Institute for the Embassy of the United States (rental).

THE NATIVITY—PIERO DELLA FRANCESCA
10 mins. Color. Britain. 1966.

Producer: Samaritan Films, London, for the Arts Council of Great Britain.

Credits: Dudley Shaw Ashton, director; Sir Philip Hendy, writer and narrator; no music.

Summary: The contemplative beauty of Piero della Francesca's *Nativity*, one of his last paintings, is explored and extolled by Sir Philip Hendy, former director of London's National Gallery. He undertakes a detailed examination of the elements of form, color, light, and the typically Renaissance characteristics to be found in this work.

U.S. distributor: The American Federation of Arts (rental); Films Incorporated (sales).

Canadian distributor: Canadian Film Institute for the National Gallery of Canada (loan).

THE NEW ABSTRACTION: MORRIS LOUIS AND KENNETH NOLAND
(*Artists*—or *U.S.A. Artists*—series)
30 mins. B&W. U.S.A. 1966.

Producer: NET and Radio Center.

Credits: Lane Slate, director; Alan Solomon, adviser; Clement Greenberg (critic), Helen Jacobson (painter who studied under Morris Louis), Marcella Brenner (Louis' widow), Helen Frankenthaler and Kenneth Noland (painters), participants.

Summary: Color-field painting is the subject of this film and of comments made by the specialists interviewed. Works by Morris Louis, Kenneth Noland, and Helen Frankenthaler are shown. Louis and Noland almost simultaneously developed the same conception of the lyrical potential of pure color and symmetrical painting. Noland analyzes the influence of Pollock and Frankenthaler on his own work.

U.S. distributor: Indiana University (sales and rental).

Canadian distributor: Canadian Film Institute for the National Gallery of Canada (loan).

NEW ARTS
16 mins. Color. U.S.A. 1971.

Producer: The American Film Board for the Los Angeles County Museum of Art and the Container Corporation of America.

Credits: Eric Saarinen and Howard Chesley, directors; Gill Melle, music.

Summary: The New Art exhibit contains reflections from the art and technology program of the Los Angeles County Museum. Twenty-four artists obtained financial and technical support from forty large corporations to prospect new directions in art through the media of space age technology. Eight of them are shown in this film, consecutively as eight news items. Their names and those of their sponsors are listed below.
Tony Smith (cardboard), Container Corporation of America;
Robert Withman and John Forkmer, Philco-Ford Corporation;
Newton Harrison, Jet Propulsion Laboratories;
Rockne Krebs (laser), Hewitt-Packard;
Roy Lichtenstein (films), Universal City Studios;
Andy Warhol, Cowles Communications;
Boyd Mefferd, Universal Television;
Claes Oldenburg (ice bag), Gemini GEL.

U.S. distributor: Pyramid (sales and rental).

Canadian distributor: International Tele-Film Enterprises (sales and rental).

THE NEW NATIONAL GALLERY IN BERLIN (*Die neue Nationalgalerie von Berlin*)
18 mins. Color. Federal Republic of Germany. 1968.

Producer: Fernsehgesellschaft der Berliner Tageszeitungen.

Credits: Horst Schnare, writer.

Summary: The building and opening of the New National Gallery in Berlin, the first museum to be built by the famous architect Mies van der Rohe. This informative study deals with the actual construction of the outstanding gallery, completed in 1968, as well as visiting the art treasures displayed in it.

U.S. distributor: Modern Talking Pictures for the Embassy of the Federal Republic of Germany (loan).

Canadian distributor: Canadian Film Institute for the Embassy of the Federal Republic of Germany (loan).

NO TIME FOR UGLINESS
26 mins. Color. U.S.A. 1965.

Producer: Nova Studios for the American Institute of Architects.

Credits: Peter Young, director.

Summary: "An appraisal of the American city by the American Institute of Architects." Good and bad design are presented to stimulate awareness of the difference, to show what communities are doing, and to suggest some things that any community can do to improve its physical environment.

U.S. distributor: American Institute of Architects (sales and loan).

NOGUCHI: A SCULPTOR'S WORLD
28 mins. Color. U.S.A. 1972.

Producer: Arnold Eagle.

Credits: Arnold Eagle, director; Patia Isaku, music (voices, Japanese instruments, and piano).

Summary: A document on Isamu Noguchi and the diverse influences which shaped his art. Interviews with the sculptor are filmed in his Unesco Park in Paris, the Billy Rose Gardens in Jerusalem, his plaza setting for the Chase Manhattan Bank in New York, and at the Osaka World Exposition, for which he designed spectacular fountains.

U.S. distributor: Arnold Eagle (sales and rental); Museum at Large (sales and rental).

Canadian distributor: Canadian Film Institute for the National Gallery of Canada (loan).

THE NORMAN CONQUEST OF ENGLAND—THE BAYEUX TAPESTRY
(*La conquête de l'Angleterre*)
20 mins. Color. Originally 35mm. France. 1955.

Producer: Les Films Roger Leenhardt, Paris.

Credits: Roger Leenhardt and J.-P. Vivet, directors; Guy Bernard, music.

Summary: The famous so-called tapestry of Queen Mathilde, wife of William of Normandy, which dates from about the end of the eleventh century. A strip of linen 229½ feet (70 meters) long embroidered in wool in eight colors, it very much resembles a film itself as it follows the chronological description of the invasion of England by William I of Normandy, culminating in the Battle of Hastings, where the English King Harold was killed by a chance arrow in the eye.

Distributor: Film Images (sales and rental).

NOTRE-DAME DE PARIS, JOYAU DE FRANCE
20 mins. Color. France. 1961.

Producer: Pathé Cinéma, Paris.

Credits: Pierre Baculard, director; Léonce de St. Martin, music (organ).

Summary: A result of the filmmaker's ten years of close contact with the artistic, religious, and musical aspects of the Cathedral. Its sculpture and architecture are seen against the changing background of the seasons, with the immense nave flooded with light from its stained-glass windows.

U.S. distributor: FACSEA (rental).

Canadian distributor: Embassy of France (loan).

THE NUREMBERG CHRONICLE
22 mins. B&W. U.S.A. 1967.

Producer: John Frazer and Russell T. Limbach for Wesleyan University, Davidson Art Center.

Summary: As the camera explores the handsome woodcuts that illustrate this famous incunabulum, the narration gives an account of history (as envisaged in 1493) from the Creation to the Final Judgment, predicted to be imminent. The film creates a vivid impression of people's hopes, fears, and beliefs at a time in history when, as today, old ways and ideas were changing radically.

U.S. distributor: Connecticut Films (sales and rental).

ON LOAN FROM RUSSIA: FORTY-ONE FRENCH MASTERPIECES
30 mins. Color. U.S.A. 1973.

Producer: A. H. Perlmutter, WNET-TV.

Credits: Gardner Compton, director; Lou Solomon, writer; Larry Keith, Dan Resin, Pierre Epstein, narrators; John Rewald, consultant; John Adams, music supervisor.

Summary: A presentation of the exhibition "Impressionist and Post-Impressionist Painting from the U.S.S.R." at the National Gallery of Art in 1973. The film contains behind-the-scenes preparations and provides historical background on the paintings, which were selected from the Hermitage and Pushkin Museums.

U.S. distributor: National Gallery of Art (loan).

OPEN SPACE (ROCKEFELLER PLAZA, N.Y.) (*Essays: I. M. Pei* series)
4 mins. Color. U.S.A. 1969.

Producer: Rick Hauser for WGBH Educational Foundation with a grant from the Massachusetts Council for the Humanities.

Credits: Rick Hauser, Joyce Chopra, directors; Peter Hoving, photographer; Rick Hauser, narrator.

Summary: The first of five film essays in which famed architect I. M. Pei gives his views on aspects of building. Here he guides the viewer through Rockefeller Plaza, which "may be the most successful open space in the entire world." He shows us a human space where people can go to talk, relax, eat, skate, listen to a summer concert, or just sit and sense the excitement of New York City.

U.S. distributor: Museum at Large (sales and rental, singly or in set).

THE OPEN WINDOW (*La fenêtre ouverte*)
18 mins. Color. Originally 35mm. Britain, France, and Benelux. 1952. (Re-issue 1966.)

Producer: Artifex Film with Prociné, Brussels, Crown Film Unit, London, and Les Films d'Ariel.

Credits: Henri Storck, director; Jean Cassou, art adviser; Cyril J. Knowles, photographer; Georges Auric, music; Alan Wheatley, narrator.

Summary: Landscape painting in Belgium, France, Luxembourg, the Netherlands, and the United Kingdom is the subject of this joint project of members of the Brussels Treaty Organization. Fifty-nine works from the most important museums in the countries concerned re-create the history of the genre. Covering the scenery of the six European countries, the paintings include Flemish primitives, Dutch artists of the Golden Age, the British school with Constable and Turner, and the French Impressionists.

U.S. distributor: International Film Bureau (sales and rental); Royal Netherlands Embassy (rental).

Canadian distributor: Educational Film Distributors (rental); Canadian Film Institute for the National Gallery of Canada (loan).

OPUS–IMPRESSIONS OF BRITISH ART AND CULTURE
29 mins. Color. Originally 35mm. Britain. 1967.

Producer: James Archibald and Associates for the Central Office of Information, Foreign Office, and Commonwealth Office.

Credits: Don Levy, director; Tristram Cary, music; no commentary.

Summary: A sophisticated approach to the upsurge of creative talent in Britain in 1967, the film and its musical score are divided in four movements highlighting different aspects of contemporary sculpture, painting, architecture, drama, and ballet. It contains glimpses of aluminum sculpture by Eduardo Paolozzi, the home of architect Colin St. John Wilson, the action paintings of Alan Davie, canvases by Francis Bacon, jewelry by Gerda Flockinger, and the sculptures of Henry Moore seen, in most cases, in natural surroundings.

U.S. distributor: Pyramid (sales and rental).

Canadian distributor: International Tele-Film Enterprises (sales and rental); Canadian Film Institute (rental).

THE ORIGINS OF ART IN FRANCE or THE ORIGINS OF FRENCH ART
(*Land of the Arts* series) (*Les origines de l'art en France*, série *Terre des Arts*).
44 mins. B&W. France. 1967.

Producer: ORTF (Office de Radiodiffusion Télévision Française).

Credits: John L'Hote, director; Max-Pol Fouchet, director, writer of commentary and narrator; modern music (Bartók and Stravinsky).

Summary: A study of Celtic art, filmed at the Musée des Antiquités Nationales of Saint-Germain-en-Laye, other French museums, and in natural sites of ancient Gaul. Many of these ancient drawings, jewelry, and ornaments reveal similarities with modern art forms; woman is seen as a symbol of beauty and fertility. The Roman conquest transformed Celtic art, but the invaders did not extinguish the Gallic spirit still evident today.

U.S. distributor: The Roland Collection (sales and rental).

THE OROZCO MURALS: QUETZALCOATL
23 mins. Color. U.S.A. 1962.

Producer: Robert Canton for Brookshire Production.

Credits: Robert Canton, director and writer; Theodore Newman, music; Joseph Marzano, narrator.

Summary: A brief biographical sketch of the Mexican painter José Clemente Orozco, followed by a description of the murals he painted in 1934 for the Baker Library of Dartmouth College, Hanover, New Hampshire. Considered one of the most important fresco achievements in the United States, the murals embody the fusion of legend, history, social comment, and personal myth characteristic of Orozco's style. They are based on the Aztec legend of Quetzalcoatl, the white messiah who bestows civilization and the humanizing arts on mankind, but leaves when his people fail him.

U.S. distributor: Macmillan (sales and rental).

Canadian distributor: Marlin Motion Pictures (sales and rental).

PAINTERS PAINTING
116 mins. Color and B&W. Originally 35mm. U.S.A. 1972.

Producer: Emile de Antonio, New Yorker Films.

Credits: Emile de Antonio, director; Ed Emswhiller, photographer.

Summary: The lives and work during the three decades from 1940 to 1970 of fourteen contemporary New York artists—Willem de Kooning, Robert Rauschenberg, Frank Stella, Larry Poons, Jackson Pollock, Helen Frankenthaler, Robert Motherwell, Kenneth Noland, Hans Hofmann, Jasper Johns, Barnett Newman, Andy Warhol, Jules Olitski, and Philip Pavia—depicted through interviews and conversations with the producer, Emile de Antonio, and many of the critics, dealers, and backers of the artists. De Kooning and Pavia speak for the painters, and outstanding among the second group are Clement Greenberg, Leo Castelli, Philip Johnson, and Hilton Kramer.

U.S. distributor: New Yorker Films (sales and rental).

Canadian distributor: New Cinema Enterprises (sales and rental).

PAINTING IN AMERICA: COPLEY TO AUDUBON
21 mins. Color. U.S.A. 1957.

Producer: Detroit Institute of Arts.

Credits: Franklin Page, director and writer; Robert Starring, narrator; folk songs sung by Rowena.

Summary: Eighteenth-century American paintings are shown. The film includes portraits by John Singleton Copley, William Dunlap, and John Trumbull; compositions by Charles Willson Peale, Gilbert Stuart, and Thomas Sully; narrative pictures by Rembrandt Peale and Washington Allston; birds and animals by John James Audubon; landscapes of the Hudson River by Thomas Doughty.

U.S. distributor: Film Images (sales and rental).

THE PAINTINGS OF CO WESTERIK (*Tableaux de Co Westerik*)
12 mins. Color. Netherlands. 1965.

Producer: Bob Kommer.

Credits: Bob Kommer, director; Otto Ketting, music.

Summary: Co Westerik, a striking figure in the world of contemporary Dutch art, describes his paintings as figurative and explains that his presentation of man reflects his own strange haunting vision. Complete paintings and details of paintings are woven into a rhythmical sequence that intensifies their expressive force.

U.S. distributor: Netherlands Government Information Services (loan).

Canadian distributor: Canadian Film Institute for the Embassy of the Netherlands (rental).

PAOLO UCCELLO
15 mins. Color. Italy. 1971.

Producer: Luce.

Credits: G.B. Girardi, director.

Summary: A documentary illustrating in great detail the works of the Italian painter who best personifies the spirit of the early Renaissance in his original and imaginative approach. Engrossed in the problems of representing three-dimensional reality on a two-dimensional surface through perspective, Uccello (so nicknamed for his love of birds) wedded science to a poetical interpretation of his subject matter. *The Rout of San Romano* and *St. George and the Dragon* are two paintings in which his gifts of form and fantasy are most clearly shown.

U.S. distributor: Istituto Italiano di Cultura (loan).

PAUL CEZANNE–A MAN OF CONTRADICTIONS
(*Pioneers of Modern Painting* series, no. 2)
40 mins. Color. Britain. 1972.

Producer: Colin Clark for Independent Television Corporation.

Credits: Colin Clark, director; Lord Clark, writer and narrator.

Summary: Cézanne is the painter Lord Clark admires most since Rembrandt, but whom he finds hardest to analyze because of the many contradictions in his life and work: a rich man who lived simply, a violent romantic who became the most classical of modern artists, a rebel who turned into a timid conformist. Among the paintings shown and discussed in the film is *House in Provence* which, with its simplification of complex, disordered nature into grand, simple shapes, must be considered the first Cubist landscape.

U.S. distributor: Independent Television Corporation (sales); National Gallery of Art (loan).

Canadian distributor: ITC of Canada (sales); Canadian Film Institute for the National Gallery of Canada (loan).

PAUL GAUGUIN (1848-1903) or PAUL GAUGUIN
15 mins. B&W. France. 1950.

Producer: Panthéon Production.

Credits: Alain Resnais, director; Yannick Bellon, editor; Martin Gabel, narrator; Darius Milhaud, music.

Summary: One of the early films by Resnais, who tells Gauguin's story through his almost biographical paintings; the commentary is drawn from direct translation of his letters, journals, and other writings.

U.S. distributor: Pictura (sales and rental).

Canadian distributor: International Tele-Film Enterprises (sales and rental).

PAUL KANE GOES WEST (*Paul Kane chez les Amérindiens*)
14 mins. Color. Originally 35mm. Canada. 1972.

Producer: Robert Verrall, National Film Board of Canada.

Credits: Gerald Budner, director and writer; J. Russell Harper, consultant; John Evans, photographer; Eldon Rathburn, music.

Summary: A painter's discovery of the West in the mid-1800s, as recorded in his sketchbooks and the diary of his 9,000 mile journey through Indian territories. Kane's heroic view of the West gains even more vitality in the larger dimensions of the motion picture screen.

U.S. distributor: EBEC (sales and rental).

Canadian distributor: National Film Board of Canada (sales and loan).

PAUL KLEE
31 mins. Color. Federal Republic of Germany. 1967.

Producer: Bayerischer Rundfunk, Munich, for Telepool.

Credits: Georgia van der Rohe, director; Will Grohmann, writer; Stravinsky, music.

Summary: Some of the qualities of Grohmann's book on Klee are brought out in this document: a friendly, fervent, and intelligent approach is taken to the art of the painter. Examples from 9,000 works by Klee are grouped according to subject matter and not in chronological order. The choice of detail is never arbitrary, and the film is a good introduction to Klee's theories and to an appreciation of his sensibility.

U.S. distributor: Modern Talking Pictures for the Embassy of the Federal Republic of Germany (loan).

Canadian distributor: Canadian Film Institute for the Embassy of the Federal Republic of Germany (rental).

PEDRO LINARES, FOLK ARTIST (*Pedro Linares, Artesano Cartonero*)
22 mins. Color. U.S.A. 1975.

Producer: Robert Grant and Judith Bronowski, The Works.

Credits: Robert Grant and Judith Bronowski, directors; ethnic Mexican music.

Summary: Shows the making and use of large puppet figures and "Judases" in the Mexican tradition. Pedro Linares, with the help of his sons, creates these sculptures with bamboo and papier-maché in a poor district of Mexico City for the celebration of Good Friday. We see how he models and decorates them while giving his explanation of the traditional ceremonies. He takes some of his puppets to a village which has commissioned him to organize a firework display with its grand finale, the destruction of Judas.

U.S. distributor: The Works (sales and rental).

PEGGY GUGGENHEIM: ART IN VENICE
44 mins. Color. Italy. 1975.

Producer: Raffaele Andreassi for Mondadori Editore.

Credits: Raffaele Andreassi, director.

Summary: A remarkable collection and a remarkable collector, Peggy Guggenheim conducts us on a journey through art history, past and present. Her ancient Palazzo Venier dei Leoni on the Grand Canal, Venice, houses one of the world's great private collections of the art of this century. Works shown are by Picasso, Braque, Kandinsky, Arp, Brancusi, Mondrian, Ernst, de Chirico, Klee, Miró, Giacometti, Moore, Gorky, Pollock, de Kooning, Nicholson, Pomodoro, and many others.

U.S. distributor: Films for the Humanities (sales and rental).

Canadian distributor: Canadian Film Institute (sales).

PETER ALEXANDER (*Artists in America* series)
30 mins. Color. U.S.A. 1971.

Producer: KCET Los Angeles and the National Endowment for the Arts.

Credits: Richard S. Scott, director.

Summary: Sculptor Peter Alexander makes plastic cubes, wedges, pyramids, and strips tinted with color to create a byplay with the light surrounding his pieces. Alexander, an ex-architect, used to draw in pen and ink but has since become interested in the technical processes, materials, and the dematerializing quality in the nature of light. Currently he is working with molds and using color. He states: "Art starts in a man's thoughts and dreams, but the mechanics can be boring unless the piece surprises the artist."

U.S. distributor: Indiana University (sales and rental).

Canadian distributor: Canadian Film Institute (sales); International Tele-Film Enterprises (sales and rental).

PHILIP GUSTON

28 mins. Color. U.S.A. 1972.

Producer: Blackwood Productions.

Credits: Michael Blackwood, director.

Summary: At his Woodstock studio, the artist traces the development of his style from the figurative paintings of the late thirties and forties to his color abstractions during the height of the New York School, and his recent return to recognizable shapes. The works that Guston speaks of are shown in detail. He paints a large picture, becomes dissatisfied with it and paints it out; at the end of the film he destroys it.

U.S. distributor: Blackwood Productions (sales and rental).

THE PHOTOGRAPHER

27 mins. B&W. U.S.A. 1948.

Producer: Affiliated Film Producers.

Credits: Willard Van Dyke, director and photographer; Ben Maddow, writer; Irving Jacoby, narrator; Alexander Hammid, editor.

Summary: The cultural and artistic values of photography as seen through the life and work of American photographer Edward Weston. The film focuses on Weston's rapport with his subjects—mountain, water, dune, woman—and how it was achieved. Made by noted documentary filmmaker and photographer Willard Van Dyke.

U.S. distributor: The Museum of Modern Art (rental).

PICASSO

43 mins. Color. Originally 35mm. Italy. 1954.

Producer: Sergio Amidei, Rizzoli Film, Rome.

Credits: Luciano Emmer, director; A. Trombodori, R. Guttuso, writers of commentary; Roman Vlad, music.

Summary: The development of the work of Picasso from 1896 to the mid-fifties. The artist is caught in the act of creation at Vallauris; twisting the slender neck of an amphora so that it takes on the semblance of a dove; scraping out a design from the soft surface of an unfired platter. Nearly 500 of Picasso's designs, paintings, charcoals, and ceramics made from the ages of fourteen to seventy-eight are shown. Some were photographed at Picasso's exhibitions in Rome and Milan; the shooting opens and closes on the French Riviera.

U.S. distributor: Museum at Large (sales and rental).

Canadian distributor: Canadian Film Institute for the National Gallery of Canada (loan).

PICASSO, A PORTRAIT (*Picasso, un portrait*)
60 mins. Color. France/Britain. 1969.

Producer: Quinn Productions.

Credits: Edward Quinn, director.

Summary: Still photographs (reproduced in sepia) and a few candid shots give an intimate impression of the last fifteen years of Picasso's life at various Riviera villas. The prolific artist is shown now playful, now dedicated to his work, but always drawing new inspiration from the things around him.

U.S. distributor: New Yorker Films (sales and rental).

Canadian distributor: Faroun Films (sales and rental).

PICASSO, ARTIST OF THE CENTURY (*Picasso, peintre du siècle*)
56 mins. Color. Originally 35mm. France. 1973.

Producer: Simon Schiffrin, Filmsonor Marceau.

Credits: Lauro Venturi, director and writer; Jean Leymaire, then director of Musée National d'Art Moderne, Paris, writer of commentary; Roman Vlad, music.

Summary: Made a short time before Picasso's death, this survey of his life and work is divided into three parts:

1. PICASSO: FROM 1900 THROUGH CUBISM, 12 mins. Period photographs and other material are used as background to an analysis of his early work: his experiments with analytical and synthetic Cubism; examples from the Blue and the Rose periods; *Les demoiselles d'Avignon, The Harlequins*, and their devastating impact on the art world.

2. PICASSO: THE VOLCANIC THIRTIES, 17 mins. Picasso's departure from Paris for the sun and sea of Provence and the Côte d'Azur resulted in an explosion of paintings representing his dreams and obsessions: *The Seated Bather, Girl Before a Mirror*, and *Minotauromachy*. His agony over the Spanish Civil War inspired *Guernica*, commissioned for the Spanish Pavilion at the Paris Exhibition.

3. PICASSO: THE 1940s AND AFTER, 27 mins. His later works, beginning with *Night Fishing at Antibes, Joie de vivre*, and the *Classical Fantasies* group. His departure for Vallauris marked the increased importance of sculpture and ceramics in his work: a library sequence shows him painting on a clay vase, and the sculpture *Man with the Lamb* is examined in detail in its village setting. The film includes a visit to the Museum of Antibes and several of Picasso's houses and castles in the south of France.

U.S. distributor: Macmillan (sales and rental in full or in part).

Canadian distributor: Embassy of France (loan).

PICASSO IN HIS TIME or PICASSO, HIS LIFE AND HIS ART
60 mins. Color. Britain. 1972.

Producer: BBC-TV.

Credits: Sir Roland Penrose, Picasso, and his wife Jacqueline Roque, participants.

Summary: A television biography, made to honor Picasso on his ninetieth birthday, with special emphasis on the basic themes in his work. The printing of a recent engraving in his workshop in Mougins, followed by a variety of printing processes, is used as leitmotiv. Paintings and drawings are interspersed with photographs, documentary footage, and interviews. The glittering circle of Picasso's friends in the Paris of the twenties and the part played by women in his life are both emphasized.

U.S. distributor: Time-Life (sales and rental).

Canadian distributor: BBC-TV Enterprises (sales and rental).

PICASSO IS 90!
51 mins. Color. U.S.A. 1971.

Producer: CBS News.

Credits: Charles Collingwood, writer and reporter.

Summary: A filmed biography of Pablo Picasso: "His Life, His Loves, His Art." Representative paintings and sculptures were filmed at the Pushkin Museum, Moscow; the Hermitage, Leningrad; The Museum of Modern Art and The Metropolitan Museum, New York. Intimate glimpses of Picasso's private life are given by his son, Claude Picasso, the artist's former wife, Françoise Gilot, and his friend the renowned Spanish bullfighter, Luis Miguel Dominguin.

U.S. distributor: Carousel Films (sales and rental).

Canadian distributor: Marlin Motion Pictures (sales and rental).

PICASSO, THE SCULPTOR
27 mins. Color. Britain. 1968.

Producer: British Film Institute for the Arts Council of Great Britain.

Credits: Sir Roland Penrose, director and writer; Jill Balcon, narrator; music by Bela Bartók.

Summary: Sir Roland Penrose, Chairman and Honorary Director of the London Institute of Contemporary Art, longtime friend of Picasso, provides insight into a comprehensive exhibition of sculpture by the famous artist held at the Tate Gallery in 1967. Most of Picasso's sculpture remained in his personal collection until his death and is viewed here for the first time. From early figurative heads through to the sheet metal cutouts of the last years, Picasso's wit and magic are always evident.

U.S. distributor: The American Federation of Arts (rental); Films Incorporated (sales).

Canadian distributor: Canadian Film Institute for the National Gallery of Canada (loan).

PIERO DELLA FRANCESCA
10 mins. Color. Italy. 1970.

Producer: Romor Film.

Credits: Carlo L. Ragghianti, director and writer; Giorgio Fabor, music.

Summary: In this "critofilm" (a term originated by the director) Carlo Ragghianti studies the style of the great Renaissance painter and mathematician. First inspired by the tragic force of Masaccio and the turbulent plasticity of Donatello, his mature work reveals a powerful personality. Nature and architecture are of great importance in his compositions. The *Flagellation* now at Urbino is shown as his most accomplished achievement.

U.S. distributor: The Roland Collection (sales and rental).

PIET MONDRIAAN, A FILM ESSAY
18 mins. Color. Originally 35mm. Netherlands. 1973.

Producer: Nico Crama.

Credits: Nico Crama, director; Mart Ambry, Hans Locher, Nico Crama, writers; David Brierley, John Jory, narrators.

Summary: The development of a major Dutch painter from naturalism through Cubism to pure abstraction. The film uses some fifty paintings and drawings carefully selected with the cooperation of the Municipal Museum of The Hague, where most of Mondrian's work is on view. Photographs and documents evoke his life-style and attest his influence.

U.S. distributor: Visual Resources (sales and rental).

Canadian distributor: Faroun Films (sales and rental); Canadian Film Institute for the Netherlands Embassy (rental).

THE PINK CITY—JAIPUR, INDIA (*The Glory That Remains* series)
30 mins. Color. Britain. 1970.

Producer: Kenneth Shepherd, BBC-TV.

Credits: Kenneth Shepherd, director; Robert Erskine, writer and narrator.

Summary: Jaipur, in the Indian State of Rajasthan, is a pink city of elaborately stuccoed buildings. The film examines the history, architecture, and art objects of the palaces of the Maharajas Man Singh, Jai Singh, and Sawai Jai Singh, and discusses these three most famous rulers of Jaipur.

Canadian distributor: BBC-TV Enterprises (sales and rental).

PIONEERS OF MODERN PAINTING series
6 parts, 40 mins. each. Color. Britain. 1972.

Producer: Colin Clark for Independent Television Corporation.

Credits: Colin Clark, director; Lord Clark, writer and narrator; Martha Higgins, researcher.

Summary: Following the tremendous success of the *Civilisation* series, which J. Carter Brown, director of the National Gallery of Art, Washington, D.C. compared to a piece of "symphonic writing," this series in which Lord Clark deals with individual artists may, in its more informal treatment, be likened to "chamber music." For convenience, the six films have been entered under their individual titles:

1. EDOUARD MANET

2. PAUL CEZANNE

3. CLAUDE MONET

4. GEORGES SEURAT

5. HENRI ROUSSEAU

6. EDVARD MUNCH

The first five have been filmed in parks, galleries, and cafés of Paris and its suburbs, the French countryside and seaside; the last one was made in Norway. The paintings are from museums and private collections throughout the world.

U.S. distributor: Independent Television Corporation (sales); National Gallery of Art (loan).

Canadian distributor: ITC of Canada (sales); Canadian Film Institute for the National Gallery of Canada (loan).

POMPEII: ONCE THERE WAS A CITY
25 mins. Color. U.S.A. 1970.

Producer: Sol Kaplan and Reva Schlesinger.

Credits: Sol Kaplan and Reva Schlesinger, directors.

Summary: Everyday life in ancient Pompeii is re-created as its ruins are explored, and is compared with life in a modern American town. The giant volcanic eruption, following an era of unprecedented material prosperity, suggests disturbing contemporary parallels. (Teacher's guide available.)

U.S. distributor: Learning Corporation of America (sales and rental).

Canadian distributor: Marlin Motion Pictures (sales and rental).

PORTRAIT OF FRANS HALS (*Portret van Frans Hals*)
17 mins. Color. Originally 35mm. Netherlands. 1963.

Producer: G. F. de Clerck, Multifilm, Hilversum, for the Ministry of Education, Arts, and Sciences.

Credits: Frans Dupont, director and writer; Wim Franken, music.

Summary: Records the Frans Hals exhibition held in Haarlem in 1962 to mark his centenary. The large number of works from the Frans Hals Museum of Haarlem, and from other Dutch and foreign art collections, presented a unique opportunity for capturing on film the life of the artist and tracing the evolution of his genius.

U.S. distributor: Museum at Large (sales and rental); Netherlands Government Information Services (loan).

Canadian distributor: Canadian Film Institute for the National Gallery of Canada (loan).

POSADA
10 mins. B&W. U.S.A. 1964.

Producer: José Pavon.

Credits: José Pavon, director; Mexican folk music (guitar); no narration.

Summary: Printmaker to the Mexican people's movement, José Guadalupe Posada (1851-1913), produced over 20,000 engravings in forty-four years. Camera movements and extreme close-ups reveal his strong and graceful style. Lithographs, woodcuts, and etchings provide a satirical and violent comment on the history, politics, and events of the time. They were so widely circulated in Mexico that they became known simply as *posadas*.

U.S. distributor: Film Images (sales and rental); The Museum of Modern Art (rental).

Canadian distributor: Canadian Film Institute for the National Gallery of Canada (loan).

THE POSSIBILITIES OF AGAM
28 mins. Color. U.S.A. 1967.

Producer: Warren Forma.

Credits: Warren Forma, director; Yaacov Agam, narrator; Daniel Pinsky, music.

Summary: The work of Yaacov Agam, Israeli artist of the optic-kinetic school is shown. He is seen in several locales in the United States and abroad. He speaks of the possibilities of expression of movement, space, time, and the multiple aspects of life. "Contrapuntal" paintings are seen from left to right or right to left, affording the actual changing visual effect intended by the artist. "Sound tactile paintings" are also shown; here the transformation of the image depends on the tone of the sound.

U.S. distributor: Forma Art Associates (sales and rental).

POUSSIN—THE SEVEN SACRAMENTS or MIND OF NICOLAS POUSSIN— A STUDY OF HIS PAINTINGS—SEVEN SACRAMENTS
20 mins. Color. Originally 35mm. Britain. 1968.

Producer: Samaritan Films, London, for the Arts Council of Great Britain.

Credits: Dudley Shaw Ashton, director; Sir Anthony Blunt, writer and narrator; Renaissance music (Giovanni da Palestrina).

Summary: Poussin's second version of the *Seven Sacraments* was painted in France between 1644 and 1648 for Paul Freart de Chantelou. The seven paintings now form part of the Duke of Sutherland's collection at the National Gallery of Scotland, Edinburgh. Sir Anthony Blunt's skillful analysis illuminates the symbolic and liturgical significance of their content.

U.S. distributor: The American Federation of Arts (rental); Films Incorporated (sales).

Canadian distributor: Canadian Film Institute for the National Gallery of Canada (loan).

EL PRADO—MASTERPIECES AND MUSIC (*The Bell Telephone Hour* series)
60 mins. Color. U.S.A.

Producer: Bell Telephone.

Credits: Andrés Segovia, music (guitar).

Summary: A one-hour long visit to the El Prado Museum, Madrid. Emphasis is placed on the great classical masters of Spanish painting: El Greco, Velázquez, and Goya.

U.S. distributor: AT&T (rental).

PRE-COLUMBIAN ART OF COSTA RICA: POINT OF CONVERGENCE
15 mins. Color. Costa Rica. 1972.

Producer: Organization of American States.

Credits: José Goméz-Sicre and Angel Hurtado, directors; José Goméz-Sicre, writer; John Gavin, narrator; Bernal Flores, music.

Summary: An extensive panorama of pre-Columbian artifacts from Costa Rica is presented. José Goméz-Sicre organized an exhibition "Two Thousand Years of Columbian Art," which has been shown in the United States and in five European countries.

U.S. distributor: Pan American Development Foundation (sales).

THE PRECURSORS: CEZANNE, GAUGUIN, VAN GOGH (*Les Précurseurs: Cézanne, Gauguin, Van Gogh*) (*Pathways of Modern Painting* series, no. 2)
26 mins. Color. Originally 35mm. France. 1970.

Producer: Jacqueline Jullien, Les Films du Cyprès, and International Film Bureau.

Credits: Pierre Alibert, director; Bernard Dorival, consultant; Philip Gaunt, narrator; Francis Seyrig, music.

Summary: A sequel to *Impressionism and Neo-Impressionism* in the same series. A study of the different paths followed by Cézanne, Gauguin, and Van Gogh after 1880, all three affected by Impressionism and profoundly influencing the development of modern art. Divided into three parts, the first and most important deals with Cézanne, contrasting his fresh techniques for painting an apple with traditional and Impressionist treatment of the same subject. Gauguin, to whom bright, heightened color was important, considered the picture as an independent reality created by man; Van Gogh used his art to convey an emotion or a state of mind.

U.S. distributor: International Film Bureau (sales and rental).

Canadian distributor: Educational Film Distributors (sales and rental).

PREHISTORIC IMAGES—THE FIRST ART OF MAN (*Images préhistoriques*)
17 mins. Color. Originally 35mm. France. 1954.

Producer: Les Films de Saturne and Renaissance du Film, Montrouge.

Credits: Arcady and Thomas L. Rowe, directors; Thomas L. Rowe, writer; Arcady, music.

Summary: Paintings in the prehistoric caves of France and Spain dating from the age of the glaciers ten to forty thousand years ago. Animals and other subjects are seen in detail on the walls of the caves of Pech Merle, Lascaux, Trois Frères and Niaux in the Dordogne, and Altamira and El Castillo in northern Spain. The animated sequence does not add appreciably to the impact of the film.

U.S. distributor: Macmillan (sales and rental).

Canadian distributor: Marlin Motion Pictures (sales and rental).

THE PRE-RAPHAELITE REVOLT
30 mins. Color. Originally 35mm. Britain. 1967.

Producer: Samaritan Films, London, for the Arts Council of Great Britain.

Credits: David Thompson, director and writer; John Wood, Freda Dowie, narrators; Elisabeth Lutyens, music.

Summary: Some of the most widely familiar paintings in the history of English art were produced by the Pre-Raphaelite Brotherhood (1848 to early 1850s). They stand out as one of the most intensely romantic aspects of the Victorian era. Over thirty paintings and nearly fifty drawings by Ford Madox Brown, John Everett Millais, John Ruskin, Holman Hunt, Arthur Hughes, and Dante Gabriel Rossetti have been filmed from originals in both public and private collections. The commentary includes poems by Tennyson, Dante Gabriel and Christina Rossetti.

U.S. distributor: The American Federation of Arts (rental); Films Incorporated (sales).

Canadian distributor: Visual Education Centre (sales and rental); Canadian Film Institute for the National Gallery of Canada (loan).

PROSPECT FOR A CITY
25 mins. Color. Originally 35mm. Britain.

Producer: Films of Scotland for the Corporation of Edinburgh and the Scottish Arts Council.

Credits: Henry Cooper, director; Colin McWilliams, writer; Tom Fleming, narrator; Eric Roberts and the Pro Arte Orchestra of Edinburgh, music.

Summary: Documents the planning and growth of Edinburgh since the eighteenth century. James Craig's plan of three main thoroughfares and two great squares was followed by the City Architects William Sibbald and Robert Reid. Among the outstanding buildings shown and discussed are: Robert Adam's University, Thomas Hamilton's Royal High School, and Playfair's Art Galleries.

U.S. distributor: Sherman Films (sales and rental).

R. B. KITAJ
20 mins. Color. Britain. 1967.

Producer: Maya Film Productions, London, for the Arts Council of Great Britain.

Credits: James Scott, director; R. B. Kitaj and Christopher Finch, narrators.

Summary: Kitaj, an early Pop painter, views painting as an extension of political commitment and awareness. The film explores the sources of his ideas and their growth from first sketches to final painting. Some of his photographic material, the basis of his work, is shown. Kitaj places art in society and illustrates with examples from mass media.

U.S. distributor: The American Federation of Arts (rental); Films Incorporated (sales and rental).

Canadian distributor: Canadian Film Institute for the National Gallery of Canada (loan).

RAG TAPESTRY or A RAG TAPESTRY BY 25 CHILDREN
11 mins. Color. U.S.A. 1968.

Producer: Julien Bryan.

Credits: George and Sherry Zabriskie, directors and photographers.

Summary: Twenty-five children, eight to twelve years old, in a course at the Metropolitan Museum of Art design and complete a tapestry with the Jackson shuttle, a crude early American instrument used in rug hooking. The leader of the experimental workshop is Ms. Ann Wiseman. The subject of the tapestry: New York. It is a do-it-yourself activity. The tapestry now hangs in the Children's Museum.

U.S. distributor: International Film Foundation (sales and rental); International Film Bureau (sales and rental).

Canadian distributor: Educational Film Distributors (rental).

RAPHAEL (*Canvas* series no. 4–*Personal Reflections on Great Paintings*)
20 mins. Color. Britain. 1966.

Producer: John Furness, BBC-TV.

Credits: Leslie Megahey, director; Leonard Rosoman, R.A., participant, writer and narrator.

Summary: From the Victoria and Albert Museum, London, Leonard Rosoman communicates his enthusiasm for *The Miraculous Draught of Fishes*, one of the tapestry designs made by Raphael for the Sistine Chapel. He shows the importance of the tapestries in the decoration of this famous shrine, and explains Raphael's challenge to the weavers of Brussels, who had to cut the canvas into pieces in order to prepare the tapestry. This, which is designed in reverse, is compared with Raphael's restored canvas. The last sequence of the film is a brief survey of Raphael's work.

U.S. distributor: Time-Life (sales only).

Canadian distributor: BBC-TV Enterprises (sales and rental).

THE REALITY OF KAREL APPEL (*De Werkelijkheid van Karel Appel*)
16 mins. Color. Originally 35mm. Netherlands. 1961.

Producer: Piet van Moock for Nederlandse Filmproductie Maatschappij, Rotterdam.

Credits: Jan Vrijman, director; Dizzie Gillespie, Karel Appel, music.

Summary: Accompanies the Dutch action painter Karel Appel, member of the "Cobra" group, along the streets and bridges of Paris to his studio where he flings, drips, and jabs paint on a huge canvas. He comments on his work: "If I paint like a barbarian, it is because I live in a barbarous age."

U.S. distributor: Netherlands Government Information Services (loan).

Canadian distributor: Canadian Film Institute for the National Gallery of Canada (loan).

THE REBEL ANGEL (JOSEPH MALLORD TURNER, 1775-1851)
50 mins. Color. Britain. 1975.

Producer: BBC-TV and Reiner Moritz.

Credits: John Read, director and writer; Andrew Wilton, script consultant; Frank Duncan, narrator.

Summary: Made to celebrate the bicentenary of J. M. W. Turner, generally recognized as England's greatest painter, this production fulfills his expressed desire that his work should be viewed as a whole. Sketchbooks, watercolors, and oils bequeathed to the nation are presented in chronological order, accompanied by views of the actual landscapes painted by the artist on his lengthy travels in Britain and Europe. The film includes work never shown during Turner's lifetime, much of it in storage since his death, revealing him to have been in many ways in advance even of the Impressionists.

Canadian distributor: BBC-TV Enterprises (sales and rental); Canadian Film Institute for the National Gallery of Canada (loan).

RECLINING FIGURE (Henry Moore's Sculpture for the UNESCO Building in Paris)
16 mins. Color. Britain. 1959.

Producer: The British Council and the Arts Council of Great Britain.

Credits: Dudley Shaw Ashton, director; Sir Philip Hendy, writer and narrator.

Summary: Shows how the idea of UNESCO is captured and its ideals symbolized in the powerful carved stone figure by Henry Moore that stands before the UNESCO building in Paris. Restrained narration and perceptive camera work outline the various stages from original conception to completed work. The design is followed through a series of maquettes, the half-size plaster model, and the execution of the sculpture in travertine, quarried at Carrara.

Canadian distributor: Canadian Film Institute for the National Gallery of Canada (loan).

RED STONE DANCER
5 mins. B&W. Britain. 1967.

Producer: Firebird Films, London and Sydney, Australia.

Credits: Arthur Cantrill, director, writer, and photographer; electronic sound.

Summary: A contemplative film devoted to a single sculpture by Gaudier-Brzeska. It can be considered as a complement to a longer film on the artist (see HENRI GAUDIER-BRZESKA). Starting from his statement "Sculptural feeling is the appreciation of masses in relation," the film insists on the formal and rhythmic subtleties of *The Red Stone Dancer*, one of his major works.

U.S. distributor: Film Images (sales and rental).

REFLECTIONS—Enamels of Artist-Craftsman Paul Hultberg
(*The Artist and His Craft* series)
14 mins. Color. U.S.A. 1967.

Producer: George Ancona for the American Crafts Council.

Credits: George Ancona, director.

Summary: A study of Paul Hultberg creating his enamel-on-copper art. Familiar scenes and influences from nature are blended by the fire of the craftsman's vision and technique into new and personal images.

U.S. distributor: ACI (sales and rental); New York University Film Library (rental).

Canadian distributor: Marlin Motion Pictures (sales and rental); Canadian Film Institute for the National Gallery of Canada (loan).

REMBRANDT or REMBRANDT AND THE BIBLE (*The Human Dimension* series)
30 mins. Color. U.S.A. 1971.

Producer: Aram Boyajan, ABC Public Affairs.

Credits: Aram Boyajan, director; Cecile Starr, writer; John Cunningham, narrator; Alexander Vlas Datzenko, music.

Summary: Rembrandt's career is traced through more than a hundred of his paintings. Throughout his life the Bible was the main source of his inspiration, and his religious preoccupations deepened with his growth in artistic maturity.

U.S. distributor: Graphic Curriculum (sales and rental).

REMBRANDT'S THREE CROSSES
15 mins. Color. Britain. 1969.

Producer: Balfour Films, London, for the Arts Council of Great Britain.

Credits: Dudley Shaw Ashton, director; Christopher White, writer and narrator.

Summary: The development of a print considered to be Rembrandt's crowning achievement as printmaker. Four successive states are examined, the artist varying his effects by the use of different papers and different inking techniques. Nearly a decade later, Rembrandt totally reworked the plate, altering both the representation and the actual movement in the story line illustrated.

U.S. distributor: The American Federation of Arts (rental); Films Incorporated (sales).

Canadian distributor: Visual Education Centre (sales and rental); Canadian Film Institute for the National Gallery of Canada (loan).

RENOIR
23 mins. Color. U.S.A. 1953.

Producer: Jerry Winters, Auerbach Film Enterprises.

Credits: Otto Peter Radl, director and writer; Justin Hine and Jerry Winters, co-writers; George Ives, narrator.

Summary: A chronological description of Renoir's entire painting career, using many examples of his work in the United States. His personality, development of style, experiments in Impressionism, and deep love for the world and its people are portrayed, using fifty of his outstanding works. The commentary devotes more time to description of the painter's life than to the analysis of his work and its meaning.

U.S. distributor: Jerry Winters (sales and rental).

THE RESPONSIVE EYE
26 mins. B&W. U.S.A. 1965.

Producer: Midge Mackenzie, Zodiac Associates, New York, for WCBS-TV and Eastern Airlines.

Credits: Brian De Palma, director and photographer; Mike Wallace, narrator; Gordon Powell, music (jazz).

Summary: By balancing scholarly opinion against public reaction, the film provides an insight into optical art and at the same time communicates the explosive excitement of a big New York art opening. It features interviews with various authorities, including William Seitz, who put together the exhibition "The Responsive Eye" at The Museum of Modern Art. The following artists are represented in the film: Josef Albers, Richard Anuszkiewicz, David Hockney, Philip Johnson, Al Leslie, Mon Levinson, Marisol, Larry Rivers, Jeffrey Steele.

Canadian distributor: Canadian Film Institute for the National Gallery of Canada (loan).

RICHARD HAMILTON
26 mins. Color. Britain. 1969.

Producer: Maya Film Productions, London, for the Arts Council of Great Britain.

Credits: James Scott and Richard Hamilton, directors.

Summary: Richard Hamilton, one of the originators of Pop Art, took part in the making of this film, which was conceived like his paintings, as a collage. It draws on images of twentieth-century popular culture to produce a shock of recognition in the viewer. Newsreel footage complements references to Marilyn Monroe and the trial of pop singer Mick Jagger.

U.S. distributor: The American Federation of Arts (rental); Films Incorporated (sales).

Canadian distributor: Canadian Film Institute for the National Gallery of Canada (loan).

RICHARD HUNT, SCULPTOR (*The Black Achievement in America* series)
14 mins. Color. U.S.A. 1969.

Producer: Encyclopaedia Britannica Corporation.

Credits: Louise Dunn Yochim, collaborator.

Summary: Study of a black American artist, a junk sculptor who enriches the urban environment by transforming discarded articles into art. He is seen working on a figure of John Jones, the first Negro to be elected to public office in Illinois.

U.S. distributor: EBEC (sales and rental).

ROAD TO SANTIAGO: FRANCE (Part 1)
30 mins. Color. Britain. 1967.

ROAD TO SANTIAGO: SPAIN (Part 2)
21 mins. Color. Britain. 1967.

Producer: Pilgrim Films, London.

Credits: Mary Kirby, director, photographer, and editor; Catherine Blue, writer; period music.

Summary: A journey following the steps of the pilgrims of the twelfth century to the Shrine of St. James at Santiago de Compostela. The four routes through France are marked by the Church of St. Sernin at Toulouse, the sculpture and relics of Conques, the Abbey of Cluny, and the tympanum of Moissac. The roads converge at Puenta la Reina in Spain, revealing examples of Mozarabic and Romanesque art along the way.

U.S. distributor: International Film Bureau (sales and rental).

Canadian distributor: Educational Film Distributors (sales and rental); Canadian Film Institute for the National Gallery of Canada (loan).

ROBERT INDIANA PORTRAIT
25 mins. Color. U.S.A. 1973.

Producer: Huszar Productions.

Credits: John Huszar, director, writer, photographer, and editor; David Baily, narrator; music by Virgil Thomson.

Summary: A cinéma vérité account of the famous Pop artist at work, at play, walking, and talking. This portrait includes a detailed visit to his studio and the analysis of some of his paintings, and his "Love" sculpture while on exhibition in New York's Central Park. In conversation with the filmmaker, Indiana gives his views on his own art and on life in general.

U.S. distributor: Huszar Productions (sales and rental).

ROBERT MOTHERWELL
28 mins. Color. U.S.A. 1972.

Producer: Blackwood Productions.

Credits: Michael Blackwood, director.

Summary: Motherwell opens a show in St. Gall, Switzerland, and is seen at work in his studios at Greenwich and Provincetown. He also appears as a member of the Guggenheim painting and sculpture committee and editor of Viking Press. He discusses the issue of Abstract Expressionism as it evolved in New York following World War II, as well as its coexistence with the new styles that emerged in the sixties. He is seen working on *Elegies to the Spanish Republic* and the *Open Series*.

U.S. distributor: Blackwood Productions (sales and rental).

ROBERT RAUSCHENBERG (*Artists*—or *U.S.A. Artists*—series)
30 mins. B&W. U.S.A. 1966.

Producer: NET and Radio Center.

Credits: Lane Slate, director; Alan Solomon, writer; Norman Rose, narrator.

Summary: The winner of the 1964 Venice Biennale International Art competition, Rauschenberg was caught at the moment when he decided to stop painting to experiment in dance, sculpture, and film. Excerpts from his dance composition "Pelican," and his film *Canoe* are used to illustrate the reasons he advances for his decision. Several of his canvases are shown with comments by art dealer Leo Castelli.

U.S. distributor: Indiana University (sales and rental).

Canadian distributor: Canadian Film Institute for the National Gallery of Canada (sales and loan).

RODIN: THE BURGHERS OF CALAIS
18 mins. Color. U.S.A. 1969.

Produced for the Fogg Art Museum, Harvard University.

Credits: Robin Jones and Robert Kuretsky, directors and writers; Bill Cavness, narrator.

Summary: An historical and esthetic examination of one of the great sculptural monuments of the nineteenth century, and its importance in Rodin's career. The film records the monument's evolution from the first plaster sketch, through intermediate studies, to the final casting and installation. Use is made of the artist's own writings and other contemporary sources, including photographs, prints, and drawings.

U.S. distributor: Film Images (sales and rental).

ROMANTIC VERSUS CLASSIC ART series
One 50 min. and fourteen 26 min. films. Color. Britain. 1973.

Producer: Colin Clark for Visual Programme Systems; John Brabourne Productions, with W. H. Smith and Sotheby's.

Credits: Colin Clark, director; Lord Clark, writer and narrator.

Summary: This series based on Sir Kenneth Clark's book *The Romantic Rebellion* may not have the astonishing impact of *Civilisation* or even of *Pioneers of Modern Painting*, and though the weight of the various parts differs, all provide excellent material for discussion.

THE ROMANTIC REBELLION (50 mins.). An introductory program that discusses the general principles of Romantic and Classic art, with examples from the works of artists represented in the series.

1. JACQUES LOUIS DAVID. The first revolt against Classicism. Emphasis is on the political aspect of David's paintings, and its impact on the public.

2. GIAN-BATTISTA PIRANESI, HENRY FUSELI. Piranesi's ruins of Rome are compared with the world of Kafka. Fear and sex are represented in Fuseli's graphic works as part of the darker side of Romanticism.

3. WILLIAM BLAKE. In his visionary compositions he expresses an important aspect of Romanticism—the need for a new approach to religion. His dream-like art combines poetry and prophesy.

4. FRANCISCO GOYA. First known for lighthearted tapestries, Goya became court painter and a sought-after portrait artist. Following an illness causing total deafness, he was haunted by the hideous deformed monsters shown in the series of etchings *Los Caprichos.* Horrified by the atrocities of the French occupation of Spain, he represented human cruelty with a freedom then unknown in European art.

5 & 6. JEAN AUGUSTE DOMINIQUE INGRES. A two-part study of this superlative draftsman. In the first half, Lord Clark finds more Oriental than Classical influence in Ingres' sinuous lines; the second part follows the success in 1814 of his *Grande Odalisque.* Subsequently Ingres turned to portraiture and religious painting.

7. THEODORE GERICAULT. Painter of movement and of a perverse and destructive Nature. Shows one of his favorite subjects—horses; his masterpiece—*The Raft of the Medusa*; and his last works—portraits of lunatics.

8. JOHN CONSTABLE. A minor painter when young, Constable found his inspiration in nature and became a master of landscape painting. He anticipated by half a century the secret of representing light.

9 & 10. JOSEPH MALLORD WILLIAM TURNER. Lord Clark reviews the artist's lesser-known watercolors, many done during trips to Europe, which reveal Turner's understanding of nature and his skill as a landscape painter. The second film discusses his use of color; Lord Clark states that he was "the first artist to realize that color could communicate to us directly and independently of subject matter."

11. EUGENE DELACROIX. Revealer of the Dionysiac side of the Romantic movement—boundless energy and ferocity are balanced by a great faith in the human spirit that made him possibly the greatest religious painter of the nineteenth century.

12. JEAN-FRANCOIS MILLET. Lord Clark joins many eminent authorities in thinking Millet one of the greatest painters of the mid-nineteenth century. His choice of subject, often country folk at work in their fields, and his humanitarian beliefs provoked charges of socialism and subversion.

13. AUGUSTE RODIN. Last of the great Romantic sculptors, Rodin was a modeler not a carver; his instruments of power were his fingers. Lord Clark concludes that Rodin is greatest "when not working from a given subject but from a chance pose or movement that fired his imagination."

14. EDGAR DEGAS. "Possibly the last great Classical artist in European painting," says Lord Clark, though his themes—horse racing and the ballet—led him far from "the plastic realism of Academic Classicism. . ."

U.S. distributor: Pyramid (sales and rental).

Canadian distributor: International Tele-Film Enterprises (sales and rental).

RUBENS
45 mins. Initially 65 mins. B&W. Originally 35mm. Belgium. 1948.

Producer: Ministry of Education and Ministry of Communications, Belgium.

Credits: Paul Haesaerts and Henri Storck, directors; Paul Haesaerts, writer; Raymond Chevreuille, music.

Summary: Paul Haesaerts' first contact with film, strongly supported by the masterly art of Henri Storck. The approach to Rubens' works is lyrical and analytical with a fresh contribution to art criticism by film. There are many technical innovations in this production which uses split-screen, crosscutting, superimposition, micro-photography, distortion, and animated diagrams to reveal the intrinsic nature of Rubens' painting, its sources, structures, and evolution.

U.S. distribution: International Film Bureau (sales and rental).

Canadian distributor: Canadian Film Institute for the National Gallery of Canada (loan).

RUBENS (*Rubens en Liberté*) (*The Flemish Renaissance* series)
26 mins. Color. Originally 35mm. Belgium. 1973.

Producer: Resobel, Brussels; International Film Bureau, Chicago.

Credits: Jean Cleinge, director, writer and editor.

Summary: Works from the last years of his life strongly express Rubens' freedom and his love of painting. They include the portraits of Hélène Fourment, his second wife, and landscapes and scenes from peasant life. In contrast some earlier commissioned paintings are analyzed in a flashback. The commentary is based on Rubens' letters and theoretical writings. Music by Monteverdi and other Baroque composers from Italy and Flanders helps to revive the period.

U.S. distributor: International Film Bureau (sales and rental).

Canadian distributor: Educational Film Distributors (sales and rental); Canadian Film Institute (loan).

RUFINO TAMAYO: THE SOURCES OF HIS ART
27 mins. Color. U.S.A. 1972.

Producer: Alcon Films.

Credits: Gary Conklin, director; Octavio Paz, writer of commentary and poetry; John Huston, narrator; music by J. S. Bach and Carlos Chávez.

Summary: Life in the crowded streets of Mexico City, the Mexican landscape, its temples and stone carvings, the art and the crafts of Mexico—pottery, music, and poetry—are sensitively interpreted as the source material of Rufino Tamayo's achievement. The artist in his studio talks about his experiences, works on a painting, and begins the preparation of a lithograph. The closing sequences revisit his works from 1930 to the present.

U.S. distributor: Alcon Films (sales and rental).

Canadian distributor: Canadian Film Institute for the Canadian Centre for Films on Art (loan).

RUSSELL DRYSDALE
15 mins. Color. Australia.

Producer: Collings Productions for QANTAS Airways Ltd.

Credits: Dahl Collings, director.

Summary: Russell Drysdale is the most widely acclaimed painter of the more factual aspects of the Australian outback. This documentary traces the development of his work, emphasizing its sparkle and linear vitality.

U.S. distributor: QANTAS Airways (loan).

Canadian distributor: QANTAS Airways (loan); Canadian Film Institute for the National Gallery of Canada (loan).

RUSSIAN LUBOK (*Folk Painting and Woodcut Art*)
10 mins. Color. U.S.S.R. 1971.

Producer: Filmexport Film Studio.

Summary: A glimpse of the little-known Russian folk art of the eighteenth century, showing its development from purely religious subjects and icon painting to embrace folk legend and pagan lore, and often recording historical events of the time. Examples of contemporary wood carving show that the charm and vivid coloring of the folklore style have endured into the twentieth century.

U.S. distributor: Carousel Films (sales).

SACRED ART OF TIBET
28 mins. Color. U.S.A. 1972.

Producer: Larry Jordan (Lama Tarthang Tulka, executive producer) for the Tibetan Nyingmapa Meditation Center with financing by a Guggenheim Fellowship.

Credits: Larry Jordan, director; Lama Chogyam Trubgpa, narrator; ritual music.

Summary: A constant change of images and colors gives to this experimental documentary the charm of fireworks. A wide range of special effects is used: animation, superimposition, stroboscopic flips, dissolves, fades. The role of the gods and their symbols is explained in various separate "chapters." Traditional paintings and the sculpture of Tibet take part in a subtle ballet accompanied by chanted mantras and religious music.

U.S. distributor: The American Federation of Arts (sales and rental); Canyon Cinema Cooperative (rental).

ST. ADOLPH II
20 mins. Color. Britain. 1971.

Producer: Rosebrook Productions Ltd. for the Arts Council of Great Britain.

Credits: Lionel Miskin, director.

Summary: The art of a schizophrenic artist, Adolf Wölfli, who believed he was both God and the Devil, St. Adolph II, a star-traveler, and a potentate with many wives. His paintings represent a highly ordered world of brilliant colors and ornamentation. Interviews with specialists and with people who have met him throw some light on his strange case.

U.S. distributor: The American Federation of Arts (rental); Films Incorporated (sales).

SAINT-URBAIN IN TROYES (*Saint-Urbain de Troyes*)
28 mins. Color. Canada. 1972.

Producer: François Séguillon, National Film Board for the National Gallery of Canada.

Credits: Yves Leduc, director and editor; Frances Hyland, narrator.

Summary: Commissioned by the National Gallery of Canada in the context of its exhibition "Art of the Courts, 1259-1328." This is not only an exploration of the pure Gothic basilica, its gargoyles, and great colored windows, but a visit to the marketplace and the old town where people live and work. Other churches are presented for comparison: Notre-Dame de Dijon, Saint-Sulpice de Favière, and Sainte-Chapelle in Paris.

U.S. distributor: International Film Bureau (sales and rental).

Canadian distributor: National Film Board (sales and loan); Educational Film Distributors (sales and rental).

SAM FRANCIS
52 mins. Color. U.S.A. 1975.

Producer: Blackwood Productions.

Credits: Michael Blackwood, director.

Summary: This production takes place in France, Tokyo, and Los Angeles, where Sam Francis lives and works. Francis talks about his beginnings in Paris after World War II, his discovery of the Orient, his art, and his down-to-earth relationship with Los Angeles. Among other personal revelations by Francis: the importance of his dreams vis-à-vis his art; his love of poetry, alchemy, Jungian philosophy; his feelings about color, lithography, self-portraits. Important works from the 1950s on are shown.

U.S. distributor: Blackwood Productions (sales and rental).

SCENES SEEN WITH ALLEN JONES
28 mins. Color. U.S.A. 1971.

Producer: Blackwood Productions.

Credits: Michael Blackwood, director.

Summary: Allen Jones is filmed in a variety of scenes selected to illustrate his multifarious activities and interests. He visits a London tailor where his wife has a fitting for the latex and vinyl costumes he has designed for the film *A Clockwork Orange*. He paints in his studio, talks about lithography, his pin-up postcard collection, and his recent graphics, drawings, and sculpture.

U.S. distributor: Blackwood Productions (sales and rental).

SCHAWINSKY 1969
11 mins. Color. U.S.A. 1971.

Producer: Fred Salaff.

Credits: Fred Salaff, director; no narration.

Summary: An experimental film on the art of the Bauhaus painter and teacher, Xanti Schawinsky. The filmmaker has made a fascinating and spellbinding visual exercise from the brush of the dynamic master artist.

U.S. distributor: Fred Salaff.

A SCULPTOR SPEAKS: CHAIM GROSS (The *American Artists* collection)
15 mins. Color. U.S.A. 1958.

Producer: Lewis Jacobs.

Credits: Lewis Jacobs, director.

Summary: The life, work, and ideas of the American sculptor Chaim Gross, are intelligently presented by Lewis Jacobs. Working in his studio, Gross discusses his theoretical approach to sculpture, and many examples in wood and stone are presented both in their preliminary stages and completed form. Special attention is paid to the artist's brilliant technique.

U.S. distributor: Film Images (sales and rental).

SCULPTURE BY LIPTON
15 mins. B&W. U.S.A. 1954.

Producer: Nathan Boxer.

Credits: Nathan Boxer, director; Morton Feldman, music.

Summary: This American metal constructionist-sculptor, always in search of new materials, creates a fresh world with his own technique and tools. Lipton is shown in his studio, where he declares his dedication to the forces of nature while carrying out a production using metal shears, welding torches, goggles, and hammers. Eight finished pieces are presented in an open-air display.

U.S. distributor: Film Images (sales and rental).

THE SCULPTURE OF RON BOISE
9 mins. Color. U.S.A. 1966.

Producer: Leland Auslender Films.

Credits: Leland Auslender, director; Ron Boise, music.

Summary: A short document on metal sculptor Ron Boise, made shortly before his death in 1966. The first section shows him collecting "available" materials for the figure of a woman, and then, working from a model, cutting, shaping, and welding the various pieces to complete the figure. The last part is a montage of elements of the sculptor's works in an abstract cinepoem.

U.S. distributor: Leland Auslender Films (sales and rental).

Canadian distributor: International Tele-Film Enterprises (sales and rental).

THE SECRET WORLD OF ODILON REDON
30 mins. Color. Britain. 1973.

Producer: Kevala Films for the Arts Council of Great Britain.

Credits: Stephen Cross, director; Alun Hoddinott, music.

Summary: This film is an attempt to explain the dream world of Odilon Redon. His journal "A soi-même" is effectively used as commentary accompanying rare photographs of the artist, the house in the country where he was born, and the sea he loved with its strange and changing colors. By virtue of the editing, his work is placed in its biographical context, and the frescoes *Night and Day* are seen first in the creative stages and then completed in the Abbaye de Fontfroide.

U.S. distributor: The American Federation of Arts (rental); Films Incorporated (sales).

SENTINELS OF SILENCE (*Ruins of Ancient Mexico*) (*Centinelas del Silencio*)
19 mins. Color. Mexico. 1971.

Producer: Producciones Concord, Mexico City.

Credits: Manuel Arango, director; Robert Amran, writer; Dr. Ignacio Bernal, Director of the National Institute of Anthropology and History, Mexico City, consultant; James Freeman, photographer; Mariano Moreno, music; Orson Welles, narrator.

Summary: A panorama of Mexico's pre-Columbian ruins shot entirely from a helicopter. Among the archaeological sites viewed are Teotihuacán, Monte Alban, Mitia, Tulum, Palenque, and Uxmai. (Teacher's guide available.)

U.S. distributor: EBEC (sales and rental).

Canadian distributor: Mexican Tourist Council (loan, under title ANCIENT MEXICO).

THE SHADOW CATCHER—Edward S. Curtis and the North American Indian
88 mins. Partly Color and Partly B&W. Canada. 1974.

Producer: Teri C. McLuhan.

Credits: Teri C. McLuhan, director and writer; Dennis Wheeler, co-writer; Robert Fiore, cinematography; Donald Sutherland (Curtis' voice) and Patrick Watson, narrators.

Summary: Edward S. Curtis was a photographer, anthropologist, and filmmaker who spent thirty-four years of his life (1896-1930) among the North American Indians. This feature-length documentary uses his own film footage (1906-1912), his photographs, and his diaries, together with original Indian music combined with recent interviews, to retrace his journeys through New Mexico, Arizona, California, British Columbia, and Vancouver Island.

U.S. distributor: Phoenix (sales and rental).

Canadian distributor: International Tele-Film Enterprises (sales and rental).

SHALOM OF SAFED (*The Innocent Eye of a Man of Galilee*)
28 mins. Color. U.S.A. 1967.

Producer: Daniel Doron, Arnold Eagle.

Credits: Daniel Doron, director and writer; Stephan Chodorov, co-writer; Shulamit Ram, music.

Summary: An impression of Shalom, watchmaker, toymaker, carver, and engraver who, at the age of seventy, turned to painting. The Hassidic heritage from which his work is derived is evoked in the naive but beautifully concise paintings in which he retells the ancient stories of the people of Israel.

U.S. distributor: Daniel Doron (sales and rental); Alden Films (rental).

Canadian distributor: International Tele-Film Enterprises (sales and rental); Canadian Film Institute for the National Gallery of Canada (loan).

SHE SHALL BE CALLED WOMAN (*Elle sera appelée femme*)
14 mins. B&W. Belgium. 1954.

Producer: Gérard De Boe.

Credits: Gérard De Boe, director; Emile Degelin, writer; Flora Robson, narrator; André Souris, music.

Summary: Carvings of Zaire (Belgian Congo at the time of production) selected from the rich collections of the Tervueren Museum (near Brussels). The script is based on woman's place in primitive African society, and the role she has played in Negro art. The original region and the period are not identified. This experimental film uses light effects to heighten the dramatic qualities of the various pieces shown, which are selected to illustrate the Biblical account of the creation of woman, her place in society, and her influence in family and community life.

U.S. distributor: Macmillan (sales and rental).

Canadian distributor: Canadian Film Institute for the National Gallery of Canada (loan).

SIDNEY NOLAN
21 mins. Color. Australia. 1963.

Producer: Geoffrey Collings, Collings Productions for QANTAS Airlines.

Credits: Dahl Collings, director.

Summary: Nolan's explosive yet poetic vision is revealed through paintings dealing with Australian myth and legend, including the *Ned Kelly* series.

U.S. distributor: QANTAS Airways (loan).

Canadian distributor: QANTAS Airways (loan); Canadian Film Institute for the National Gallery of Canada (loan).

SIENA (*The Treasury of Tuscany* series)
20 mins. Color. U.S.A. 1965.

Producer: Clifford B. West.

Credits: Clifford B. West, director, writer, and photographer.

Summary: The beautiful Medieval city of Siena, a living museum full of color. Piazzas, palaces, and public buildings are visited while their artistic style and social history are explained. In the Baptistry the magnificent font with sculptured panels by Donatello and Jacopo della Quercia rivets attention.

U.S. distributor: Film Images (sales).

SONAMBIENTS: THE SOUND SCULPTURE OF HARRY BERTOIA
16 mins. Color. U.S.A. 1970.

Producer: Kenesaw Films.

Credits: Jeffrey Eger, director; Harry Bertoia, music.

Summary: A cinéma vérité document on the well-known American sculptor Harry Bertoia, who explains his concept of sound sculpture. His studio is full of wires of varying sizes, metal tubes, and other elements which, when touched by the artist, fill the room with musical sound. Bertoia does not call it "music," but considers the sounds analogous to those of nature.

U.S. distributor: Kenesaw Films (sales); The Museum of Modern Art (rental).

THE SONG OF THE EARTH (*Le chant du monde*)
17 mins. Color. France. 1965.

Producer: Roger Mercanton, Telefilms Productions.

Credits: Pierre Birot and Victoria Mercanton, directors; Jean Lurçat, writer of commentary; Pierre Henry, music.

Summary: The production of the last and most important tapestry of Jean Lurçat, who died the following year. This great work which may be regarded as Jean Lurçat's artistic testament is shown in detail, and the film also reveals some aspects of his life. In a final sequence the activities of the craftsmen in Aubusson, the famous old center of tapestry where Lurçat had his studio, are shown and suggested.

U.S. distributor: FACSEA (rental).

Canadian distributor: Embassy of France (loan).

SORT OF A COMMERCIAL FOR AN ICEBAG (CLAES OLDENBURG)
16 mins. Color. U.S.A. 1971.

Producer: Gemini G.E.L.

Credits: Michel Hugo, director; Erik Saarinen, photographer.

Summary: The genesis and evolution of the *Giant Soft Icebag* produced by Gemini G.E.L. for Osaka's Expo 70. Oldenburg makes many preliminary drawings for this work, his first kinetic sculpture and largest to date. (A twenty-six-minute version of this film is available from Museum at Large, sales and rental, under the title *Claes Oldenburg: Ice Bag*.)

U.S. distributor: Benchmark Films (sales and rental); Castelli-Sonnabend (sales and rental); The Museum of Modern Art (rental).

Canadian distributor: Marlin Motion Pictures (sales and rental).

SOTO
15 mins. Color. Venezuela. 1972.

Producer: Instituto Nacional de Cultura y Bellas Artes and Organization of American States.

Credits: Angel Hurtado, director, photographer, and editor; William P. Clark, Herbert Morales, narrators; Antonio Esteves, music.

Summary: A tribute to the Venezuelan kinetic artist, Jésus Rafael Soto. Scenes of his hometown, Ciudad Bolivar, and many of his works are shown—his early paintings done while at the Academy of Caracas, and others in Venezuela and in Paris, where an important retrospective exhibit was held. The commentary uses excerpts from articles written by the French critics Pierre Restany and Jean Clay.

U.S. distributor: Pan American Development Foundation (sales).

SPIRAL JETTY
35 mins. Color. U.S.A. 1970.

Producer: John Weber Gallery and Visual Resources.

Credits: Robert Smithson, director.

Summary: Construction from start to finish of the largest earthwork of a number conceived by Robert Smithson: a spiral jetty jutting into the shallows off the shore of the Great Salt Lake of Utah. The sculptor-filmmaker shot the film from a car, forward and backward, and from a helicopter. There are sequences using a red filter, slow motion in negative, comparisons with the mouth of an active volcano, the huge skeleton of a dinosaur, and also geographical maps. Smithson's gigantic project has inspired a poetic film.

U.S. distributor: Visual Resources (sales and rental).

STANLEY WILLIAM HAYTER—THE ARTIST AS A TEACHER
25 mins. Color. U.S.A. 1970.

Producer: Ohio State University, Department of Photography and Cinema.

Summary: On the occasion of his visit to Ohio State University, Hayter, outstanding printmaker and founder-director of the famous Paris studio, Atelier 17, demonstrates his innovative techniques—etching, inking, and printing intaglio plates. While he works he comments on his methods and discusses printmaking and art in general.

U.S. distributor: Ohio State University (sales and rental).

UNE STATUETTE
11 mins. Color. Originally 35mm. France. 1971.

Producer: Société Nouvelle Pathé Cinéma.

Credits: Carlos Vilardebo, director, writer, and photographer; André Bouchourechliev, music.

Summary: A visual poem devoted to a terracotta statuette belonging to the Teotihuacán civilization. It was recently discovered in Michoacan, Mexico, and is now preserved in Montreal. It represents a man with articulated arms and a detachable clay piece forming the breast. Inside the body, a man with a club and a shield faces the inside of the covering plate representing a man in ceremonial dress. The camera plays with the statuette, which can look either like a tragic divinity or like a doll.

U.S. distributor: McGraw-Hill Films (sales and rental).

Canadian distributor: McGraw-Hill Ryerson (sales and rental); Canadian Film Institute for the National Gallery of Canada (loan).

SUMI ARTIST

11 mins. Color. U.S.A. 1954.

Producer: Lobett Productions.

Summary: A demonstration of Japanese brush painting by Chiura Obata. The camera placed behind his left shoulder shows the various strokes and brushes used. Sumi art is the ancient method of painting with pigment made from lampblack. Finished examples of Obata's work are shown.

U.S. distributor: Lobett Productions (sales).

SUPER ARTIST, ANDY WARHOL

22 mins. Color. U.S.A. 1966.

Producer: Torbet Films and Film Services.

Credits: Bruce Torbet, director; Henry Geldzahler, The Metropolitan Museum of Art, writer of commentary.

Summary: A visit to Andy Warhol's Factory and a free impressionistic, satirical portrait of the "super artist" who expounds his views on Pop art, his environment, and his image. He is shown with his actors making a film and spending a typical day. Henry Geldzahler places Warhol's art in its contemporary context.

U.S. distributor: Grove Press Film Division (sales and rental).

SURREALISM (AND DADA)

18 mins. Color. U.S.A. and Italy. 1970.

Producer: Texture Films and RAI.

Credits: Guido Guerrasio, director; Adriano Bernacchi, photographer.

Summary: The Surrealist-Dadaist movements following World War I were in part reactions against nineteenth-century rationalism. The artists celebrated the "outrageous gesture," the irrational, the fantastic, as exemplified here in the works of Duchamp, Man Ray, Arp, Miró, Klee, de Chirico, Magritte, Matta, Tanguy, Giacometti, Ernst, Dali, and others. The sound track reproduces the startling music of the period, including the "Pre-Syllabic Sonata" by painter-composer Kurt Schwitters.

U.S. distributor: Texture Films (sales and rental).

Canadian distributor: International Tele-Film Enterprises (sales and rental).

THE SWORD AND THE FLUTE
24 mins. Color. U.S.A. 1959.

Producer: James Ivory.

Credits: James Ivory, director and writer; Saeed Jaffrey, narrator; Ravi Shankar, music.

Summary: Life and thought in sixteenth-century India are seen through exquisite miniature paintings of the period. They capture the splendid pageantry of courtly life under the Muslim emperor Akbar and the idealization of both asceticism and romantic love by the Hindus.

U.S. distributor: Film Images (sales and rental).

Canadian distributor: Canadian Film Institute for the National Gallery of Canada (loan).

THE TEMPLE OF APOLLO AT BASSAE
16 mins. Color. Britain. 1970.

Producer: Malcolm R. McBride and Derek Stewart for the British Film Institute.

Credits: Malcolm R. McBride, director; Dr. Jacob Bronowski, narrator and writer.

Summary: A reconstruction of this celebrated Greek temple is shown by using animation sequences. The Doric temple, created by Ictinus, who later designed the Parthenon, contained the first known Corinthian column. The marble frieze depicts the stories of the Athenians' battle against the Amazons and the battle of the Lapiths and the Centaurs. The film was shot on the temple site and at the British Museum, where the Bassae Frieze is preserved.

U.S. distributor: International Film Bureau (sales and rental).

Canadian distributor: Educational Film Distributors (sales and rental).

THAI IMAGES OF THE BUDDHA (*Arts of the Orient* series)
14 mins. Color. U.S.A. 1962.

Producer: Indiana University Audio-Visual Center with the Arts of Thailand Exhibition Committee of Participating Institutions (Theodore A. Bowie, chairman).

Summary: This film traces the transformation of the Buddha image in the arts of Thailand from the representation of a revered teacher to that of a supreme deity, paralleling the course of Buddhism itself. For the first time, sculpture from the National Museum of Bangkok is displayed in the United States with selections from American museums. The film is uniquely useful for study despite some deterioration in color quality.

U.S. distributor: Indiana University (sales and rental).

Canadian distributor: Canadian Film Institute for the National Gallery of Canada (sales and loan).

THIS IS BEN SHAHN

17 mins. Color. U.S.A. 1965.

Producer: CBS News.

Credits: Jack Landau, director and writer.

Summary: A discussion of the painter's humanistic philosophy, illustrating his thinking with examples. Much of the content of his work derives from his involvement with current affairs (the Sacco and Vanzetti case, for example), revealing him as a great humanist who has found a very personal form for the expression of his involvement. (Teacher's guide available.)

U.S. distributor: BFA (sales and rental).

Canadian distributor: Holt, Rinehart and Winston (sales and rental).

THE TITAN: THE STORY OF MICHELANGELO (*Michel Angelo—das Leben eines Titanen*)

67 mins. B&W. Originally 35mm. Germany-Switzerland. 1938-1940.

Producer: Original German version: Pandora-Film, Zurich. Revised U.S. version (1949): Robert Flaherty and Robert Snyder.

Credits: Curt Oertel, director and photographer; Curt and Franz Oertel, J. B. Malina and Werner Pleister, writers; Alois Melichar, music.
U.S. version: Richard Lyford, director and editor; Norman Borisoff, writer; Fredric March, narrator.

Summary: This was one of the most successful and certainly the most innovative of the earlier films on art. The life and achievement of Michelangelo were re-created without the use of actors. The turbulence, suffering, and creative outpouring of the High Renaissance are powerfully reflected in the film.

U.S. distributor: Michelangelo Company.

TO OPEN EYES

32 mins. Color. U.S.A. 1971.

Producer: ACI for Union College and State University of New York at Albany.

Credits: Carl Howard, director.

Summary: A film document on octogenarian Josef Albers. It contains footage on his first years of teaching at Black Mountain College and Yale, to which he had come after the closing of the Bauhaus in 1933; recent scenes in his workshop, and a visit to the 1968 exhibition at the Sidney Janis Gallery in New York. This experimental artist and teacher, sometimes called "the Father of Op Art," explains his theories on the interaction of colors and on the role of the artist in society.

U.S. distributors: ACI Films (sales and rental).

Canadian distributor: Marlin Motion Pictures (sales and rental).

THE TORCH AND THE TORSO: THE WORK OF MIGUEL BERROCAL (*Miguel Berrocal*)
11 mins. B&W. Originally 35mm. France. 1965.

Producer: Specta Films.

Credits: Jules Engel, director; Andréa Harran, co-director and writer; Francis Seyrig, music; no narration.

Summary: The sculpture of this Spanish artist is based on the dissociative principle: it may be dismantled and reassembled. Berrocal is seen at work in his studio with his helpers, and production is followed right up to the molding stages and the casting in bronze. A selection of his work is shown on view at the Venice Biennale.

U.S. distributor: Film Images (sales and rental).

THE TOTEM POLE (*American Indian Films* series)
27 mins. Color. U.S.A. 1964.

Producer: University Extension, University of California at Berkeley.

Credits: A. L. Kroeler and S. A. Barrett, directors; Wilson Duff and C. B. Smith, consultants; traditional Kwakiutl music.

Summary: The origin, development, and significance of the totem poles of the Kwakiutl and Haida Indians of Canada's West Coast. Sometimes reaching a height of eighty feet, the totems proclaimed the rank, lineage, wealth, and prestige of their owners. Two famous sculptors, Mungo Martin, chief of the Kwakiutl, and Henry Hunt, are shown carving and painting.

U.S. distributor: University of California (sales and rental).

Canadian distributor: International Tele-Film Enterprises (sales and rental); Canadian Film Institute for the National Gallery of Canada (loan).

TREASURES FROM EL PRADO series
8 films 4-15 mins. Color. Originally 35mm. Spain. 1970.

Producer: Audio-Brandon.

Credits: Vincente Lluch, director; Mario Bistagne, photographer; James Macdonald, David Tucker, adaptation.

Summary: Masterpieces from El Prado Museum in Madrid have been filmed with unusual magnification and clarity. The smallest brushstroke is visible and the painters' techniques are made as clear as anything short of a studied examination of the canvas itself could produce.

1. GOYA TREASURES, 15 mins.

2. TITIAN TREASURES, 6 mins.

3. BOSCH TREASURES, 12 mins.

4. RIBERA TREASURES, 4 mins.

5. RUBENS TREASURES, 8 mins.

6. MURILLO TREASURES, 9 mins.

7. VELAZQUEZ TREASURES, 9 mins.

8. EL GRECO TREASURES, 5 mins.

U.S. distributor: Macmillan (sales and rental).

Canadian distributor: Marlin Motion Pictures (sales and rental).

TREASURES OF SAN MARCO: THE STORY OF A CATHEDRAL or THE BASILICA OF SAINT MARK (*San Marco*)
40 mins. Color. Italy. 1975.

Producer: Raffaele Andreassi for Mondadori Editore.

Credits: Raffaele Andreassi, director and photographer; period music.

Summary: Famous for its location and decoration, San Marco in Venice is one of the most spectacular buildings in the world. It is a curious mingling of Romanesque and Byzantine features, golden mosaics from the Orient, and painstaking Medieval craftsmanship. The camera work underlines the variety in style and ornamentation of this cathedral at the artistic crossroads of East and West.

U.S. distributor: Films for the Humanities (sales and rental).

Canadian distributor: Canadian Film Institute (sales).

A TRIP WITH CURRIER AND IVES
11 mins. Color. U.S.A. 1963.

Producer: Bronstein, Van Veen, and Bailey, Trident Films.

Credits: René Bras, director; George K. Arthur, participant; Tom Glazer, folksinger; no narration.

Summary: America in the second half of the nineteenth century shown through the hand-colored lithographs published by Currier and Ives. The camera focuses on scenes typical of the period: clipper ships and the whaling trade, frosty winters in New England, steamboat races on the Mississippi, wagon trains and early steam engines moving West. Nostalgia for American ways of life a century ago is heightened by old folk songs: "Long Long Ago," "Mary Jane and Michael Roy," "Blow, Blow, Blow," "Nellie Was a Lady," "Working on the Railroad," and "Sweet Betsy from Pike."

U.S. distributor: The American Federation of Arts (rental).

TURNER
28 mins. Color. Originally 35mm. Britain. 1966.

Producer: Samaritan Films, London, for the Arts Council of Great Britain with the help of Showways Limited and the British Council.

Credits: David Thompson, director and writer; Michael Hordern, narrator; Elisabeth Lutyens, music.

Summary: Turner's sensitivity to patterns of light on air, land, and water is accurately and vividly conveyed in this impressive artistic documentary. It is divided into three parts: the first contrasts a storm at sea with the peacefulness of the English countryside; the second opposes the great cities of history and legend to scenes of catastrophe; the third deals with the paintings of his last twenty years. All his major works are covered, including the last great paintings of pure light and color.

U.S. distributor: The American Federation of Arts (rental); Films Incorporated (sales).

Canadian distributor: Visual Education Centre (sales and rental); Canadian Film Institute for the National Gallery of Canada (loan).

TWENTIETH CENTURY ART—A BREAK WITH TRADITION (*History Through Art* series)
20 mins. Color. U.S.A. 1965.

Producer: Alemann Films.

Credits: Johanna Alemann, director.

Summary: A review of the art of the first half of the century, with its revolutionary use of color and reaction against the rules created by the Renaissance: a useful introduction to modern art appreciation. Works by Picasso, the German Expressionists, Fauves, French Cubists, Surrealists and painters of the New York School are successively shown. Following the history of contemporary art, we are led through distortion and the symbolic use of color before World War I to the many dynamic developments and new forms of expression covered by the term abstract art.

U.S. distributor: Alemann Films (sales and rental).

Canadian distributor: International Tele-Film Enterprises (sales and rental).

2,100-YEAR-OLD TOMB EXCAVATED
30 mins. Color. People's Republic of China. 1972.

Producer: Documentary Films Studios, Peking.

Summary: A record of an important archeological discovery and a study of the meaning of the tomb, the body, and the burial accessories. These well-preserved relics will contribute to the study of the history, culture, handicrafts, agriculture, and medicine of China twenty-one hundred years ago.

U.S. distributor: Grove Press Film Division (sales and rental).

UKIYO-E (*Prints of Japan*)
27 mins. Color. U.S.A. 1960.

Producer: Audio-Brandon Films for the Art Institute of Chicago and the Japan Society, New York.

Credits: Francis Haar, photographer; Oliver Statler, writer; Margaret O. Gentles, Associate Curator of Oriental Arts and Keeper of the Buckingham Collection of Japanese Prints, the Art Institute of Chicago, consultant; James A. Michener, narrator.

Summary: Prints by twelve famous artists of the seventeenth and eighteenth centuries in Japan from the collection of the Art Institute of Chicago. Moronobu, Kaigetsudo, Kiyomasu, Masanobu, Kiyomitsu, Harunobu, Shunsho, Kiyonaga, Utamaro, Sharaku, Hokusai, and Hiroshige represent the age of Ukiyo-e, i.e. the "pictures of the floating world." Their subjects are the fashions and the foibles of feudal Japan.

U.S. distributor: Macmillan (sales and rental).

Canadian distributor: Marlin Motion Pictures (sales).

UKIYOE: THE FABULOUS WORLD OF JAPANESE PRINTS
30 mins. Color. Japan. 1973.

Producer: NHK (Japanese Broadcasting System).

Summary: Works of Sharaku, Utamaro, Hokusai, and Hiroshige are shown with commentaries on the social role of the art and the development of printmaking. The invention of multicolored printing in the eighteenth century brought about a revolution in the Ukiyo-e and created a color art unparalleled anywhere else in the world.

U.S. distributor: Films Incorporated (sales and rental).

UNDER THE BLACK MASK (*Sous le masque noir*)
50 mins. Color. Originally 35mm. Belgium. 1958.

Producer: Art et Cinéma, Brussels.

Credits: Paul Haesaerts, director and writer; Tom Prideaux, American adapter; Central African music.

Summary: The variety and imaginative force of the work of the native carvers of the Belgian Congo (now Zaïre), presented in their local settings and accompanied by regional music. The sculpture, masks, and artifacts of four tribes—the Ba-Kuba, Ba-Mbala, Ben Lula, Ba-Yaka—reflect their traditional view of the origin of the world and the influence of art in their daily lives. The film is divided into three parts: The Birth of the World; Styles and Influences; and Power of Kings—Power of Magicians. Scenes of tribal life contribute to a better understanding of African art.

U.S. distributor: Macmillan (sales and rental).

Canadian distributor: Canadian Film Institute for the National Gallery of Canada (loan).

L'UNIVERS D'UTRILLO (*Utrillo*)
20 mins. Color. Originally 35mm. France. 1955.

Producer: Francinex and Gallus Films.

Credits: Georges Régnier, director; Maurice Jarre, music.

Summary: The main interest of this biographical film is the sequence showing the artist at home a few months before his death. An attempt is made to re-create his youth emphasizing the influence of his mother, Suzanne Valadon. A brief survey of his work concentrates on the Montmartre paintings, alternating photographed views with the painter's actual canvases from Boston and New York museums and the collection of Utrillo's dealer, Pétridès.

U.S. distributor: FACSEA (rental).

VAN EYCK: FATHER OF FLEMISH PAINTING (*The Flemish Renaissance* series) (*Van Eyck, Père de la Peinture Flamande*)
27 mins. Color. Originally 35mm. Belgium. 1973.

Producer: Resobel, Brussels; International Film Bureau, Chicago.

Credits: Jean Cleinge, director, writer, and editor.

Summary: A detailed analysis of the work of the founder of the Flemish school of painting. Liberated from the conventions and restrictions of manuscript illumination, Van Eyck's panels attain imposing proportions without losing the sense of minute detail. A large number of close-ups and complex camera movements lead to an intimate insight into this mystical painting and an understanding of its symbols.

U.S. distributor: International Film Bureau (sales and rental).

Canadian distributor: Educational Film Distributors (sales and rental); Canadian Film Institute (loan).

VAN GOGH
17 mins. B&W. Originally 35mm. France. 1948.

Producer: Pierre Braunberger, Films du Panthéon, Paris.

Credits: Alain Resnais and Gaston Diehl, directors and writers; Robert Hessens, co-writer; Martin Gabel, narrator; Jacques Besse, music.

Summary: One of the first films by Alain Resnais: the drama of Van Gogh told through his paintings. Emphasis throughout is on his life rather than his work. This early black-and-white film continues to be of great visual as well as historical interest.

U.S. distributor: Pictura (sales and rental).

Canadian distributor: Embassy of France (loan).

VAN GOGH
14 mins. B&W. Britain. 1964.

Producer: BBC-TV.

Credits: C. Day Lewis, narrator.

Summary: The development of Van Gogh's style and interests, revealed through his drawings and excerpts from his letters read by poet C. Day Lewis.

U.S. distributor: Time-Life (sales only).

Canadian distributor: BBC-TV Enterprises (sales and rental).

VAN MEEGEREN'S FAKED VERMEERS (*J'ai peint des Vermeer*)
27 mins. B&W. Belgium. 1952.

Producer: Sofedi, Brussels.

Credits: G. A. Magnel and Jan Botermans, directors; P. B. Coremans, Director of the Central Laboratory of the Museums of Belgium, adviser.

Summary: The micro-chemical analysis of one of the faked Vermeers, which exposed the forgery. The film traces the character of Jan Van Meegeren, who was responsible. P. B. Coremans, one of the leading experts who studied the famous faked paintings, took part in the production.

U.S. distributor: Macmillan (sales and rental).

VENICE BE DAMNED
52 mins. (In 2 parts, 24 and 28 mins.) Color. U.S.A. 1971.

Producer: Lou Hazam for NBC News.

Credits: Tom Priestly, director and photographer; Lou Hazam, writer; José Ferrer, narrator; John Wells Delegation, music.

Summary: The destruction of Venice by water erosion, air pollution, and worst of all, lack of planning and concern. In this living museum of Western man's cultural history, too many inhabitants are more concerned with a strong economy and the expansion of industries that pollute their environment than with their crumbling sculptures and deteriorating art treasures.

U.S. distributor: Films Incorporated (sales and rental).

Canadian distributor: Visual Education Centre (sales and rental).

VENICE, THEME AND VARIATIONS
30 mins. Color. U.S.A. 1957.

Producer: James Ivory for the University of Southern California.

Credits: James Ivory, director, writer, and photographer; Stelios Roccos, additional photographer and editor; Alexander Scourby, narrator; period music.

Summary: Venice today shown through the perceptive art of filmmaker James Ivory, and Venice as seen by artists from the thirteenth to twentieth centuries. Beginning with the anonymous Italo-Byzantine mosaicists of San Marco, the life and pageantry of the city through the years is shown in the paintings of Veneziano, Bellini, Carpaccio, Longhi, and Guardi, approaching the present day via Whistler and Steinberg.

U.S. distributor: Film Images (sales and rental).

Canadian distributor: Canadian Film Institute for the National Gallery of Canada (loan).

VERMEER (*Canvas* series no. 3—*Personal Reflections on Great Paintings*)
20 mins. Color. Britain. 1966.

Producer: John Furness, BBC-TV.

Credits: Derek Trimby, director; Patrick Nuttgens, participant, writer and narrator.

Summary: *The Guitar Player* by Vermeer is analyzed in detail by Patrick Nuttgens at Kenwood House, Hampstead. He also studies the artist's work in the perspective of the golden age of Dutch painting. The expert advances the hypothesis that Vermeer may have used the camera obscura to produce his canvases. He speaks of their impact on the Impressionists and mentions that they have been favorite subjects of copyists.

U.S. distributor: Time-Life (sales and rental).

Canadian distributor: BBC-TV Enterprises (sales and rental).

VERSAILLES (*Kinetic Art* collection)
19 mins. Color. Originally 35mm. France. 1966.

Producer: Films Montsouris, Paris.

Credits: Albert Lamorisse, director; Roger Glachant, writer of commentary; Henri Alekan, photographer; seventeenth-century music (Pachelbel).

Summary: An aerial tour of the splendors of King Louis XIV's palace and gardens at Versailles. Lamorisse specialized in shooting film from helicopters using a system which counterbalanced the vibrations. (He died a few years later when using the same dangerous process in Iran.) Sweeping low over canals, circling hidden woodland springs, hovering face-to-face with statuary high on the palace façade, or floating over fantastic sparkling fountains, the film reveals aspects never before witnessed of the beautiful garden estate.

U.S. distributor: Films Incorporated (sales and rental).

Canadian distributor: Visual Education Centre (sales and rental).

VILLARD DE HONNECOURT, BUILDER OF CATHEDRALS
(*Villard de Honnecourt, bâtisseur de cathédrales*)
15 mins. B&W. France. 1964.

Producer: Productions de Touraine, France.

Credits: Georges Rebillard, director; Christian Pouillon, writer of commentary; thirteenth-century Troubadour songs.

Summary: Based on the notebook of the famous thirteenth-century architect, now preserved in the National Library in Paris. The film combines drawings, sketches, and plans with actual views of the cathedrals of France (Chartres, Rheims, Laon), Switzerland (Lausanne), and Hungary. We discover the ardent world of the Gothic builders.

U.S. distributor: The Roland Collection (sales and rental).

VINCENT VAN GOGH: A SELF-PORTRAIT
54 mins. Color. U.S.A. 1961.

Producer: Lou Hazam, NBC News.

Credits: Ray Garner, director; Lou Hazam, writer; Dr. Mark Tralbaut (Belgium), consultant; Jacques Belasco, music.

Summary: The life of Vincent Van Gogh, traced through his drawings, paintings, and many revealing letters (written primarily to his brother Theo), and further illuminated by interviews with two people who had known him. Permission was obtained from the artist's nephew to reproduce, for the first time on motion picture film, many of the works in the extensive collection under his control. Photographed in the Netherlands, Belgium, and France, many of the actual landscapes seen in Van Gogh's canvases are shown, then followed by and blended into his paintings of the same subject. (Teacher's guide available.)

U.S. distributor: McGraw-Hill Films (sales and rental).

VIOLENCE AND VISION—FROM WORLD EXPRESSIONISM TO EXPRESSIONISTIC ART IN FLANDERS or BELGIUM'S CONTRIBUTION TO EXPRESSIONISM (*Cri et Connaissance–de l'expressionnisme dans le monde à l'expressionnisme en Flandre*)
40 mins. B&W. Originally 35mm. Belgium. 1963.

Producer: Art et Cinéma.

Credits: Paul Haesaerts, director and writer; Hugo Claus, co-writer; Louis De Meester, music.

Summary: The history of Expressionism in art from frescoes in prehistoric caves till today, with special emphasis on the movement in Flanders. The film includes paintings by Munch, Chagall, Kokoschka, Bacon, and the Belgian painters Permeke, Brusselmans, De Smet, and Oscar Jespers.

U.S. distributor: Embassy of Belgium (loan).

Canadian distributor: Canadian Film Institute for the National Gallery of Canada (loan).

THE VISION OF WILLIAM BLAKE
29 mins. Color. Originally 35mm. Britain. 1958.

Producer: Blake Film Trust, British Film Institute's Experimental Production Fund, British Council, and Arts Council of Great Britain.

Credits: Guy Brenton, director and writer; Basil Wright, Sir Anthony Blunt, and V. de S. Pinto, advisers; Bernard Miles and Robert Speight, narrators; Ralph Vaughan Williams, music.

Summary: A tribute to William Blake, poet, painter, and engraver, commemorating the bicentenary of his birth. It illustrates the story of Blake's spiritual journey, as he seeks to reconcile the ideal world of the spirit with the harsh realities of the industrial revolution, social injustice, and war. The film includes works from the British Museum, the Victoria and Albert Museum, the Tate Gallery, and the Fitzwilliam Museum in Cambridge.

U.S. distributor: Films Incorporated (sales and rental).

Canadian distributor: Canadian Film Institute for the National Gallery of Canada (loan).

VISITING THE INDIANS WITH GEORGE CATLIN
24 mins. Color. U.S.A. 1973.

Producer: University of Iowa.

Summary: The different life-styles of four tribes in the 1830's, viewed through the original lithographs and maps of George Catlin. The film reacts against commonly held stereotypes of the frontier Indians and provides the ethnographic view of tribal cultures necessary for an understanding of prehistory.

U.S. distributor: Iowa State University (rental); University of Iowa (rental).

WALLS OF FIRE
82 mins. Color. U.S.A. 1971.

Producer: Gertrude Ross Marks and Edmund F. Penney.

Credits: Herbert Kline, director; Arthur Ross, writer.

Summary: Made as a tribute to three of Mexico's greatest artists, José Clemente Orozco, Diego Rivera, and David Alfaro Siqueiros (Los Tres Grandes), whose lives are shown to be as spirited and revolutionary as the murals they created. The last interview footage shot of David Siqueiros is included in the film.

U.S. distributor: RBC Films (lease and rental).

WAYS OF SEEING
4 parts, 30 mins. each. Color. Britain. 1973.

Producer: Michael Dibb for BBC-TV.

Credits: Michael Dibb, director; John Berger, writer and narrator.

Summary: In a series of four programs the well-known art critic and author, John Berger, examines our past and present attitudes toward paintings. He shows how reproductions, which destroy the unique quality of a painting, can also, when seen under varying conditions, alter its impact on the viewer. He discusses attitudes toward the nude; how the realism of the traditional oil painting aroused the viewer's desire to possess the object painted; and he draws a parallel between this aspect of traditional art and present-day advertising and publicity. (Teacher's guide available.)

U.S. distributor: Time-Life (sales and rental).

Canadian distributor: BBC-TV Enterprises (sales and rental); Canadian Film Institute for the National Gallery of Canada (loan).

THE WEAPONS OF GORDON PARKS (*Artists at Work* series)
28 mins. Color. U.S.A. 1966.

Producer: Warren Forma.

Credits: Warren Forma, director; Gordon Parks, participant and music.

Summary: A sensitive homage to Gordon Parks, based on his photographs and on his auto-biography, *A Choice of Weapons*. The fifteenth child of a poor black Southern family, he overcame the difficulties of his youth in Harlem to become one of *Life* magazine's most noted photographers. His pictures were a powerful documentation of the impossible living conditions of the poor, and conveyed a message of love rather than hatred. An impressive exhibition of his photographs concludes the film.

U.S. distributor: Forma Art Associates (sales and rental).

THE WEST OF CHARLES RUSSELL (*Project 20* series)
53 mins. Color. U.S.A. 1970.

Producer: Donald B. Hyatt, NBC News.

Credits: Donald B. Hyatt, director; Richard Hanser, writer; Milburn Stone, narrator; Robert Russell Bennett, music.

Summary: The art of Charles Russell, cowboy, painter, and commentator on the Western era. Historic stills and films, as well as Russell's own paintings and writings, are used to illustrate the ideas and personality of the artist. Russell, who went to Montana in 1880 at the age of sixteen, saw the West from the Indian's point of view and resented the crushing of primitive ways by the white settlers.

U.S. distributor: Films Incorporated (sales and rental).

Canadian distributor: Visual Education Centre (sales and rental).

WHERE TIME IS A RIVER
18 mins. Color. U.S.A. 1966.

Producer: Radrick Production.

Credits: Gay Matthaei and Jewel Bjork, directors; Richard Peaslee, music; no narration.

Summary: An introduction to art appreciation in which emotion and imagination are stimulated by means of skillfully selected visuals to help children as well as adults make personal contact with paintings and so add a new dimension to their lives. Four examples have been selected: Rousseau's jungle pictures, the Russia of Chagall's youth, Gauguin's Tahitian paradise, and the mechanistic world of Léger.

U.S. distributor: New York University Film Library (rental); Museum of Modern Art (rental).

Canadian distributor: International Tele-Film Enterprises (sales and rental).

WHO IS: VICTOR VASARELY or VICTOR VASARELY (*Who Is* series)
30 mins. Color. Britain and U.S.A. 1968.

Producer: Alan King Associates, London, and Roger Graef for NET.

Credits: Dick Fontaine, Mark Peploe, and Stephen Milne, directors.

Summary: Victor Vasarely, considered the founder of Op Art, believes that the truths of our time are represented by relativity, the speed of light, and the weight of an atom. To this end he has moved from representational abstraction through kinetic experiment, to what he terms an abstract geometrical alphabet. Many of his pictures are prototypes designed for unlimited reproduction.

U.S. distributor: Indiana University (sales and rental).

WHY LEGER? (*Why Léger, Is He the Major Painter of Modern Times?*)
25 mins. B&W. Britain. 1965.

Producer: Michael Gill, BBC-TV.

Credits: Michael Gill, director; John Berger, writer and narrator.

Summary: In the setting of a gallery exhibition of Léger's paintings, the film presents a dialogue between John Berger, British film critic, and a skeptic, David Kronig, in which Berger argues passionately for Léger as the major artist of modern times. To support his views, Berger takes his audience to the south of France to tour the Léger Museum at Biot and the places which inspired so much of his work.

U.S. distributor: Time-Life (sales only).

Canadian distributor: BBC-TV Enterprises (sales and rental); Canadian Film Institute for the National Gallery of Canada (loan).

WILL ART LAST? or HORIZON: WILL ART LAST?
32 mins. Color. Britain. 1967.

Producer: Michael Heckford, BBC-TV.

Credits: Michael Heckford, director; Michael Clarke, writer; Christopher Chataway, narrator.

Summary: The preservation and restoration of works of art are shown. The materials used by artists, now and formerly, are discussed in this film, which includes a demonstration of the restoration of Titian's *Bacchus and Ariadne* at the National Gallery of London, using X-rays, reflected light photography, cleaning, varnishing, and retouching.

Canadian distributor: BBC-TV Enterprises (sales and rental).

WILLEM DE KOONING, THE PAINTER
13 mins. Color. U.S.A. 1966.

Producer: Hans Namuth and Paul Falkenberg.

Credits: Hans Namuth and Paul Falkenberg, directors; Morton Feldman, music.

Summary: A film essay on Netherlands-born artist Willem de Kooning, who appears throughout the film painting and commenting on the challenges that confront a painter with each new project. He correlates his observations and solutions with his brushwork and use of color to illustrate the points being evaluated.

U.S. distributors: Museum at Large (sales and rental); Film Images (sales and rental).

Canadian distributor: Canadian Film Institute for the National Gallery of Canada (loan).

WILLIAM DOBELL
21 mins. Color. Australia. 1961.

Producer: Geoffrey Collings Productions for QANTAS Airways Ltd.

Credits: Dahl Collings, director; Laurie Thomas, writer; Herbert Marks, music.

Summary: The career of the Australian portrait and character painter is covered from his early days of struggle in London to the present. Dobell is interviewed in his studio while he paints. Some eighty-five of his paintings are shown, including many portraits, works from his trip to New Guinea in 1952, abstract paintings and sketches from Hong Kong, 1961. These last drawings have a calligraphic style and show great economy of line. (The color of the print has faded.)

U.S. distributor: QANTAS Airways (loan).

Canadian distributor: QANTAS Airways (loan); Canadian Film Institute for the National Gallery of Canada (loan).

WILLIAM HOGARTH (*Artists' Notebooks* series)
30 mins. B&W. Britain. 1965.

Producer: Barbara Parker for BBC-TV.

Credits: Barbara Parker, director.

Summary: Notebooks, diaries, letters, and other sources give an insight into the life, work, and aspirations of this eighteenth-century English painter. The film places Hogarth in the artistic and social context of his time, and the commentary makes extensive use of his own writings. His passionate commitment to realism is discussed and illustrated through engravings and paintings photographed in American and British museums.

U.S. distributor: Time-Life (sales only).

WITH THESE HANDS—THE REBIRTH OF THE AMERICAN CRAFTSMAN
60 mins. Color. U.S.A. 1971.

Producer: Daniel Wilson Productions for Johnson Wax Company.

Credits: Daniel Wilson, director; David Wayne, narrator.

Summary: The following eight artist-craftsmen demonstrate the creative process and discuss their thoughts and ideas about their work, emphasizing the trend toward personal accomplishment in the folk arts: James Tanner, glassblower; Harry Nohr, wood-carver; Corian Zachai, weaver; Clayton Bailey, sculptor of clay, rubber, and plastic; Peter Voulkos, sculptor of metal and clay; and Toshiko Takaezu, weaver and potter.

Paul Solonor

U.S. distributor: Daniel Wilson Productions (sales and rental).

WOODBLOCK MANDALA: THE WORLD OF SHIKO MUNAKATA
30 mins. Color. Japan. 1973.

Producer: N.H.K. International Productions (Nippon Hoso Myokai, Japanese Broadcasting System).

Summary: The process of printmaking is presented from start to finish. Although now almost blind, Shiko Munakata creates at a furious pace: drafting the design, carving the block, making the print, and applying the colors. He states that the block is not only his chosen medium—it is the very flesh and blood of the finished print—and he is merely a tool of the Buddha who does the work for him.

U.S. distributor: Films Incorporated (sales and rental).

WORKS IN SERIES: JOHNS, STELLA, WARHOL
30 mins. Color. U.S.A. 1973.

Producer: Blackwood Productions.

Credits: Barbara Rose, director and writer.

Summary: Shot in 1973 at the opening of an exhibition by Jasper Johns, Frank Stella, and Andy Warhol at the Art Museum of South Texas, Corpus Christi. The film opens with a roundtable discussion involving the three artists, David Whitney—the architect of the Museum, and Barbara Rose—the noted art critic and filmmaker. After a tour of the new and functional building, Miss Rose interviews the artists in their studios, where the discussion centers on some of their latest paintings.

U.S. distributor: Blackwood Productions (sales and rental).

WORKS OF CALDER
20 mins. Color. U.S.A. 1950.

Producer: Burgess Meredith, New World Film Productions for the Museum of Modern Art.

Credits: Herbert Matter, director and photographer; Burgess Meredith, John Latouche, narrators; John Cage, music.

Summary: A poetic approach to Calder's mobiles, free forms in free movement, rhythm, and reflection. Shown in comparison with familiar shapes, their interplay with motion and light constitute an art whose deceptive appearance of spontaneity half conceals its calculation and brilliant invention.

U.S. distributor: The Museum of Modern Art (lease and rental).

Canadian distributor: Canadian Film Institute for the National Gallery of Canada (loan).

THE WORLD OF ANDREW WYETH
26 mins. Color. U.S.A. 1968.

Producer: Al Schwartz and Hal Wallace with the Art Institute of Chicago and the Whitney Museum of New York for ABC-TV.

Credits: Al Schwartz and Hal Wallace, directors; Nicholas Wyeth, adviser; Henry Fonda, participant.

Summary: Forty-nine paintings by Andrew Wyeth are examined, giving the viewer both an overall impression of each canvas and a close-up of specific details of his technique. Significant facts in Wyeth's life and actual scenes from the Pennsylvania and Maine countryside complete the discovery of Andrew Wyeth's world.

U.S. distributor: International Film Bureau (sales and rental).

Canadian distributor: Educational Film Distributors (sales and rental).

THE WORLD OF PAUL DELVAUX (*Le monde de Paul Delvaux*)
12 mins. B&W. Belgium, 1946.

Producer: Le Séminaire des Arts, Brussels.

Credits: Henri Storck, director; René Micha, writer; André Souris, music; Paul Eluard's poem spoken by himself (in French); no other narration.

Summary: A lyrical approach to the Surrealist compositions of the Belgian painter Paul Delvaux. Its production brought a new dimension to the film on art. Slow camera movement, accompanied by an inspired musical score and the voice of one of France's greatest poets, gives a strong impression of the dreams and obsessions of this disquieting artist.

U.S. distributor: Grove Press Film Division (sales and rental).

Canadian distributor: Canadian Film Institute for the National Gallery of Canada (loan, under French title).

THE WORLD SAVES ABU SIMBEL (*Abou-Simbel: journal d'une résurrection*)
28 mins. Color. UNESCO. 1967.

Producer: Herbert Meyer-Franck for UNESCO and Joint Venture Abu Simbel.

Credits: Herbert Meyer-Franck, director.

Summary: When work began on the Aswan High Dam in Upper Egypt, the two temples of Abu Simbel, carved in the living rock along the Nile, were threatened with complete destruction. In following the course of the International Campaign launched by UNESCO in 1960, these temples have been dissected and removed stone by stone to higher ground. The film records this operation and explains the archaeological significance of the temples of Abu Simbel.

U.S. distributor: UNESCO (loan).

Canadian distributor: Canadian Film Institute for UNESCO (loan).

THE WYETH PHENOMENON
26 mins. Color. U.S.A. 1967.

Producer: Harry Morgan for CBS.

Credits: Harry Morgan, director; Harry Reasoner, writer; Charles Mack, photographer; Glenn Paxton, music.

Summary: An examination of the world, cult, and art of Andrew Wyeth, made with the participation of the artist himself, his son Jamie, and Harry Reasoner, CBS newsman. Appreciations of Wyeth's painting are provided by interviews with his sister, Mrs. Peter Hurd, herself an artist, and *New York Times* art critic John Canaday. Samples of his work illustrate his skill and strength in the portrayal of traditional American subjects, and scenes of Chadds Ford, Pennsylvania, where three Wyeth generations have lived and painted, complete a penetrating portrait of the so-called Wyeth Dynasty.

U.S. distributor: BFA (sales and rental).

Canadian distributor: Holt, Rinehart and Winston (sales and rental); Canadian Film Institute for the National Gallery of Canada (loan).

YANKEE PAINTER: THE WORK OF WINSLOW HOMER
26 mins. Color. U.S.A. 1964.

Producer: Radio-TV Bureau, University of Arizona, Tucson.

Credits: Harry Atwood, director, photographer, and editor; Robert M. Quinn, writer of commentary and narrator; Robert Muczynski, music.

Summary: A chronological and critical appraisal of the paintings of Winslow Homer based on a 1963 retrospective exhibition of his works at the University of Arizona Museum of Art. Drawings, watercolors, and oils illustrate his artistic development and the great breadth of his interests.

U.S. distributor: International Film Bureau (sales and rental).

Canadian distributor: Canadian Film Institute for the National Gallery of Canada (loan).

THE YEAR 1200
19 mins. Color. Originally videotape. U.S.A. 1970.

Producer: CBS News.

Summary: Records an important exhibition at The Metropolitan Museum of Art, New York. Objects included were carefully chosen from collections around the world not only to represent a period but to delineate a style, "The Style 1200." During this period, dramatic creativity in the artists was in evidence for almost the first time since the ancient Greek and Roman eras.

U.S. distributor: BFA (sales and rental).

Canadian distributor: Holt, Rinehart and Winston (sales and rental).

INDEXES

Subject Index

MODERN ART—SCULPTURE

MOSAICS

Artist Index

Name and dates of birth and death	Title of film, or films, in which the artist is represented
Braque, Georges (1882-1963)	Un autre regard, 42 Cubism, 60 Georges Braque, 78 Gertrude Stein: When This You See, Remember Me, 79 Peggy Guggenheim: Art in Venice, 123
Brauner, Victor (1903-)	From Dada to Surrealism, 75
Brickell, Barry	Barry Brickell, Potter, 44
Brown, Ford Madox (1821-1893)	The Pre-Raphaelite Revolt, 131
Bruegel, Pieter (1525-1569)	Bruegel and the Follies of Men: Babel, 50 Bruegel and the Follies of Men: Dulle Griet, 50
Brusselmans, Jean (1884-1953)	Violence and Vision—from World Expressionism to Expressionistic Art in Flanders, 159
Burchfield, Charles E. (1893-1967)	Charles Burchfield: Fifty Years of His Art, 52
Burra, Edward (1905-)	Edward Burra, 67
Burri, Alberto (1915-)	Alberto Burri, 23
Calder, Alexander (1898-1976)	Alexander Calder: from the Circus to the Moon, 25 American Sculpture of the Sixties, 29 The Calder Man, 51 Calder's Circus, 51 Contemporary American Sculpture in the Collection of the Art Institute of Chicago, 58 Works of Calder, 164
Canaletto, Bernardo Bellotto (1697-1768)	The Age of Rococo, 22
Caravaggio (1573-1610)	He Is Risen, 86
Carolus-Duran, Charles (1837-1917)	The Charm of Life, 53
Carpaccio, Vittore (c.1460-c.1525)	Venice, Theme and Variations, 157
Casson, Jackie	Art of the Sixties, 39
Catlin, George (1796-1872)	Visiting the Indians with George Catlin, 160
Cayo, Hermogenes	Imaginero, 92
Cézanne, Paul (1839-1906)	Impressionism and Neo-Impressionism, 93 The Impressionists, 93 Journey into a Painting, 99 Paul Cézanne, 121 The Precursors, 131
Chagall, Marc (1887-)	From Dada to Surrealism, 75 The Gift, 80

Name and dates of birth and death	Title of film, or films, in which the artist is represented
Chagall, Marc (1887-)	Violence and Vision—from World Expressionism to Expressionistic Art in Flanders, 159 Where Time Is a River, 161
Chamberlain, John (1927-)	American Sculpture of the Sixties, 29 Contemporary American Sculpture in the Collection of the Art Institute of Chicago, 58
Chirico, Giorgio de (1888-)	The Egg and the Eye, 67 From Dada to Surrealism, 75 Peggy Guggenheim: Art in Venice, 123 Surrealism (and Dada), 149
Christo, Javacheff (1935-)	Christo: Four Works in Progress, 54 Christo's Valley Curtain, 54 Christo: Wrapped Coast, 55
Conner, Bruce (1933-)	American Sculpture of the Sixties, 29
Constable, John (1776-1837)	Corot, 59 The Open Window, 119 *Romantic versus Classic Art* series, no. 8, 138, 139
Copley, John Singleton (1738-1815)	Painting in America: Copley to Audubon, 120
Coplins, John (1920-)	Artist's Proof, 41
Le Corbusier (Charles Edouard Jeanneret) (1887-1965)	The Chapel of Ronchamp, 52 Le Corbusier, 59
Corinth, Lovis (1858-1925)	Lovis Corinth—a Life in Pictures, 105
Cornell, Joseph (1903-1973)	American Sculpture of the Sixties, 29
Corot, (Jean-Baptiste) Camille (1796-1875)	Corot, 59
Costa, Lucio (1902-)	Brasilia, 48
Courbet, Gustave (1819-1877)	Gustave Courbet, the First Realist, 85
Craig, James (d. 1795)	Prospect for a City, 132
Cranach, Lukas the Elder (1472-1553)	Lukas Cranach: the Reformation Artist, 105
Creeft, José de (1884-)	José de Creeft, 99
Cross, Henri-Edmond (1856-1910)	Impressionism and Neo-Impressionism, 93
Cunningham, Imogen (1883-1976)	Imogen Cunningham, Photographer, 93
Currier, Nathaniel (1813-1888)	America: the Artist's Eye, 26 A Trip with Currier and Ives, 153
Curtis, Edward S. (1896-1930)	The Shadow Catcher, 145
Dali, Salvador (1904-)	The Egg and the Eye, 67 From Dada to Surrealism, 75 La maison aux images, 108 Surrealism (and Dada), 149

Name and dates of birth and death	Title of film, or films, in which the artist is represented
Daudelin, Charles (1920-)	Bronze, 49
Daumier, Honoré (1808-1879)	1848 or The Revolution of 1848, 67 Daumier, Eye-Witness of an Epoch, 61
David, Gérard (1460-1523)	Flanders in the Fifteenth Century—the First Oil Paintings, 73
David, Jacques-Louis (1748-1825)	Monsieur Ingres, 114 *Romantic versus Classic Art* series, no. 1, 138, 139
Davie, Alan (1920-)	Opus—Impressions of British Art and Culture, 119
Davis, Ronald (1937-)	American Art in the Sixties, 27
Davis, Stuart (1894-1964)	The American Image, 28 American Realists, 29
Decamps, Alexandre (1803-1860)	1848 or The Revolution of 1848, 67
Degas, Edgar (1834-1917)	Degas, 62 Impressionism and Neo-Impressionism, 93 The Impressionists, 93 *Romantic versus Classic Art* series, no. 14, 138, 139
De Kooning, Willem (1904-)	Art of the Sixties, 39 Painters Painting, 120 Peggy Guggenheim: Art in Venice, 123 Willem De Kooning, the Painter, 163
Delacroix, Eugène (1798-1863)	1848 or The Revolution of 1848, 67 Civilisation series, no, 12, 55, 56 *Romantic versus Classic Art* series, no. 11, 138, 139
Delaunay, Robert (1885-1941)	Cubism, 60 Fauvism, 72
Delvaux, Paul (1897-)	From Dada to Surrealism, 75 The World of Paul Delvaux, 165
Demuth, Charles (1883-1935)	American Realists, 29
Derain, André (1880-1954)	Un autre regard, 42 Fauvism, 72 La maison aux images, 108
De Smet, Gustave (1877-1943)	Violence and Vision—from World Expressionism to Expressionistic Art in Flanders, 159
Dine, Jim (1936-)	Jim Dine, 98
Dobell, William (1899-)	William Dobell, 163
Donatello (1386-1466)	Piero della Francesca, 127
Doughty, Thomas (1793-1856)	Painting in America: Copley to Audubon, 120

Name and dates of birth and death	Title of film, or films, in which the artist is represented
Drysdale, Russell (1912-)	Russell Drysdale, 141
Duchamp, Marcel (1887-1968)	Anemic Cinema, 33 The Art Show that Shocked America, 40 Dada, 60 Fauvism, 72 Surrealism (and Dada), 149
Duchamp-Villon, Raymond (1876-1918)	Un autre regard, 42
Dufy, Raoul (1877-1953)	Fauvism, 72
Dunlap, William (1766-1839)	Painting in America: Copley to Audubon, 120
Dunoyer de Segonzac, André (1884-1974)	La maison aux images, 108
Dürer, Albrecht (1471-1528)	Albrecht Dürer (BBC), 24 Albrecht Dürer (1471-1528), 24
Eakins, Thomas (1844-1916)	America: the Artist's Eye, 26
Epstein, Sir Jacob (1880-1959)	An Act of Faith, 20 Epstein, 69
Ernst, Max (1891-1976)	Dada, 60 From Dada to Surrealism, 75 Peggy Guggenheim: Art in Venice, 123 Surrealism (and Dada), 149 Twentieth Century Art—a Break with Tradition, 154
Escher, Maurits Cornelis (1898-1972)	Adventures in Perception, 21
Evans, Merlyn (1910-)	Artist's Proof, 41
Eyck, Jan van (1390-1440)	Flanders in the Fifteenth Century—the First Oil Paintings, 73
Feininger, Lyonel (1871-1956)	The Expressionist Revolt, 72
Field, Erastus Salisbury	Around the World in Eighty Feet, 36
Flavin, Dan (1933-)	American Art in the Sixties, 27
Flockinger, Gerda	Opus—Impressions of British Art and Culture, 119
Fon, Ree Woo	Japan: the New Art, 96
Forbes, Edwin (1839-1895)	America: The Artist's Eye, 26
Forkmer, John	New Arts, 116
Francesca, Piero della (see Piero della Francesca)	
Francis, Sam (1923-)	American Art in the Sixties, 27 Sam Francis, 142
Frankenthaler, Helen (1928-)	American Art in the Sixties, 27 The New Abstraction: Morris Louis and Kenneth Noland, 115 Painters Painting, 120

Name and dates of birth and death	Title of film, or films, in which the artist is represented
Fresnaye, Roger de la (1885-1925)	Cubism, 60
Fuseli, Henry (1741-1825)	*Romantic versus Classic Art* series, no. 2, 138, 139
Gainsborough, Thomas (1727-1788)	The Age of Rococo, 22 Gainsborough, 76
Gallego, Fernando (1466-1507)	A Masterpiece of Spanish Painting, 110
Garnier, Robert (c.1545-1590)	The Charm of Life, 53
Gaudi, Antonio (1852-1926)	Antoni Gaudi, 34 Antonio Gaudi, 35
Gaudier-Brzeska, Henri (1891-1915)	Un autre regard, 42 Henri Gaudier-Brzeska, 87 Red Stone Dancer, 134
Gauguin, Paul (1848-1903)	Gauguin in Tahiti: The Search for Paradise, Paul Gauguin (1848-1903), 122 The Precursors, 131 Where Time Is a River, 161
Gavarni, Paul (1804-1866)	1848 or The Revolution of 1848, 67
Gaza, Dragan (1930-)	The Funeral of Stef Halacek, 76
Generalic, Ivan (1914-)	The Funeral of Stef Halacek, 76
Géricault, Théodore (1791-1824)	*Romantic versus Classic Art* series, no. 7, 138, 139
Gerö, Maria	About a Tapestry, 19
Giacometti, Alberto (1901-1966)	Alberto Giacometti, 23 Alberto Giacometti, 1901-1966, 23 Giacometti, 80 Giacometti (*Canvas* series), 80 Peggy Guggenheim: Art in Venice, 123 Surrealism (and Dada), 149
Giotto di Bordone (c.1266-1337)	Giotto and the Pre-Renaissance, 81
Gleizes, Albert (1881-1953)	Albert Gleizes, 22 Cubism, 60
González, Julio (1876-1942)	Un autre regard, 42
Gorky, Arshile (1904-1948)	Peggy Guggenheim: Art in Venice, 123
Gottlieb, Adolph (1903-1974)	Art of the Sixties, 39
Goya y Lucientes, Francisco José de (1746-1828)	The Glory of Goya, 82 Goya (by Ben Berg), 82 Goya (by David W. Powell), 82 Goya (*Museum Without Walls* Collection), 83 Goya: Disasters of War, 83 El Prado—Masterpieces and Music, 130 *Romantic versus Classic Art* series, no. 4, 138, 139 *Treasures from El Prado* series, 152

Name and dates of birth and death	Title of film, or films, in which the artist is represented
Grant, Alistair (1925-)	Artist's Proof, 41
Grant, Duncan (1885-)	Duncan Grant at Charleston, 64
El Greco (Domenikos Theotokopoulos) (1541-1614)	El Prado—Masterpieces and Music, 130 *Treasures from El Prado* series, 152
Gris, Juan (1887-1927)	Cubism, 60
Gropius, Walter (1883-1969)	The Bauhaus: Its Impact on the World of Design, 45
Gross, Anthony (1905-)	Artist's Proof, 41 Expressionism, 71
Gross, Chaim (1904-)	A Sculptor Speaks: Chaim Gross, 143
Guardi, Francesco (1712-1793)	Venice, Theme and Variations, 157
Guillaumin, Armand (1841-1927)	Impressionism and Neo-Impressionism, 93
Guston, Philip (1913-)	Philip Guston, 124
Hals, Frans (1584-1666)	Portrait of Frans Hals, 129
Hamilton, Richard (1922-)	Richard Hamilton, 136
Harris, Paul (1925-)	American Sculpture of the Sixties, 29
Harrison, Anthony (1931-)	Artist's Proof, 41
Harrison, Newton (1932-)	New Arts, 116
Hartung, Hans (1904-)	Hartung, 86
Harunobu, Suzuki (1725-1770)	Ukiyo-e, 154
Hayter, Stanley William (1901-)	Stanley William Hayter—the Artist as a Teacher, 148
Heckel, Erich (1883-1970)	Expressionism, 71
Hepworth, Barbara (1903-1975)	Barbara Hepworth, 43 Barbara Hepworth at the Tate, 44 Figures in a Landscape, 73
Hiroshige, Ando Tokitaro (1797-1858)	Ukiyo-e, 154 Ukiyoe: the Fabulous World of Japanese Prints, 155
Hirschberg, Martin (1937-)	Electric Gallery Plus Three, 68
Hockney, David (1937-)	David Hockney's Diaries, 61 The Responsive Eye, 136
Hofer, Karl (1878-1955)	Expressionism, 71
Hofmann, Hans (1886-1966)	The Americans: Three East Coast Artists at Work, 30 Painters Painting, 120
Hogarth, William (1697-1764)	The London of William Hogarth, 103 William Hogarth, 163
Hokusai, Katsushika (Natajima Tet-Sujiro) (1760-1849)	Ukiyo-e, 154 Ukiyoe: the Fabulous World of Japanese Prints, 155

Name and dates of birth and death	Title of film, or films, in which the artist is represented
Holbein, Hans (the Younger) (1497-1543)	At the Turn of the Age—Hans Holbein, 42
Homer, Winslow (1836-1910)	American Realists, 29 Yankee Painter: the Work of Winslow Homer, 166
Hopper, Edward (1882-)	The American Image, 28
Hughes, Arthur (1832-1915)	The Pre-Raphaelite Revolt, 131
Hugo, Ian (1898-)	Ian Hugo: Engraver and Filmmaker, 91
Hultberg, Paul	Reflections—Enamels of Artist-Craftsman Paul Hultberg, 134
Hunt, Henry (1923-)	The Totem Pole, 152
Hunt, Richard (1935-)	Richard Hunt, Sculptor, 136
Hunt, William Holman (1827-1910)	The Pre-Raphaelite Revolt, 131
Indiana, Robert (1928-)	Robert Indiana Portrait, 137
Ingres, Jean-Auguste Dominique (1780-1867)	Monsieur Ingres, 114 *Romantic versus Classic Art* series, nos. 5 and 6, 138, 139
Inness, George (1825-1894)	American Realists, 29
Irwin, Robert (1928-)	American Art in the Sixties, 27
Ives, James Merritt (1824-1895)	America: the Artist's Eye, 26 A Trip with Currier and Ives, 153
Jarvis, Roland	Artist's Proof, 41
Jenkins, Paul (1923-)	The Ivory Knife, 95
Jespers, Oscar (1887-)	Violence and Vision—from World Expressionism to Expressionistic Art in Flanders, 159
Johns, Jasper (1930-)	American Art in the Sixties, 27 Jasper Johns, 97 Jasper Johns: Decoy, 97 Painters Painting, 120 Works in Series: Johns, Stella, Warhol, 164
Johnson, Philip (1906-)	The Responsive Eye, 136
Jones, Allen (1914-)	Scenes Seen with Allen Jones, 143
Jones, Howard (1922-)	Howard Jones, 90
Judd, Donald (1928-)	American Art in the Sixties, 27 American Sculpture of the Sixties, 29 Art of the Sixties, 39
Kaigetsudo	Ukiyo-e, 154
Kandinsky, Vassily (1866-1944)	Expressionism, 71

Name and dates of birth and death	Title of film, or films, in which the artist is represented
Kandinsky, Vassily (1866-1944)	The Expressionist Revolt, 72 Peggy Guggenheim: Art in Venice, 123 Twentieth Century Art—a Break with Tradition, 154
Kane, Paul (1810-1871)	Paul Kane Goes West, 122
Katz, Alex (1927-)	Alex Katz, One Flight Up, 25
Kelly, Ellsworth (1923-)	American Art in the Sixties, 27
Kenojuak (1927-)	Eskimo Artist: Kenojuak, 69
Kienholz, Ed (1927-)	American Art in the Sixties, 27 American Sculpture of the Sixties, 29 Kienholz on Exhibit, 100
Kingman, Dong (1911-)	Dong Kingman, 63
Kirchner, Ernst Ludwig (1880-1938)	Expressionism, 71 The Expressionist Revolt, 72
Kitaj, R. B. (1932-)	R. B. Kitaj, 132
Kiyomasu (1694-1716)	Ukiyo-e, 154
Kiyomitsu (1735-1785)	Ukiyo-e, 154
Kiyonaga (1742-1815)	Ukiyo-e, 154
Klee, Paul (1879-1940)	Expressionism, 71 The Expressionist Revolt, 72 From Dada to Surrealism, 75 Paul Klee, 122 Peggy Guggenheim: Art in Venice, 123 Surrealism (and Dada), 149 Twentieth Century Art—a Break with Tradition, 154
Kline, Franz (1910-1962)	American Art in the Sixties, 27 Art of the Sixties, 39
Kofi, Vincent	Bronze Casting: Vincent Kofi, 49
Kokoschka, Oskar (1886-)	Expressionism, 71 The Expressionist Revolt, 72 Violence and Vision—from World Expressionism to Expressionistic Art in Flanders, 159
Krebs, Rockne (1938-)	New Arts, 116
Kuhn, Walt (1877-1949)	American Realists, 29
Laboureur, Jean-Emile (1877-1943)	La maison aux images, 108
La Fresnaye, Roger de (1885-1925)	Cubism, 60
Lancret, Nicolas (1690-1743)	The Age of Rococo, 22
Laurencin, Marie (1885-1956)	Gertrude Stein: When This You See, Remember Me, 79

Name and dates of birth and death	Title of film, or films, in which the artist is represented
Laurens, Jean-Paul (1838-1921)	The Charm of Life, 53
Leach, Bernard (1887-)	Bernard Leach: a Potter's World, 46
Le Corbusier (Charles-Edouard Jeanneret) (1887-1965)	The Chapel of Ronchamp, 52 Le Corbusier, 59
Léger, Fernand (1881-1955)	Ballet mécanique, 43 Cubism, 60 Fernand Léger in America—his New Realism, 72 Where Time Is a River, 161 Why Léger?, 162
Leonardo da Vinci (1459-1519)	*Civilisation* series—no. 5, 55, 56 The Drawings of Leonardo da Vinci, 63 Leonardo: to Know How to See, 102
Leslie, Al (1927-)	The Responsive Eye, 136
Levine, Jack (1915-)	The American Image, 28 Jack Levine, 95
Levine, Les (1935-)	Art of the Sixties, 39
Levinson, Mon (1926-)	The Responsive Eye, 136
Lichtenstein, Roy (1923-)	Lichtenstein in London, 102 New Arts, 116
Linares, Pedro	Pedro Linares, Folk Artist, 123
Lipchitz, Jacques (1891-1973)	The Artist at Work—Jacques Lipchitz, Master Sculptor, 40 Chaim Soutine, 52 Gertrude Stein: When This You See, Remember Me, 79 Jacques Lipchitz, 96
Lippi, Fra Filippo (c.1406-1469)	The Adoration of the Magi, 20
Lipton, Seymour (1903-)	Sculpture by Lipton, 143
Lloyd, Charles	The Incised Image, 94
Longhi, Pietro (1702-1785)	Venice, Theme and Variations, 157
Lorrain, Claude (Claude Gellée) (1600-1682)	The Art of Claude Lorrain, 38
Louis, Morris (1912-1962)	American Art in the Sixties, 27 The New Abstraction: Morris Louis and Kenneth Noland, 115
Lowry, L. S. (1887-)	L. S. Lowry "The Industrial Artist," 101
Lucebert (Lubertus Jacobus Swaanswyk) (1924-)	A Film for Lucebert, 73
Lurçat, Jean (1892-1966)	A propos des Gobelins, 19 The Song of the Earth, 147
Lye, Len (1901-)	Art of the Sixties, 39

Name and dates of birth and death	Title of film, or films, in which the artist is represented
MacIver, Loren (1909-)	Loren MacIver, 104
Mackintosh, Charles Rennie (1868-1928)	Mackintosh, 106
Magritte, René (1898-1967)	From Dada to Surrealism, 75 Magritte, 106 Magritte: the False Mirror, 107 Magritte or the Object Lesson, 107 Surrealism (and Dada), 149
Maillol, Aristide (1861-1944)	Dina in the King's Garden, 62 Maillol, 107
Malevitch, Casimir (1878-1935)	Malevitch Suprematism, 108
Manessier, Alfred (1911-)	Manessier, 109
Manet, Edouard (1832-1883)	Edouard Manet, 65 The Impressionists, 93
Mantegna, Andrea (c.1431-1506)	Mantegna—the Triumph of Caesar, 109
Marc, Franz (1880-1916)	Expressionism, 71 The Expressionist Revolt, 72
Marin, John (1870-1953)	American Realists, 29 John Marin, 98
Marini, Marino (1901-)	Marino Marini, 109
Marisol (Escobar) (1930-)	The Responsive Eye, 136
Marquet, Albert (1875-1947)	Marquet, 110
Marsh, Reginald (1898-1954)	American Realists, 29
Martin, Mungo (1881-1956)	The Totem Pole, 152
Masaccio (Tommaso di Giovanni) (1401-1428)	Piero della Francesca, 127
Masson, André (1896-)	La maison aux images, 108
Matisse, Henri (1869-1954)	The Art Show that Shocked America, 40 Un autre regard, 42 Fauvism, 72 Henri Matisse, 87 The Henri Matisse Centennial at the Grand Palais, 87 Matisse, 111 Matisse—a Sort of Paradise, 111 Twentieth Century Art—a Break with Tradition, 154
Matta, Echaurren (1912-)	Surrealism (and Dada), 149
Mayakovsky, Vladimir Vladimirovich (1893-1930)	Mayakovsky—the Poetry of Action, 112
Mefferd, Boyd	New Arts, 116
Memling, Hans (c.1433-1494)	Memling: Painter of Bruges, 112
Metzinger, Jean (1883-1956)	Cubism, 60

Name and dates of birth and death	Title of film, or films, in which the artist is represented
Michelangelo Buonarroti (1475-1546)	*Civilisation* series, no. 5, 55, 56 Michelangelo: the Last Giant, 113 The Titan: the Story of Michelangelo, 151
Mies van der Rohe, Ludwig (1886-1969)	The Bauhaus: Its Impact on the World of Design, 45 The New National Gallery in Berlin, 116
Millais, John Everett (1829-1896)	The Pre-Raphaelite Revolt, 131
Millet, Jean-François (1814-1875)	Corot, 59 *Romantic versus Classic Art* series, no. 12, 138, 139
Miró, Joan (1893-)	Around and about Joan Miró, 36 From Dada to Surrealism, 75 Gertrude Stein: When This You See, Remember Me, 79 Joan Miró Makes a Color Print, 98 La maison aux images, 108 Peggy Guggenheim: Art in Venice, 123 Surrealism (and Dada), 149
Modigliani, Amedeo (1884-1920)	Amedeo Modigliani, 26 Un autre regard, 42
Moholy-Nagy, Laszlo (1895-1946)	Light-Play: Black-White-Gray, 102
Mondriaan, Piet Cornelis (1872-1944)	Peggy Guggenheim: Art in Venice, 123 Piet Mondriaan: a Film Essay, 127
Monet, Claude (1840-1926)	Avec Claude Monet, 43 Claude Monet, 57 Impressionism and Neo-Impressionism, 93 The Impressionists, 93 Monet in London, 113
Moore, Henry Spencer (1898-)	Henry Moore, 88 Henry Moore at the Tate Gallery, 88 I Think in Shapes—Henry Moore, 91 Opus—Impressions of British Art and Culture, 119 Peggy Guggenheim: Art in Venice, 123 Reclining Figure, 134
Morandi, Giorgio (1890-1964)	Giorgio Morandi, 81
Moreau, Gustave (1826-1898)	The Age of Rococo, 22
Morisot, Berthe (1841-1895)	Impressionism and Neo-Impressionism, 93
Moronobu, Hishikawa (1625-1694)	Ukiyo-e, 154
Morris, Robert (1931-)	American Art in the Sixties, 27
Moses, Grandma Anna Mary Robertson, (1860-1961)	Grandma Moses, 84
Motherwell, Robert (1915-)	Painters Painting, 120 Robert Motherwell, 137

Name and dates of birth and death	Title of film, or films, in which the artist is represented
Mucha, Alfons Maria (1860-1939)	Art Nouveau, 38
Munakata, Shiko (1903-)	Woodblock Mandala: the World of Shiko Munakata, 164
Munch, Edvard (1863-1944)	Edvard Munch—the Norwegian Master of Expressionism, 66 Edvard Munch: Paintings, 66 Edvard Munch: Prints, 66 Expressionism, 71 Violence and Vision—from World Expressionism to Expressionistic Art in Flanders, 159
Murillo, Bartolomé (1618-1682)	*Treasures from El Prado* series, 152
Myers, Jerome (1867-1940)	Artist in Manhattan—Jerome Myers, 41
Nakanishi	The Egg and the Eye, 67
Nakian, Reuben (1897-)	American Sculpture of the Sixties, 29
Narita, Katsuhiku	Japan: the New Art, 96
Nattier, Jean-Marc (1685-1766)	The Age of Rococo, 22
Nevelson, Louise (Beliansky) (1904-)	American Sculpture of the Sixties, 29 Contemporary American Sculpture in the Collection of the Art Institute of Chicago, 58 Louise Nevelson, 104
Newman, Barnett (1905-1970)	Art of the Sixties, 39 Barnett Newman, 44 Painters Painting, 120
Nicholson, Ben (1894-)	Peggy Guggenheim: Art in Venice, 123
Niemeyer, Oscar (1907-)	Brasilia, 48
Niviaksiak (1920-1959)	The Living Stone, 103
Noguchi, Isamu (1904-)	American Sculpture of the Sixties, 29 Isamu Noguchi, 95 Noguchi: a Sculptor's World, 117
Nohr, Harry	With These Hands—the Rebirth of the American Craftsman, 164
Nolan, Sidney (1917-)	Sidney Nolan, 146
Noland, Kenneth (1924-)	American Art in the Sixties, 27 The New Abstractions: Morris Louis and Kenneth Noland, 115 Painters Painting, 120
Nolde, Emil (1867-1956)	Emil Nolde, 68 Expressionism, 71 The Expressionist Revolt, 72 Twentieth Century Art—a Break with Tradition, 154

Name and dates of birth and death	Title of film, or films, in which the artist is represented
Rivers, Larry (1923-)	American Art in the Sixties, 27 Larry Rivers, 101 The Responsive Eye, 136
Rodin, Auguste (1840-1917)	Homage to Rodin, 90 Rodin: the Burghers of Calais, 138 *Romantic versus Classic Art* series, no. 13, 138, 139
Rossetti, Dante Gabriel (1828-1882)	The Pre-Raphaelite Revolt, 131
Rouault, Georges (1871-1958)	Georges Rouault, 78 Miserere, 113
Rousseau, Henri (le Douanier) (1844-1910)	Henri Rousseau, 88 Where Time Is a River, 161
Rousseau, Théodore (1812-1867)	Corot, 59
Rubens, Pieter Paulus (1577-1640)	Rubens, 140 Rubens (Rubens en liberté), 140 *Treasures from El Prado* series, 152
Ruscha, Edward (1937-)	American Art in the Sixties, 27
Ruskin, John (1819-1900)	The Pre-Raphaelite Revolt, 131
Russell, Charles M. (1864-1926)	The West of Charles Russell, 161
Ryder, Albert Pinkham (1847-1917)	American Realists, 29 The Art Show that Shocked America, 40
Schawinsky, Xanti	Schawinsky 1969, 143
Schmidt, Clarence (d. 1975)	Clarence Schmidt—the Woodstock Environment, 57
Schmidt-Rottluff, Karl (1884-1976)	Expressionism, 71 The Expressionist Revolt, 72
Schöffer, Nicholas (1912-)	Art for Tomorrow, 37
Segal, George (1924-)	American Art in the Sixties, 27 Art of the Sixties, 39 Contemporary American Sculpture in the Collection of the Art Institute of Chicago, 58
Sekine, Nobuo	Japan: the New Art, 96
•Seurat, Georges (1859-1891)	Georges Seurat, 79 Impressionism and Neo-Impressionism, 93 The Impressionists, 93
Shahn, Ben (1898-1969)	American Realists, 29 This is Ben Shahn, 151
Shalom of Safed	Shalom of Safed, 145
Sharaku, Toshusai	Ukiyo-e, 154

Name and dates of birth and death	Title of film, or films, in which the artist is represented
Takis, Vassilakis (1925-)	Art for Tomorrow, 37
Tamayo, Rufino (1899-)	Rufino Tamayo: the Sources of His Art, 140
Tanguy, Yves (1900-1955)	Surrealism (and Dada), 149
Tanner, James (1941-)	With These Hands—the Rebirth of the American Craftsman, 164
Ting, Walasse (1929-)	Encre, 68
Tinguely, Jean (1925-)	Art for Tomorrow, 37 Breaking It Up at the Museum, 48 Homage to Jean Tinguely, 89
Tintoretto, Jacopo Robusti (1518-1594)	He Is Risen, 86
Titian (Tiziano Vecellino) (c.1477-1576)	*Treasures from El Prado* series, 152 Will Art Last?, 162
Tobey, Mark (1890-1976)	Mark Tobey Abroad, 110
Toulouse-Lautrec, Henri de (1864-1901)	The Impressionists, 93 Litho, 103
Trémois (1921-)	La maison aux images, 108
Trumbull, John (1756-1843)	America: the Artist's Eye, 26 Painting in America: Copley to Audubon, 120
Tsai, Wen-Ying (1928-)	Art for Tomorrow, 37
Turner, Joseph Mallord William (1775-1851)	The Open Window, 119 The Rebel Angel, 133 *Romantic versus Classic Art* series, nos. 9 & 10, 138, 139 Turner, 153
Tworkov, Jack (1900-)	The Americans: Three East Coast Artists at Work, 30
Uccello, Paolo (c.1396-1479)	Paolo Uccello, 121
Utamaro, Kitagawa (1754-1806)	Ukiyo-e, 154 Ukiyoe: the Fabulous World of Japanese Prints, 155
Utrillo, Maurice (1883-1955)	L'Univers d'Utrillo, 155
Van der Zee, James	Black Has Always Been Beautiful, 46
Van Dyck, Sir Anthony (1599-1641)	He Is Risen, 86
Van Eyck, Jan (1390-1441)	Van Eyck: Father of Flemish Painting, 156
Van Gogh, Vincent (1853-1890)	The Art Show that Shocked America, 40 The Impressionists, 93 The Precursors, 131 Van Gogh (by Alain Resnais), 156 Van Gogh (BBC), 156 Vincent Van Gogh: a Self-Portrait, 159
Van Meegeren, Henricus (1889-1947)	Van Meegeren's Faked Vermeers, 157

Name and dates of birth and death	Title of film, or films, in which the artist is represented
Vasarely, Victor de (1908-)	A propos des Gobelins, 19 Art for Tomorrow, 37 Who Is: Victor Vasarely, 162
Velazquez, Diego Rodriguez de Silva (1599-1660)	El Prado—Masterpieces and Music, 130 He Is Risen, 86 *Treasures from El Prado* series, 152
Veneziano, Lorenzo Domenico (d.1461)	Venice, Theme and Variations, 157
Vermeer, Jan Johannes (1632-1675)	Vermeer, 158
Villard de Honnecourt (13th c.)	Villard de Honnecourt, Builder of Cathedrals, 158
Villon, Jacques (Gaston Duchamp) (1875-1963)	Cubism, 60
Virius, Mirko (1889-1943)	The Funeral of Stef Halacek, 76
Vlaminck, Maurice de (1876-1958)	Un autre regard, 42 Fauvism, 72
Voulkos, Peter (1924-)	With These Hands—the Rebirth of the American Craftsman, 164
Wallis, Alfred (1855-1943)	Alfred Wallis—Artist and Mariner, 25
Warhol, Andy (1930-)	American Art in the Sixties, 27 Andy Warhol, 33 New Arts, 116 Painters Painting, 120 Super Artist, Andy Warhol, 149 Works in Series: Johns, Stella, Warhol, 164
Washington, Allston (1779-1843)	Painting in America: Copley to Audubon, 120
Watkins, Franklin Chenault (1894-)	Franklin Watkins, 75
Watteau, Jean-Antoine (1684-1721)	The Age of Rococo, 22
Westerik, Co (1924-)	The Paintings of Co Westerik, 121
Westermann, H. C. (1922-)	American Sculpture of the Sixties, 29
Weston, Edward (1886-1958)	The Photographer, 124
Weyden, Rogier van der (1400-1464)	Flanders in the Fifteenth Century—the First Oil Paintings, 73
Whistler, James Abbott McNeill (1834-1903) (1834-1903)	Venice, Theme and Variations, 157
White, Norman (1938-)	Electric Gallery Plus Three, 68
Whitney, David	Works in Series: John, Stella, Warhol, 164
Wilson, Colin St. John (1931-)	Opus—Impressions of British Art and Culture, 119
Withman, Robert	New Arts, 116
Wölfli, Adolf (1864-1930)	St. Adolph II, 142

Name and dates of birth and death	Title of film, or films, in which the artist is represented
Wyeth, Andrew Nevell (1917-)	American Realists, 29 The World of Andrew Wyeth, 165 The Wyeth Phenomenon, 166
Yoshihara, Jiro (1905-)	Japan: the New Art, 96
Youngerman, Jack (1926-)	American Art in the Sixties, 27
Zachai, Dorian	With These Hands—the Rebirth of the American Craftsman, 164
Zadkine, Ossip (1890-1968)	Un autre regard, 42
Zapf, Hermann (1918-)	The Art of Hermann Zapf, 38

Alphabetical Index

List of Sources

A ACI Films
35 West 45th Street
New York, New York 10036

Alcon Films
90 Mar Vista
Pasadena, California 91106

Alden Films
7820–20th Avenue
Brooklyn, New York 11214

Alemann Films
P.O. Box 76244
Los Angeles, California 90076

American Educational Films
132 Lasky Drive
Beverly Hills, California 90212

The American Federation of Arts
41 East 65th Street
New York, New York 10021

American Friends of the Plantin-
Moretus Museum
120 Broadway Room 2751
New York, New York 10005

American Institute of Architects
Audio-Visual Library
1735 New York Avenue N.W.
Washington, D.C. 20006

Arnold Eagle Productions
41 West 47th Street
New York, New York 10036

Art Institute of Chicago
Michigan Avenue at Adams Street
Chicago, Illinois 60603

Association Films, Inc.
866 Third Avenue
New York, New York 10022

Association Films, Inc.
333 Adelaide Street W.
Toronto, Ontario M5V 1R6

AT&T (American Telephone and
Telegraph Company) Public Relations

195 Broadway Room 511
New York, New York 10007

Audio-Brandon Films
See Macmillan Films, Inc.

Australian High Commission
First Secretary (Information)
90 Sparks Street
Ottawa, Ontario K1P 5B4

Australian Information Service
Australian Consulate General
636 Fifth Avenue
New York, New York 10020

Australian Press & Information Office
Australian Consulate General
360 Post Street Union Square
San Francisco, California 94108

AV-ED Films
7934 Santa Monica Blvd.
Hollywood, California 90046

B Barry Downes Productions
269 West 72nd Street
New York, New York 10023

BBC-TV Enterprises (British Broadcasting
Television Enterprises) Corporation
BBC Film Sales
Manulife Centre
55 Bloor Street West, Suite 510
Toronto, Ontario M4W 1A5

Bellevue Film Distributors
277 Victoria Street
Toronto, Ontario M5B 1W6

Benchmark Films, Inc.
145 Scarborough Road
Briarcliff Manor, New York 10510

BFA Educational Media
2211 Michigan Avenue (P.O. Box 1795)
Santa Monica, California 90404

Blackwood Productions, Inc.
58 West 58th Street
New York, New York 10019

British Council
British High Commission
80 Elgin Street
Ottawa, Ontario K1P 5K7

C   Canadian Film Institute
303 Richmond Road
Ottawa, Ontario K1Z 6X3

Canadian Filmmakers' Distribution Centre
406 Jarvis Street
Toronto, Ontario M4Y 2G6

Canfilm Screen Service Ltd.
583 Ellice Avenue
Winnipeg, Manitoba R3B 1Z7

Canyon Cinema Cooperative
Industrial Center Building   Room 220
Sausalito, California 94965

Carman Educational Associates
Box 205
Youngstown, New York 14174

Carman Educational Associates
Pine Grove, Ontario L0J 1J0

Carousel Films, Inc.
1501 Broadway, Suite 1503
New York, New York 10036

Castelli-Sonnabend Tapes and Films, Inc.
420 West Broadway
New York, New York 10012

CBS Publishing Group
600 Third Avenue
New York, New York 10016

Chuck Olin Associates
1728 North Wells Street
Chicago, Illinois 60614

Churchill Films
662 North Robertson Blvd.
Los Angeles, California 90069

Colonial Williamsburg Foundation
A-V Distribution Section Box "C"
Williamsburg, Virginia 23185

Connecticut Films, Inc.
6 Cobble Hill Road
Westport, Connecticut 06880

Contemporary/McGraw-Hill
See McGraw-Hill Films

D   Daniel Doron
58 West 68th Street
New York, New York 10023

Daniel Wilson Productions
300 West 55th Street
New York, New York 10001

E   EBEC (Encyclopaedia Britannica
Educational Corporation)
425 North Michigan Avenue
Chicago, Illinois 60611

Educational Film Distributors, Ltd.
285 Lesmill Road
Don Mills, Ontario M3B 2V1

Elizabeth Wiener
161 West 10th Street
New York, New York 10014

Embassy of Belgium
Film Department
3330 Garfield Street, N.W.
Washington, D.C. 20008

Embassy of the Czechoslovak
Socialist Republic
171 Clemow Avenue
Ottawa, Ontario K1S 2B3

Embassy of France
Film Services
464 Wilbrod Street
Ottawa, Ontario K1N 6M8

Embassy of Greece
Chateau Laurier Hotel Suite 110
Ottawa, Ontario K1N 8S7

Embassy of Japan
2520 Massachusetts Avenue N.W.
Washington, D.C. 20008

Embassy of Japan
75 Albert Street Suite 1005
Ottawa, Ontario K1P 5E7

Embassy of Switzerland
2900 Cathedral Avenue N.W.
Washington, D.C. 20008

Embassy of Switzerland
5 Marlborough Avenue
Ottawa, Ontario K1N 8E6

Embassy of Yugoslavia
17 Blackburn Avenue
Ottawa, Ontario K1N 8A2

F FACSEA (French American Cultural
Service and Educational Aid)
Audio-Visual Department
972 Fifth Avenue
New York, New York 10021

Faroun Films (Canada) Ltd.
136A St. Paul Street East
Montreal, P.Q. H2Y 1G6

Film Classic Exchange
1926 South Vermont Avenue
Los Angeles, California 90007

Film Images/Radim Films
17 West 60th Street
New York, New York 10023

Film Images/Radim Films
1034 Lake Street
Oak Park, Illinois 60301

Film-makers' Cooperative
175 Lexington Avenue
New York, New York 10016

Films for the Humanities
P.O. Box 2053
Princeton, New Jersey 08540

Films Incorporated
1144 Wilmette Avenue
Wilmette, Illinois 60091

Forma Art Associates
141 East 55th Street
New York, New York 10022

Fred Salaff Productions
154 Mantling Avenue
Tarrytown, New York 10591

G Gordon Watt Films
865 Shepherd Avenue W.
Downsview, Ontario M3H 2T4

Graphic Curriculum, Inc.
P.O. Box 565   Lenox Hill Station
New York, New York 10021

Grove Press Film Division
196 West Houston Street
New York, New York 10014

H Hallmark Films and Recordings
1511 East North Avenue
Baltimore, Maryland 21213

Harold Becker
N. Lee Lacy Associates, Ltd.
160 East 61st Street
New York, New York 10021

Holt, Rinehart and Winston of Canada Ltd.
55 Horner Avenue
Toronto, Ontario M8Z 4X6

Hobel-Leiterman Productions Ltd.
43 Britain Street
Toronto, Ontario M5A 1R7

Huszar Productions
420 East 55th Street
New York, New York 10022

I Illumination Film
6812 Treasure Trail
Los Angeles, California 90068

Imperial Oil Divisional Office (Québec)
4980 Bucham Street
Montreal, P.Q. M4P 1S9

Imperial Oil Divisional Office (Maritimes)
P.O. Box 220
Halifax, Nova Scotia B3J 2N6

Independent Television Corporation
555 Madison Avenue
New York, New York 10022

Independent Film Producers Co.
P.O. Box 501
Pasadena, California 91102

Indiana University
Audio-Visual Center
Bloomington, Indiana 47401

International Education Films Ltd.
Chateau Maisonneuve, Suite 558
4999 St. Catherine Street West
Montreal, P.Q. H3Z 1T3

International Film Bureau
332 South Michigan Avenue
Chicago, Illinois 60604

International Film Foundation
475 Fifth Avenue   Suite 916
New York, New York 10017

International Tele-Film Enterprises
47 Densley Avenue
Toronto, Ontario M6M 5A8

Iowa State University
Media Resources Center
121 Pearson Hall
Ames, Iowa 50010

Istituto Italiano di Cultura
686 Park Avenue
New York, New York 10021

ITC of Canada Ltd.
(Independent Television Corporation)
Manulife Centre   Suite 803
55 Bloor Street West
Toronto, Ontario M4W 1A5

J Jane Morrison Productions
218 Thompson Street
New York, New York 10012

Japan Foundation
600 New Hampshire Ave., N.W.   Room 430
Washington, D.C. 20037

Joe Kelley Film Productions
4806 Avenue C
Corpus Christi, Texas 78410

K Kenesaw Films
500 Central Avenue
Union City, New Jersey 07087

L Laura Singer
41 Central Park West
New York, New York 10023

Learning Corporation of America (LCA)
1350 Avenue of the Americas
New York, New York 10019

Leland Auslender Films
6036 Comey Avenue
Los Angeles, California 90034

Living Artists Productions
21 West 58th Street
New York, New York 10019

Lobett Productions
2002 Taraval Street
San Francisco, California 94116

M Macmillan Films, Inc.
(Audio-Brandon Films)
34 MacQuesten Parkway South
Mt. Vernon, New York 10550

Marlin Motion Pictures Ltd.
47 Lakeshore Road East
Port Credit, Ontario L5G 1C9

Martha Jackson Gallery
521 West 57th Street
New York, New York 10019

Maysles Films
1697 Broadway
New York, New York 10019

McGraw-Hill Films
1221 Avenue of the Americas
New York, New York 10020

McGraw-Hill Ryerson Ltd.
Film Division
330 Progress Avenue
Scarborough, Ontario M1P 2Z5

Mexican Tourist Council
1 Place Ville-Marie, Suite 2409
Montreal, Quebec

Michelangelo Company
Paramount Building
1501 Broadway   Suite 1511
New York, New York 10036

Modern Talking Picture Service
Modern Film Rentals
2323 Hyde Park Road
New Hyde Park, New York 11040

Modern Talking Picture Service
Modern Film Rentals
1145 North McCadden Place
Los Angeles, California 90038

Modern Talking Picture Service
Modern Film Rentals
1875 Leslie Street
Don Mills, Ontario M3B 2M6

Modern Talking Picture Service
1590 West 4th Avenue
Vancouver, B.C. V6J 1L7

Monument Film Corporation
P.O. Box 315
Franklin Lakes, New Jersey 07417

Museum at Large
157 West 54th Street
New York, New York 10019

The Museum of Modern Art (MOMA)
Department of Film
11 West 53rd Street
New York, New York 10019

N National Film Board of Canada
P.O. Box 6100
Montreal, P.Q. H3C 3H5

National Film Board of Canada (U.S.A.)
1251 Avenue of the Americas   16th Floor
New York, New York 10020

National Gallery of Art
Extension Service
Washington, D.C. 20565

Netherlands Government
Information Services
Royal Netherlands Embassy
4200 Linnean Avenue N.W.
Washington, D.C. 20008

New Cinema Enterprises
35 Britain Street
Toronto, Ontario M5A 1R7

New York University Film Library
26 Washington Place
New York, New York 10003

New Yorker Films
43 West 61st Street
New York, New York 10023

O Ohio State University
Department of Photography and Cinema
156 West 19th Avenue
Columbus, Ohio 43210

Oxford Films
1136 North Las Palmas Avenue
Hollywood, California 90038

P Pan American Development Foundation
Organization of American States
17th Street and Constitution Avenue N.W.
Washington, D.C. 20006

Pathe′ Cinema Corporation
4 West 58th Street
New York, New York 10019

Pennebaker, Inc.
56 West 45th Street
New York, New York 10036

Phoenix Films, Inc.
470 Park Avenue South
New York, New York 10016

Pictura Films Distribution Corporation
43 West 16th Street
New York, New York 10011

Pyramid Films
P.O. Box 1048
Santa Monica, California 90406

Q QANTAS Airways Ltd.
360 Post Street
San Francisco, California 94108

QANTAS Airways
900 West Georgia Street
Vancouver, B.C. V6C 1P9

R RBC Films
933 North Labrea Avenue
Los Angeles, California 90038

RJM Productions
7012 LaPresa Drive
Hollywood, California 90028

RMI Film Productions, Inc.
Film Order Department
4916 Main Street
Kansas City, Missouri 64112

The Roland Collection
1825 Willow Road
Northfield, Illinois 60093

Royal Netherlands Embassy
4200 Linnean Avenue N.W.
Washington, D.C. 20008

Royal Netherlands Embassy
275 Slater Street
Ottawa, Ontario K1P 5H9

Rudy Burckhardt
50 West 29th Street
New York, New York 10001

S   Serious Business Company
1609 Jaynes Street
Berkeley, California 94703

(A1) Sherman Films Inc.
P.O. Box 6   Cathedral Station
New York, New York 10025

T   Texture Films
1600 Broadway
New York, New York 10019

Thomas Bouchard
Stony Brook Road   West Brewster
Cape Cod, Massachusetts 02631

Time-Life Multimedia
Time-Life Films, Inc.
100 Eisenhower Drive
Paramus, New Jersey 07652

U   UNESCO
United Nations Building
New York, New York 10017

Universal Education and Visual Arts
Department MU
100 Universal City Plaza
Universal City, California 91608

Universal Education and Visual Arts
2450 Victoria Park Avenue
Willowdale, Ontario M2J 4A2

University of Arizona
Bureau of Audio-Visual Services
Tucson, Arizona 85721

University of California
Extension Media Center
Berkeley, California 94720

University of Iowa
Audio-Visual Center
Media Library
C-5 East Hall
Iowa City, Iowa 52242

V   Viking Films, Ltd.
525 Denison Street
Markham, Ontario L3R 1B8

Vision Quest
7715 North Sheridan Road
Chicago, Illinois 60626

Visual Education Centre (VEC)
115 Berkeley Street
Toronto, Ontario M5A 2W8

Visual Resources, Inc.
1 Lincoln Plaza
New York, New York 10023

Vorpal Reproductions
450 Gough
San Francisco, California 94102

W   West Coast Audio-Visual, Ltd.
2790 Arbutus Street
Vancouver, B.C. V3J 3Y6

Jerry Winters
254 Giralda Avenue
Coral Gables, Florida 33134

Woelm-Polister
1741 Glenview Avenue
St. Paul, Minnesota 55112

The Works
1659—18th Street
Santa Monica, California 90404

Y   Yugoslav Information Center
488 Madison Avenue
New York, New York 10022